Obiter Dicta

Obiter Dicta

Opinions, Judicious and Otherwise,

on Lawyers and the Law

―――――

Joseph W. Bishop, Jr.

―――――

Atheneum

NEW YORK

1971

The author gratefully acknowledges permission to reprint articles first published in the following periodicals:

AMERICAN SPEECH: Copyright © 1946 by Columbia University Press.

HARVARD LAW REVIEW; Vol. 78, p. 1510: Copyright 1965 by The Harvard Law Review Association.

THE NEW REPUBLIC: Copyright © 1961 by Harrison-Blaine of New Jersey, Inc. Reprinted by permission of The New Republic.

TRANS-ACTION: Copyright © 1970 by Trans-Action, Inc.

VILLANOVA LAW REVIEW; Vol. 12, No. 1, pp. 211–216: Copyright 1966 by Villanova University.

YALE LAW JOURNAL; Vol. 67, p. 343; Vol. 69, pp. 193 and 925; Vol. 70, p. 1028; Vol. 72, p. 614; Vol. 74, p. 193: Copyright © 1957, 1959, 1960, 1961, 1963, 1964 by The Yale Law Journal Company, Inc. Reprinted by permission of The Yale Law Journal Company and Fred B. Rothman & Company.

For my wife,

*who is not responsible for the opinions herein
expressed*

Foreword

The pieces in this collection were written at irregular intervals and deal with a variety, or hodge-podge, of subjects. I cannot detect any unifying theme except that nearly all have something to do with law. More than half took the form of book reviews, but in each case I reviewed the book because I had ideas of my own about its author, its subject, or both.

I wrote for a variety of reasons, some creditable, some less so. Vanity was, of course, a major factor, as it is with any literary work more ambitious than *Typical Electric Bills, 1969* (Government Printing Office, $1.25). Money was not. I do not, of course, have a soul above money. I would have one of the world's great collections of it, if I knew how. I agree with Dr. Johnson's observation that "there are few ways in which a man can be more innocently employed than in getting money." I hope he exaggerated when he said that "no man but a blockhead ever wrote except for money." Contributors to law reviews (and other scholarly journals) are never paid a cent, although I am not entirely certain that this fact by itself confutes the Doctor. What I got for the other articles convinced me that lawyering, or even the professor business, pays better hourly wages than free-lance writing.

Neither did I publish in order not to perish academically, for even the ones which appeared in law reviews, and were loaded to the gunwales with footnotes, were parodies of the sort of thing which qualifies professors for tenure, name chairs, and foundation grants. I knew how to parody such stuff, because I had written so much of it. Those compositions are embalmed and buried elsewhere.

Some of the articles were motivated by a pedagogical urge to elucidate a controversial and more or less complex legal problem which had been thoroughly obfuscated by polemicists on both sides of the controversy. Examples are the pieces on wiretapping, the Warren Court, West Berlin, and military justice. None of them was a brief; that is, I did not sit down to write them with the intention of persuading readers to a particular conclusion, although I argued myself into various judgments as I went along. Mainly, however, I tried to lay out what I believed were the facts and the law. This did not, of course, change the polemicists' thinking (if that is the right word) or endear me to them, but I was writing for people who were willing to read enough facts and law to make their own judgment on the merits.

I enjoyed the mail, too. The response to a regular law-review article seems to consist largely of letters from lawyers whose clients have problems of the sort discussed in the article and who want to get the author's advice without paying him for it. The controversial pieces produced mail which was an enjoyable change from the usual flow of textbook advertisements, announcements that lawyers I never heard of have become members of firms I never heard of, and manifestos needing professorial signatures and cash so that they can be published in the *Times* on Sunday and save the world by Monday. Most of the letters could be classified as (a) fan, (b) hate, or (c) nut. There was naturally a good deal of overlapping between (b) and (c) and possibly between (a) and (c). Many of those in category (c) were entertaining and instructive. There was, for example, the lady who typed several single-spaced pages chiding me for failing to perceive

that the Warren Court was part of a nefarious plot against
the United States, concocted not only by Communists,
which I had already learned from several other readers, but
also by Masons. Unwisely, I wrote her that, while I knew
very little about the Masonic Order, I did know, as a one-
time resident of Alexandria, Virginia, that George Washington had been the master of the lodge in that city. I got
back several more single-spaced pages proving either that
Washington had been duped by the Masons or that he was
part of the plot, I forget which. I gathered that George's
affiliation had long been troublesome to the anti-Masons,
but that they had developed a satisfactory explanation. I
would never have acquired this esoteric information if I had
stuck to my legal last.

My strongest motivation (other than vanity) was impa-
tience with the flood of cant, fustian, and emotional nonsense which pollutes the intellectual atmosphere. I probably
exaggerate its incidence and its deleterious effect on the Republic, for I live in New Haven, a university town which
sometimes seems to rival California in the production of
such noisome effluvia. Many of my students and colleagues
inhale it in great draughts and with every appearance of
pleasure. I have been gasping, coughing, and growing testier
for the past decade.

I was trained in the Harvard Law School of thirty years
ago. In that time and place the prevailing doctrine was that
a lawyer should try, so far as his natural wits permitted, to
think like Brandeis and Holmes. I early learned the lesson
that the first, and by far the hardest, job is to get the facts
straight. The books, speeches, and press releases of the likes
of Joe McCarthy, Richard Nixon (before he finally got to
the top of the greasy pole), William Kunstler, George Wallace, and William O. Douglas affected me in much the same
way that hard-core pornography affects a Hardshell Baptist.

These were not half-educated undergraduates or illiterate slum youths, who can be forgiven for supposing that they express a reasoned opinion when they spray "Off the Pigs" on a wall. All of them are lawyers; two, Nixon and Douglas, *good* lawyers. (The case of Mr. Justice Douglas is particularly depressing, because when he is dealing with a subject he actually understands, such as corporation finance, and when he is not trying to establish his eligibility for honorary life membership in the Youth Movement, he can still marshal the relevant facts with uncommon skill.)

It will be noticed that, as the years went on, I found more targets of opportunity on my left than on my right. This may, of course, be attributable to normal hardening of the political arteries. But I do not think I have become reactionary, or even particularly conservative. It gradually dawned on me, as it dawned on many other liberals of my generation and persuasion, that the lesson which a lot of left-wingers had really taken to heart in the Joe McCarthy era was that the use of Joe's weapons is emotionally satisfying and frequently effective.

If here and there the reader finds remarks which are unkind, or even unfair, I can only plead that I wrote more in anger than in sorrow. I will make one more extenuating statement: I believe this to be the only collection of nonponderous legal writing which does not contain a single quotation from *Alice in Wonderland*.

JOSEPH W. BISHOP, JR.

Contents

———

xi

I

Judges, Juries, and Lawyers

William Kunstler
and the New Bar

The United States, long pre-eminent in the production of spectacular criminal trials, is today staging some which must be unique in legal history. A highly visible and audible section of the defense bar (with the unintended cooperation of a few judges) seems to have set out to demonstrate, by turning trials into combinations of political rally and five-ring circus, that the adversary system of criminal justice, in which defense counsel play so prominent a role, is simply unworkable and ought to be replaced by something else whose nature they have but dimly adumbrated. The New Bar may number (by its own estimate) as many as four or five hundred lawyers (a little over one tenth of one percent of the American bar), mostly fairly youthful. Its dean and *sacer vates* is undoubtedly William Kunstler, who in the last couple of years must have received three or four times as much publicity as F. Lee Bailey, Melvin Belli, and Louis Nizer (themselves no shrinking violets) put together. He is probably the only member of the New York bar whose mere arrival on a campus can set off rejoicings and tumult comparable to the arrival of John Lennon at a rock festival or Adolf

Hitler at a Nürnberg Parteitag, circa 1938.

The custom of giving the accused a lawyer, and allowing that lawyer at least as much license as the prosecutor, is by no means so deeply rooted as most Americans assume. In a simple society, criminal procedure is also simple. The Headman, the Amir, the Ahkoond, or whatever the dispenser of justice and protector of the poor happens to be called, sits on his throne, surrounded by his catchpolls, fanning himself and swatting flies. Having heard and questioned the witnesses and the putative criminal, he strokes his beard and consults the public interest and the Canons of the Law. Anon he pronounces judgment—some picturesque and fitting variety of capital punishment, so many strokes of the bastinado, or perchance, as in the well-known custody case reported in 1 Kings 3:16–28, he calls for a sword and orders, "Divide the living child in two, and give half to the one, and half to the other" claimant. No lawyers are needed or allowed. Were the accused to appear with counsel, he would probably be awarded an extra couple of dozen lashes of the hippopotamus hide for contempt of court. This style of justice is, of course, by no means extinct. It survives not only in some of the so-called underdeveloped countries, but in many so-called civilized countries where the presumption of innocence exists in neither practice nor theory. The role of the accused in most of the Communist countries is not to assert his innocence, much less to sass back to the court, but simply to expatiate on the blackness of his guilt and attribute it to the nefarious blandishments and machinations of revisionists, dogmatists, Trotskyites and/or agents of the CIA. Even in this country, a milder variety of the primitive procedure still exists in many inferior state and city courts, where the offenses and offenders are routine, decisions are unreported and appeals infrequent, and the judge is likely to be a better politician than lawyer.

4

The Sixth Amendment's provision that "In all criminal cases, the accused shall enjoy the right . . . to have the Assistance of Counsel for his Defence" was a radical innovation in 1791. In Blackstone's time (and, indeed, until 1836) an Englishman charged with a capital crime (a category which included practically all of the modern felonies and many which today are only misdemeanors) was entitled to no more than to consult his lawyer on such legal questions as he himself might raise. His lawyer was not allowed to waste the court's time and obfuscate justice by producing or cross-examining witnesses, or arguing to (and with) the court.

Since the Bill of Rights, however, defense counsel have added both to the drama and to the fairness of criminal proceedings in the Republic. Some of them have been showmen quite as flamboyant as Kunstler. One thinks immediately of William S. Howe (of Howe & Hummel), the first to hire an appealing young woman to sit in the front of the courtroom, clutching an infant and weeping copiously while Howe pleaded for an acquittal; of Delphin Delmas, who filled the yellow press of sixty years ago with eulogies of that *chevalier sans peur et sans reproche*, Harry K. Thaw; of Bill Fallon, the Great Mouthpiece, who defended most of the eminent hoods of the Capone era. But Kunstler is to them what *Oh! Calcutta!* is to *Abie's Irish Rose*.

Kunstler and his disciples naturally prefer to compare themselves to Clarence Darrow. Indeed, Kunstler published in 1962 a commendable book, *The Case for Courage*, on ten great advocates, including Darrow, who did their damnedest for unpopular clients. But I do not think such men are the true progenitors of the New Bar. Darrow and the other lawyers who were Kunstler's heroes in 1962, though ready enough to stand up for unpopular people and unpopular ideas, operated well within the rules of court and the Canons of Ethics. Most of them had a powerful command of rhetoric, and they were not above using it to drug the intellects and rouse the emotions of jurors, but it was no part of their strategy to bait the judge, intimidate the jury, or disrupt the trial.

Moreover, they were quite willing to undertake the defense of people with whose ideas and acts they had no personal sympathy. Kunstler, on the other hand, says that "I only defend those whose goals I share. . . . I only defend those I love." The trouble with this is that there are some defendants whom practically nobody loves—Leopold and Loeb, for example, and the obscure (and mostly indigent) people accused of raping and killing little girls. It is even conceivable that some of the people Kunstler loves might prefer counsel who loved them less but knew more law: Many lawyers think that Kunstler's forensic methods, though vastly enjoyed by his clients, are not best calculated to get them off. The point is that everyone accused of crime, be he Black Panther, Ku Kluxer, or humble sneak thief, is entitled to a fair trial and the benefit of the Bill of Rights—but, in some cases, it takes a good lawyer to see that he gets them. It is hard enough for such an accused to find a lawyer sufficiently skilled to do that job, without having to find one who loves him. The New Bar never mentions, and may not know, the fact that many Wall Street lawyers have defended, without fee and without fanfare, radicals and apolitical thugs for whom they could not have had much personal affection— and defended them very ably, too.

Precedents which seem to me much more closely in point are furnished by the lawyers who in 1944 defended an assortment of home-grown and imported Nazis and by the (different) lawyers who in 1949 represented the satraps of the American Communist Party. The former got better results. After several months of obstruction and delay, a mistrial was declared because the judge suffered a fatal heart attack. The

6

government never mustered the energy to bring the defendants to trial again, and they lapsed into almost total obscurity. Who now remembers William Dudley Pelley, or Elizabeth Dilling, or even Joe McWilliams? Yet their pots were as quaintly cracked and their rhetoric as baroque and inflammatory as Abbie Hoffman's or Jerry Rubin's. *Sic transit dementia mundi.*

Harry Sacher, whose tactics in the defense of the Communist leaders were also strikingly similar to those of the Websters of the New Left, had worse luck. Although his performance had quite as much brass and brio as that of the Nazis' lawyers, he drew a durable judge who was not goaded into either a coronary occlusion or reversible error. Sacher's clients were convicted, and he himself was subsequently given six months for contempt of court (affirmed by the Supreme Court, 343 U.S. 1 [1952]) and disbarred. (It is an odd fact that the judge, Harold R. Medina, was one of Kunstler's heroes in 1962.) It is even doubtful that Sacher's clients properly appreciated his efforts, for the Old Left was always strong for Law and Order.

The Nazis' lawyers of 1944 and the Communists' lawyers of 1949 were isolated phenomena, ahead of their time. They were not held up as exemplars to law students or lionized by liberals. Kunstler, on the other hand, is a cult hero comparable to Che Guevara or Malcolm X. In any courtroom outside the backwoods he can count on an enthusiastic and leather-lunged claque, ready to whoop, dance in the aisles, and chant slogans whenever he so much as clears his throat to make an objection. He must be the only alumnus of the Columbia Law School capable of sending adolescents into Dionysiac ecstasy. The minor prophets of the new jurisprudence, such as Gerald Lefcourt, draw good houses and plenty of publicity, but they are still no more than road-company stars.

7

Their fans are by no means limited to the junior Jacobins on the campuses. Many adults, some of them very solvent, are among their admirers. The reasoning of these devotees is simple. The New Left bar and its clients are strongly opposed to war, imperialism, racism,[1] tyranny (by the wrong kind of tyrant), poverty, pollution, and probably also to spirocheta pallida and rattus norvegicus. It follows that to deny them support is to aid and abet the whole catalogue of deadly sins. There is, moreover, an ancient (and often honorable) American tradition of sympathy for people trapped in the machinery of the criminal law. Mark Twain described it in *Tom Sawyer:*

> This funeral stopped the growth of one thing—the petition to the governor for Injun Joe's pardon. The petition had been largely signed; many tearful and eloquent meetings had been held, and a committee of sappy women had been appointed to go in deep mourning and wail around the governor, and implore him to be a merciful ass and trample his duty underfoot. Injun Joe was believed to have killed five citizens of the village, but what of that? If he had been Satan himself there would have been plenty of weaklings ready to scribble their names to a pardon petition, and drip a tear on it from their permanently impaired and leaky waterworks.

Today, of course, Injun Joe's lawyer would argue that, since his client was not merely unpopular and sinister but a member of a Minority Group, he could not possibly get a fair trial and therefore should be neither tried nor punished.

1. The New Left's definition of "racism" is peculiar. It is not "racism" to hate WASPs, Irishmen, Germans, Italians, or Poles, or even Caucasians in general. Negroes, but not other people, are permitted to hate Jews. Neither is it "racism" to glorify indiscriminately Negroes, Mexicans, Indians, or other non-whites.

8

Q.E.D. The Committee, finding this logic unanswerable, would communicate its views by planting a pipe bomb in the Executive Mansion. But the psychology, and its principal exponents, are about the same as in Mark Twain's day.

The popularity of the new jurisprudence also owes much to the congenital, and probably incurable, craving of homo sapiens for irrational but beautifully simple ideas—"the substance of things hoped for, the evidence of things not seen." For most of the history of the species, of course, the demand has been met by priesthoods of one sort or another. In recent years the sale of the old reliable nostrum has been disappointing; its dispensers themselves hardly pretend to believe in its efficacy. Not many, however, are willing to abandon their calling and go to work. Thus, the reverend clergy, their natural talents improved by the thorough and systematic training in unreason provided by the nation's divinity schools, have taken their rightful place in the forefront of the Movement and are very prominent among the supporters of Kunstler and his clients. Some of them hold the keys to treasuries more tangible than St. Peter's. The new law does not pay as well as a Wall Street practice, but there is no question that very substantial sums have been collected for the defense of Black Panthers and the more picturesque of the New Bar's other clients. Moreover, some of those clients are themselves very solvent, or have very solvent parents. I strongly suspect, for example, that Dr. Spock was fully billed for the considerable value of the services of Leonard Boudin. (I should add that Boudin, though he has defended many Old and New Leftists, is a very competent lawyer whose courtroom conduct is well within the traditional bounds.)

The trial tactics of the New Bar vary greatly from case to case. Some of its members are quite willing to resort to the traditional techniques of criminal lawyers, including shrewd and hard plea-bargaining. But others, notably Kunstler, seem

9

to prefer a "political" strategy—to some extent, no doubt, because it is what their clients want. Its standard arguments and scenario go something like this:

(1) Label the prosecution as "political," and therefore in violation of the First Amendment. The fact that the defendants may have been indicted for propagating their reformist ideas by first-degree murder or by planning to blow up a random assortment of department-store customers is irrelevant, so long as their motives were "political" and pure.

(2) If the prosecution is political, it follows that the charges are patently incredible and the evidence forged or suborned. Every case is a Reichstag trial. That the defendants may have regularly and loudly proclaimed their intention to do precisely what the indictment charges them with doing does not detract from the indictment's inherent absurdity.

(3) Since the charge is a frame-up, there is by definition no chance of an acquittal or a fair trial. The prosecutor, his witnesses, the judges, both trial and appellate, and the jury are all part of the conspiracy, reading lines from a script prepared by Attorney General Mitchell, J. Edgar Hoover, Mayor Daley, and the CIA. If there is a genuine corpse of a murdered man—a corpus delicti in the most literal sense—it only shows the lengths to which the Establishment will go to put dissenters in the electric chair.

(4) Since the trial is a charade and the court of the kangaroo variety, there is no reason for the defendants to cooperate by observing the rules or focusing on what the prosecution pretends is the issue in the case—i.e., whether the accused are guilty, beyond a reasonable doubt, of having violated a constitutional law.

(5) The true role of the defense, therefore, is to expose the proceedings for what they are and the judge for what he is. Kunstler does not himself scream "Fascist pig!" at the judge, but he certainly does not discourage his clients from

doing so, along with other epithets whose transcription reduces court reporters (who are mostly middle-aged and virtuous ladies) to tears and the use of dashes or asterisks. Some of Kunstler's clients and their supporters in the audience probably could not be controlled by anything short of a police riot squad, but most lawyers in such a situation would warn their clients to control themselves or get a new lawyer. Kunstler treats it as a natural and even praiseworthy reaction to the outrages being perpetrated upon them—entirely the fault of the judge. This attitude alternates with a sort of New Left version of "Father, forgive them, for they know not what they do," which must be more infuriating than straightforward obscene abuse to elderly (and, in the case of Judge Hoffman, somewhat testy) jurists accustomed to deference, not to say soapy politeness, from counsel.

(6) Since the whole proceeding is political, defense counsel should stick to politics in his arguments. Thus, Kunstler at every opportunity orates, with or without the permission of the judge. He frequently answers the gavel by explaining that he wishes merely to add one sentence, but with him one sentence is a purely hypothetical quantity, like one martini. Kunstler's speeches are by and large neither better nor worse than the average of New Left polemics, but they are delivered *con brio* and *fortissimo*, with a maximum of emotion ("Is law so dear and order so sweet as to be purchased at the price of our brothers chained in slavery?") almost unadulterated by fact or logic. As a long-time fellow townsman of the Reverend William Sloane Coffin, Jr., I am something of a connoisseur of fustian, as a citizen of Rheims is something of a connoisseur of champagne. New Haven is the very home of it. Kunstler's is almost a greater vintage than Coffin's. But Coffin, after all, is a clergyman, and I, being a lawyer, hope for something different from lawyers. The effect which Kunstler's jeremiads produce on me is such that if he were to

11

attack venereal disease, I would find myself examining the case for gonorrhea.

Even so, Kunstler's postulates are not sheer fantasy. Most of his clients make careers of saying and doing things which are calculated to shock and repel the class of people from whom most jurors are drawn. They burn flags and threaten to burn cities and even suburbs: some of them wear bizarre and unsanitary costumes and shout obscenities still more bizarre; they yell for revolution, preferably bloody; they show no reverence for God, the Constitution, soap, or motherhood. Plainly, it is not easy to find twelve citizens who have not even a subconscious prejudice against such defendants. The defense can challenge a limited number of the panel without cause and an unlimited number for cause, but a thorough investigation of the backgrounds of prospective jurors requires a good deal of time and money. Most trial lawyers would concede that the mechanism for the exclusion of prejudiced jurors is very imperfect. Similarly, a judge can be asked to disqualify himself, but it is not easy to convince an appellate court that his refusal to do so was an abuse of discretion. The problem is aggravated by the news media's liberal use of their First Amendment freedom to report and comment on the accusations and the accused—and much of what they print and broadcast is calculated to inflame even the most cool-headed of potential jurors.

But, unless we accept the proposition that a man who makes himself sufficiently detested may violate the law *ad libitum,* all we can do is our best to see that he gets the fair trial to which the Constitution entitles him. This is primarily the job of the courts, both state and federal—for the federal courts can and do review state convictions if the defendant claims that his trial, including the selection of the jury, violated his rights under the Constitution of the United States. In recent years, at least, American courts, headed by the

Supreme Court, have by and large done a pretty good job in this respect.

A fact which the New Bar knows but does not emphasize is that the prejudice of jurors may (and often does) operate in favor of the defendants—and it takes only one to hang the jury instead of the accused. The classic examples, of course, have been the Mississippi juries which regularly refused to convict Klansmen accused of murdering Negroes or civil-rights workers. The contention of the Black Panthers that trial by a jury of their peers means trial by a jury of other Panthers, or at least other blacks, is in essence no more than a demand for the benefits long accorded to Ku Kluxers. In fact, any jury trying Black Panthers is pretty sure to include some Negroes—and a black man may need considerable courage, both moral and physical, to vote for conviction, just as it takes a brave white man to vote guilty in a Mississippi trial.

If we concede the extreme difficulty of keeping bias out of the jury box, the only alternative is to make the judge the trier of the fact as well as the law. Judges, although they are human, and often all too human, are probably by training and experience better able than most to find facts on the basis of the evidence rather than preconceptions. A number of states permit a man accused of crime to demand trial by judges instead of jurors. Connecticut has such a law; I find it interesting that the Black Panthers who are being tried in New Haven on various charges arising out of the kidnapping and murder of a suspected informer have made no such demand. Kunstler's other clients are probably somewhat less likely to find jurors who are friendly or can be intimidated, but even they can reflect that there is a good chance that at least one of the twelve will have some sympathy for the ideology of the New Left. In short, I have serious reservations about the premise that conviction is so much a foregone conclusion that a serious defense on the merits is a waste of time as well as a concession of the legitimacy of the process of railroading.

The *strategy* of the new forensics—the goals which its tactics are designed to achieve—is unclear. Whether it improves the clients' chances of staying out of jail is at least debatable. The clowning, the screaming of threats and insults, and the scuffling with marshals may alienate impartial or even sympathetic jurors. Against this drawback may be set the possibility that some judges, like Julius Hoffman, can be goaded into displays of prejudice and the commission of reversible error—which, however, usually gets the accused nothing more than a new trial. But if one starts from the assumption that ultimate conviction and punishment are part of the plot and inevitable, counsel should not worry about diminishing the nonexistent chance of acquittal.

The really important objective seems to be to make effective use of the splendid forum which a courtroom provides for the propaganda of the Movement. History is full of examples, from Socrates to Sacco and Vanzetti, of defendants whose ideas gained a better hearing in the context of a trial for the speaker's life than ever they got when he was at large and unpersecuted. The trial of Charles I made the Stuart restoration almost inevitable. Danton's eloquence might have secured his acquittal if the Committee of Public Safety had not shut him up: It certainly foreshadowed the fall of Robespierre and the Thermidorean reaction. Adolf Hitler, as many men still living can recall, made enormous political capital out of his trial for treason after the beerhall putsch of 1923. Leading off with a speech lasting four hours, he cross-examined the witnesses, interrupted the proceedings with other notable harangues, and wound up with a genuine classic of rabble-rousing—all of which, being fully reported in the entire German press, spread his name and fame far beyond the

14

borders of Bavaria. Hitler, to be sure, had the advantage of judges whose fears and sympathies conduced to extraordinary tolerance, but even if Kunstler had William O. Douglas for a trial judge, it is improbable that he would get such results. He has neither Hitler's extraordinary ability to inflame ordinary halfwits nor his demonic political genius. Kunstler, though capable of generating plenty of excitement, and by no means indifferent to the delights of being followed around by reporters and television crews, is not himself a Messiah—and apparently does not aspire to the role. He sees himself as a John the Baptist for the genuine world-shakers, such as Bobby Seale, and the seminal intellects, such as Abbie Hoffman and Jerry Rubin.

It is a truism that the first person an advocate convinces is himself. Until three or four years ago Kunstler was merely one more conventionally liberal lawyer and author, of a type which is as common on Manhattan Island as rabbits are in New South Wales. Although he now describes himself as Martin Luther King's lawyer, none of the veterans who fought the civil-rights battles of the Fifties and early Sixties seem to be able to recall any great thing which he did. None would have predicted the majestic eminence which he occupies today.

Although the New Bar is very critical of the Wall Street lawyers' subservient reflection of their clients' political views, the charge is far more applicable to themselves. The Wall Street lawyer, in fact, is likely to shape the policies of his clients, which is certainly not true of counsel to the New Left. Kunstler, for example, has progressed far beyond the milk-and-water liberalism of his early years. He now appears to believe in every single tenet of his various clients—Black Panthers, Weathermen, Yippies, Crazies, Catholic radicals, and Maoists. This takes some doing, for they do not all believe the same things: The New Left has fissioned along

15

almost as many lines as Christianity, and its members are likely to be at each other's throats whenever the cops give them a breathing space.

Kunstler's role as the Great White Father of the Black Panthers does not, to be sure, confront him with serious ideological problems, for the Panthers, although they sometimes repeat for the benefit of white contributors the clichés of the New Left, are notoriously short of ideology; with the doubtful exception of Eldridge Cleaver, they have no philosopher of even the intellectual status of Dr. Alfred Rosenberg or Dr. Herbert Marcuse. Faced with even the primitive dialectics of the Maoist faction of Students for a Democratic Society, they commonly take refuge in unimaginative obscenity. They bear less resemblance to a political movement than to the long series of slum gangs with members recruited from a particular ethnic group. The Bowery Boys, Dead Rabbits, Hudson Dusters, Gophers, and Five Pointers never discovered the advantages of carrying on their cop-fighting, extortion, and looting in the name of social justice—although the draft riots of 1863 may be an exception to this generalization—and it certainly never occurred to the literati and reformers of their day to extol their culture and leap to their defense on the occasions when the police laid them by the heels. But their *Weltanschauung* was otherwise very similar: They were wild men; their hands were against every man, and every man's hand was against them. The Panthers' political ideas do not go much beyond a feeling (for which there is considerable justification) that society has dealt unfairly with them and that they are therefore entitled to wage guerrilla war against society, beginning with the police.

The David Dellingers and Tom Haydens, on the other hand, do have an ideology, or ideologies, of sorts. They would probably describe themselves as Marxists, if only in the sense that Bishop Pike described himself as a Christian. I confess

16

that I am quite unable to expound their philosophy in detail. In the line of duty, I have tackled some of the opera of the principal philosopher of the Movement, the *doctor angelicus*, Professor Herbert Marcuse, but with indifferent success. As a lawyer, I have had some practice in deciphering impenetrable prose, but Marcuse beats anything in my experience. Such opaque sentences could be composed (in either English or German) only by one steeped in the worst stylistic traditions of German philosophy. They call to mind, indeed, the works of Dr. Alfred Rosenberg, whose ability to write lucid prose, as exemplified in *The Myth of the Twentieth Century*, was comparable to Marcuse's. The two share the knack of writing sentences like "Finite being is incomplete realization, subject to change," and "The new grasp of the world is not a dogma but an attitude." (The first quotation happens to be Marcuse and the second Rosenberg, but either sage could have written either sentence and been proud of it.) Because Marcuse does come as close as anyone to providing such philosophical underpinnings as the radical left has, including its rejection of the Bill of Rights and the rest of the bourgeois-democratic system of criminal justice, it may be relevant to examine his beliefs. Despite the peculiarities of his style, it is sometimes possible for a tough and determined reader to perceive what he is struggling to say. Here and there a sentence which is almost comprehensible catches the eye, like an only ordinarily plain woman at a D.A.R. convention. Dimly, through the *Nacht und Nebel*, the reader perceives the looming shapes of ideas, most of which can be expressed in rather simple terms. The core of his argument seems to be that industrial society has made man the slave of the machine. In capitalist countries it does so not by the direct and obvious coercion which is employed in the U.S.S.R. or China, but by instilling in the poor boob artificial wants—for television, automobiles, air-conditioning,

17

false teeth—which he can gratify only by forty hours a week of degrading toil at the machine. Left to himself, the free man (like Diogenes the Cynic) knows only natural, "biological" needs—food, shelter, sex, and a set of the works of Professor Marcuse.

Fortunately, the Sage, with some help from Plato, has discovered the way of escape from the soul-killing slavery of freedom. The proles must be cured of their artificial desires by depriving them of their specious freedom of choice—specious because they are free (and, indeed, likely) to choose wrongly. Fat ladies will no longer be allowed to choose flowered shorts in psychedelic colors, or banana splits. Mankind will no longer be free to choose between evils such as the *Times* and the *News*, or Democrats and Republicans. Choice, if there must be choice, will be restricted to things which are objectively good. Professor Marcuse categorically denies that he is an enemy of true freedom. He would not, he has made clear (or as close to clear as he makes anything), suppress every idea with which he disagrees, but only those which are objectively wrong—*i.e.*, crimethink. The restraints which he would impose would be "progressive restraints," such as the repression of air pollution or the dissemination of racist ideas. (As might be expected, he neither makes nor sees any distinction between repressing acts and repressing speech and ideas.) Indeed, this disciple of Hegel is more tolerant than his master, for he does not insist that it is the divine mission of Germans, or even of Students for a Democratic Society, to impose their particular *Kultur* on the rest of the earth's inhabitants. An eclectic *Kultur*, selected by Dr. Marcuse and other goodthinkful persons, will be perfectly satisfactory. This is consoling.

It is possible to pick other holes in the Thoughts of the great *Jugendführer*. Carried to its logical conclusion, Marcuse's anti-technological philosophy would abolish martinis,

dachshunds, air-conditioning, central heating, and dentistry
—all of them expensive artificialities forging golden chains
to bind the slave to his particular machine. I find more convincing the philosophy of Thomas Hobbes, who described
the life of man in a natural (*i.e.*, pre-technical) state as
"poor, nasty, brutish, and short." But the idyllic concept of
the natural, naturally good man naturally attracts romantics.
Most romantics are young, but it is very easy even for the
middle-aged to think wistfully of a life without TV situation
farces, go-go discothèques, op and pop art, junkyard sculp-
ture, *Ramparts*, underground movies, and above-ground
movies. But, alas, it is not certain that Marcuse's *Kulturpo-
lizei* would abolish each of these diseases of contemporary
civilization, for not even a philosopher is necessarily in-
fallible in judging the objective wrongness of other people's
ideas and tastes. I will go further: It is not even certain beyond a peradventure of a doubt that I cannot myself err in
such matters. The whole concept of outlawing crimethink,
in fact, raises disturbing memories of the last German effort
to give total power to a philosopher king.

Although the Marcusian philosophy thus diverges in some
important respects from the philosophy of the Bill of Rights,
to which Kunstler makes frequent and favorable reference,
Kunstler seems to have swallowed the ideology of this section
of his clientele without visible discomfort or difficulty. Indeed, the catholicity of his faith is such that he finds much
to admire in grotesques like Abbie Hoffman and Jerry Rubin,
whose ideology seems to consist largely of a lively appreciation of the comic potentialities of a general massacre. (Even
they are not quite without historical analogues. There is, for
example, Bertrand Barère, whose flow of jokes and general
high spirits lent a note of farce to the Terror and earned him
the sobriquet of "Anacreon of the Guillotine." Still further
back is the hangman of Louis XI, called Jean Qui Rit, who

brightened the last moments of his customers with merry jests and good-natured badinage. He had a partner, Jean Qui Pleure, who balanced the comedy with ghostly counsel to the condemned. For some reason, neither of them was really popular.)

One proposition on which Kunstler and all of his clients clearly agree is that (in Kunstler's words) "the legal sub-system itself is nothing more than the new tyrant's most reliable weapon" and that, in consequence, "those lawyers who can no longer remain their society's most complacent eunuchs must pass from passive or active acceptance to open resistance." The courts have few modern precedents to help them deal with this challenge. The Bill of Rights, and modern criminal process generally, were framed to deal with a totally different problem—the protection of the defendant and his lawyer (when he had one) from hectoring, bullying judges, such as Lord Chief Justice Scroggs and George, Baron Jeffreys, Lord Chief Justice and Lord Chancellor of England from 1684 to 1688. Jeffreys, the archetype of the hanging judge, is best remembered for the Bloody Assizes of 1685. He habitually terrorized offenders with lurid descriptions of the punishment he proposed to inflict:

> And I charge him that puts the sentence into execution to do it effectually, and particularly to take care of Mrs. Hipkins. Scourge her soundly, and the other woman . . . and since they have a mind to it this cold weather, let them be well heated.
>
> Your sentence is this—that you be carried from hence to the place from which you came, and from thence be dragged tied to a cart's tail through the streets, your bodies being stripped from the girdles upwards, and be whipped till your bodies bleed.

Nor was he much gentler to counsel: "Mr. Wallop, I observe you are in all these dirty cases; and were it not for you gentlemen of the long robe, who should have more wit and honesty than to support and hold up these factious knaves by the chin, we should not be at the pass we are at." One wonders how Kunstler would have fared in the reign of James II.

Modern judges, no matter how prosecution-minded, can hardly browbeat defendants, lawyers, and juries in the style of Scroggs and Jeffreys. Still, they are not wholly defenseless. The Supreme Court, which has not recently been accused of excessive harshness to criminal defendants, made that very clear in *Illinois v. Allen* (397 U.S. 337), decided in 1970. The constitutional right to be present at one's own trial and personally to confront witnesses does not deprive a trial judge of power to remove an obstreperous defendant from the courtroom, or to cause him to be gagged and shackled. He can punish the defendant—as well as lawyers and spectators—for contempt, although it is doubtful that such punishment can constitutionally exceed six months imprisonment even if, like Judge Hoffman, the court attempts to circumvent the restriction by inflicting separate penalties, aggregating several years in the hoosegow, for separate incidents of contempt. Even Justice Douglas concurred in the Court's decision, though he thought the Court should have waited for a genuine "political" case (Allen was a commonplace robber whose trial had no "political or subversive overtones") before laying down so much and so important law on the control of courtroom disruption.

Finally, counsel can be disbarred, as Harry Sacher learned. This presents no serious problem when the lawyer violates the Canons of Ethics by himself engaging in "undignified or discourteous conduct which is degrading to a tribunal." Things are not so simple when counsel's own conduct amounts to nothing worse than an exaggeration of ordinary forensic bad manners, as by continuing to argue and object after the judge has made a ruling and told him to sit down.

21

Most of the conduct for which Judge Hoffman punished Kunstler and his junior, Leonard Weinglass, was of this description. The court also found (with what justice a typed transcript cannot reveal) that Kunstler had shouted and pointed at the judge in a disrespectful manner. (Kunstler conceded that his tone was "angry.") He undoubtedly accused the judge of "outrageous" statements, and described his conduct as a "disgrace" and the trial as a "legal lynching," to the accompaniment of cries of "Right on!" from the spectators. Some lawyers would describe this as "discourteous conduct" within the meaning of the Canon; the New Bar would probably characterize it as mere wholesome frankness. (As Kunstler phrased it, "I was not insulting. I told you the truth this morning.")

The really serious interferences with orderly proceedings at the Chicago trial, as at others, were the work of the defendants and their supporters in the audience. Judge Hoffman found that Kunstler "encouraged and approved of such behavior" and that he "fanned the flames of the disorder with inciting comments." This may well be true, and Kunstler declared on one occasion that he approved of his clients' "groans" at some ruling of the court. But again it is hard for one who has only the bare record before him to say to what extent the defendants were egged on by counsel. It is doubtful that they needed much encouragement; most of them would probably have behaved about as they did if they had been represented by the Dean of the Harvard Law School. It does seem clear that Kunstler made little or no effort to persuade his clients to behave; but the extent of his duty to do so is less clear. The American Bar Association's Code of Professional Responsibility does not seem to deal squarely with the matter. The American College of Trial Lawyers takes the position that a lawyer has a duty to "advise any client appearing in a courtroom of the kind of behavior expected and required of him there, and to prevent

22

him, so far as lies within the lawyer's power, from creating disorder or disruption in the courtroom." I question how far it lies within the power of Kunstler or Weinglass, or any other lawyer, to compel the likes of Bobby Seale, Jerry Rubin, or Abbie Hoffman to conform to rules of decorum made for souls less free than theirs.

The New Bar is very positive that criminal law, as it exists in this country today, is simply one more instrument of tyranny which ought to be broken up and cast on the dust heap of history. But, as is commonly the case with the thinkers of the New Left, they have not described the judicial system with which they would replace it; indeed, I doubt that any of them—certainly not Kunstler—have very clear ideas on the subject. Most of their clients find much to admire in Dr. Castro's People's Courts, which are about as likely to acquit the accused as were their namesakes, the Nazi *Volksgerichtshöfe.* The New Bar and its clients would, of course, deny, and with unfeigned indignation, the accusation of fascism, whether leveled against themselves or Dr. Castro or Chairman Mao. It is true that their People's Courts would punish somewhat different sorts of crime and crimethink. It is also true that "fascist" is a word of very uncertain meaning—as an epithet, it is used as freely and loosely as "communist" was used fifteen or twenty years ago. George Orwell probably came closer than anyone else to defining it:

> By "Fascism" they [*i.e.,* ordinary people] mean, roughly speaking, something cruel, unscrupulous, arrogant, obscurantist, anti-liberal and anti-working class. . . . Almost any English person would accept "bully" as a synonym for "Fascist."

That seems to me a pretty accurate description of all the factions of the SDS, the Black Panthers, and many of the New Bar's other clients. (The nominal Marxists among them sometimes speak favorably of working people, but their real contempt for blue-collar workers is plain enough, and often explicit.) The New Bar—being, after all, lawyers—have been bred in a different tradition. In one compartment of their minds there is real respect for the Bill of Rights. But they are as a group highly emotional and impressionable, and they believe that a lawyer who does not love his clients, who does not wholeheartedly accept their values, is no better than a prostitute. To the extent that they model their thinking and their conduct on those of their clients, they bring themselves too within Orwell's definition.

Esquire, 1971

Crime, Punishment, and the
Limits of Vengeance

YALE LAW JOURNAL, 1959

———

In *Star Wormwood*, Curtis Bok, a justice of the Supreme
Court of Pennsylvania, has written an horrendous paradigm,
dedicated to the proposition that our criminal and penal system is founded on vengeance, which is a bad thing, and that
someday we shall learn to regard this system "with the same
horrified wonder as we now look back upon the Spanish In-
quisition." [1] His simple tale may be shortly summarized.
Roger, an adolescent of seventeen, brought up in the depths
of the Depression, never far from hunger and often close to
starvation, obtains temporary employment tending the furnace in a high school. On an evening when he has not eaten
for three days, he catches a rabbit in the nearby woods and,
in violation of the school rules, prepares to grill it in the furnace. Thus engaged, he is surprised by one Angela, a horrid
child of thirteen, the sister of an acquaintance. Angela's disposition, never very sweet, has been soured by the fear that
she may be pregnant by her brother, who has just broken off

1. P. 50.

an incestuous relationship of some weeks by raping her. Startled, Roger drops the rabbit on the coals, where it is quickly incinerated. Worse, Angela threatens to report his violation of the rules and have him fired. Enraged at losing his dinner and alarmed at the prospect of delation to the authorities, he seizes Angela and shakes her. She screams and struggles. To silence her, he grasps her by the throat. At this point the usual red mist of temporary insanity descends; when Roger comes to himself Angela is dead of anoxemia, fracture or dislocation of the cervical vertebrae, and asphyxia. Aware that he is in an awkward position, but unaware that a human cadaver is one of the least combustible things in the world, Roger determines to thrust her in the furnace. The top part of Angela goes in fairly easily, but the hindquarters stick. As he heaves and pushes, an arm flops out of the furnace; grasping it, he burns his fingers and thrusts them in his mouth. Thereupon events proceed as in the *Dissertation on Roast Pig*. The meat is described (on what evidence is not clear) as tender, although rare, the crackling being particularly savory. In short, Roger consumes a generous portion of Angela. Thereupon he is sick. He flees the mess in panic, wanders in a trance, is caught, and freely confesses.

So far a homely annal, and one which, bar the *outré* detail of anthropophagy, might almost be described as commonplace. Whether it actually happened or not I can't make out, but that is not very important, except to the extent that the author may intend the reader to infer that the execution of boys of eighteen is a common thing.[2] But now Roger is

2. At one point the author refers to his protagonist as "the person here called Roger Haike," p. 51, which seems to imply that the story is based on fact. I have the authority of the Supreme Court of Pennsylvania for the statement that in that Commonwealth only one person under the age of nineteen has ever suffered the death penalty. See Commonwealth v. Green, 151 A.2d 241, 246 (Pa. 1959). That person, one Alexander M. Williams, was eighteen at the time of his execution in 1931 and seventeen at the time of the murder for which he was exe-

fed into the machinery of that penal law of which Justice Bok takes so dim a view; he is indicted for murder, rape, and mutilating a dead body. The iniquities of the system are shortly manifested. The District Attorney has a paunch and a sloping forehead; [3] he leers [4] and makes coarse puns; [5] crowning outrage, he has a mustache with sharp waxed ends. [6] As for the trial judge, the less said about him the better. Having "a head full of sawdust and the soul of a man-eating shark," he intends to murder Roger; [7] he is "weak and unpredictable," [8] unlike the majority of man-eating sharks; he actually wants to be appointed to the State Supreme Court. [9] The jury's attitude to Roger is concisely stated; they want to "burn him for sure." [10] The Bad Guys win; Roger is convicted and sentenced to death. A three-judge court turns down his motion for a new trial. Besides the trial judge, it consists of one who is weak, and one who, in addition to being toothy and brisk, is the kind of Judge Jeffreys who votes to uphold a verdict if no errors appear in the record. [11] The

---

cuted, *id.* at 246 n.6; from the standpoint of chronology, he might be Roger Haike. I have been unable to find any report of Williams' case and so don't know whether his personality, his crime, or his trial resembled Roger Haike's. It is possible, of course, that Justice Bok went outside Pennsylvania for his facts. At any rate, it is obvious that Justice Bok's vivid imagination has supplied a great deal—notably as to the states of mind of the actors—which could not be documented from any legal record. If Justice Bok did start from an actual case, what he has done with it is distantly reminiscent of Theodore Dreiser's treatment, in *An American Tragedy*, of People v. Gillette, 191 N.Y. 107, 83 N.E. 680 (1908). I intend no other comparison of the two works.

3. P. 98.
4. P. 73.
5. P. 109.
6. Pp. 98, 109. The reputation of the bar for charm is partially restored by defense counsel, who is not only boyish, but has rumpled hair. Pp. 97, 124.
7. P. 43.
8. P. 77.
9. Pp. 119, 127.
10. P. 123.
11. P. 126.

Supreme Court, having "brushed aside" defense counsel's arguments, affirms in "remote and bloodless" language.[12] So Roger is electrocuted, most unpleasantly; the execution involves seven minutes of "smoking and sizzling and broiling." [13]

What moral are we to draw, what lesson do we learn, from all this Grand Guignol, aside from the obvious one that no system of justice, however enlightened, ought to be administered by such hyenas as the author has depicted? Justice Bok, whose fondness for rich, sonorous, uplifting rhetoric of a generally humanitarian cast occasionally gets the better of his fundamental common sense, draws quite a number, some probably sound, some debatable, some, I fear, palpable pishposh. Most of them are contained in the chapters of commentary which follow each section of the book (Crime, Trial, and Execution) and which are based on a series of lectures delivered by him at the University of Virginia Law School in 1957. Briefly summarized, his major conclusions seem to be:

1. The concept of punishment is evil.[14]

2. Capital punishment is particularly evil.[15]

3. There are no criminals, "but only sick men, socially or medically or both." [16]

4. The role of the courts, and of trial, in criminal cases should be limited to the assessment of facts, not including the mental condition of the accused. Indeed, the adversary trial should be abolished and replaced by "impartial inquiry" [17]—by whom is not stated.

5. After conviction, the psychiatrists, psychologists, and sociologists are to roll up their sleeves and have at the inva-

12. P. 173.   13. Pp. 183–84.
14. P. 199.   15. Pp. 102, 111, 187, 196.
16. P. 226.   17. Pp. 145–46, 150.

lid.[18] Their decision as to the appropriate therapy should have no necessary relation to the symptom of which he has been convicted; a misdemeanant may require permanent incarceration, a murderer a friendly chat with his psychiatrist.[19] In some cases, the malady may be so severe as to require that radical remedies, such as gassing or electrocution, be exhibited.[20]

6. The protection of society from further crime is the only intelligent approach. Vengeance will get us nowhere.[21]

Let us consider first the last proposition, which is fundamental to the others. For this utilitarian view of the law there is, of course, much respectable authority, none more eminent than Francis Bacon, who put it more broadly: "The end and purpose which the law ought to keep before its eyes, and at which it ought to aim its commands and penalties, is none other than that the citizens may live happily." [22] If this be accepted, as it should and probably would be by most modern lawyers, political scientists, and even politicians, there is no a priori reason (leaving aside, for the moment, the purely theological) to reject the idea of punishment as punishment; the question is simply whether fines or imprisonment or execution (or, for that matter, corporal punishment) may in some cases have something to contribute

18. P. 146.
19. Pp. 148–49, 219.
20. Pp. 194, 205–07.
21. Pp. 148, 190, 207.
22. BACON, DE AUGMENTIS SCIENTIARUM, Lib. viii, Cap. 3, Aph. 5. The translation is my own; my excuse is that the passage seems to be one of the additions which Bacon made in the process of putting his English writings into Latin and which he never got around to wording in his own English. It is part of the "*Exemplum Tractatus de Iustitia Universali, sive de Fontibus Iuris, in uno Titulo, per Aphorismos,*" which is appended to the third chapter of the eighth book. In the original it reads, "*Finis enim et scopus, quem leges intueri atque ad quem iussiones et sanctiones suas dirigere debent, non alius est, quam ut cives feliciter degant.*"

to the happiness of the citizenry, whether as a deterrent, or by ridding the community of a pest, or even by gratifying the public's desire for vengeance.[23]

Justice Bok's parable aids the objective consideration of this question not at all, for it presents a situation ideally unsuited to the use of punishment for any of the foregoing purposes. If a similar adolescent should find himself in similar circumstances, it is unlikely that he would reflect upon or be deterred by Roger's fate; Roger himself is not likely again to be dangerous to the community; and the part of the public whose desire for vengeance is gratified by the electrocution of a lonely, scared seventeen-year-old is probably not large and certainly not entitled to consideration. But what we learn about penology from Roger's case may not prove to be valid when we come to ponder what ought to be done with Al Capone or Albert B. Fall or Ernst Kaltenbrunner. *Star Wormwood*'s approach to crime and criminals may be nearly as sentimental and faulty as a general approach to the problem as the let-'em-fry attitude of a tabloid newspaper whooping up a crime wave.[24]

23. At one point (p. 150) Justice Bok says, rather inconsistently, "I am careful not to say let us abolish punishment, for the word has the root sense of penitence, but let us abolish a criminal system of laws and sanctions based on vengeance." I am not sure what the first clauses of this sentence mean. Etymologically, it would be nearer the truth to say that penitence has the root sense of punishment, for "poenitentia" is plainly a derivative of "poena." Certainly no Roman ever thought that "punire" meant to repent; in some contexts, in fact, it meant not merely to punish, but to revenge. Possibly the idea in Justice Bok's mind is that punishment may contribute to the cure of the criminal's psyche by meeting his need for atonement.

24. In all fairness, it ought to be noted that Justice Bok's actual dealings with criminals since his elevation to the Supreme Court have been considerably less starry-eyed than some of his homilies in *Star Wormwood* might cause the reader to suppose. In three cases he has voted with the majority to affirm convictions of murder and in two to affirm the dismissal of a convicted murderer's petition for a writ of habeas corpus. Commonwealth v. Wilson, 394 Pa. 588, 148 A.2d 234 (1959); Commonwealth v. Novak, 395 Pa. 199, 150 A.2d 102 (1959);

The fact is, of course, that the infliction of the death penalty, or even imprisonment, is almost always disagreeable to an intelligent, sane, and civilized man, such as Justice Bok. "Almost always," because for most of us, perhaps even for Justice Bok, there is some crime so monstrous that human wrath—that is, a plain desire for vengeance—erupts through the thickest crust of civilization. Thus, if one questions opponents of capital punishment, he discovers that a surprising number of them are willing to make an exception in favor of the Nazi war criminals. The late Mr. Justice Murphy, though not in principle opposed to punishment, was ordinarily a most clement man, anxious to give to those convicted of crime the benefit of every doubt. In one case,[25] however, he dissented sharply because he thought the conviction and punishment ought to be upheld. The criminals were three Georgia police officers who had brutally murdered a Negro accused of a minor offense—a crime which was probably outrageous beyond all others to Mr. Justice Murphy. It is interesting to speculate on the kind of tract Justice Bok might have composed if he had taken the *Screws* case for his starting point.

Moreover, it is just possible that vengeance as a motive of punishment may not always be so indefensible as most modern writers assume it to be. The rejection of vengeance as a

---

Commonwealth v. Clanton, 395 Pa. 521, 151 A.2d 88 (1959); Commonwealth *ex rel.* Norman v. Banmiller, 395 Pa. 232, 149 A.2d 881 (1959); Commonwealth *ex rel.* Bolish v. Banmiller, 151 A.2d 480 (Pa. 1959). In two cases he has concurred with the majority in reversing convictions of murder and in one in vacating a sentence of death and directing the imposition of life imprisonment. Commonwealth v. Edwards, 394 Pa. 335, 147 A.2d 313 (1959) (defendant aged fourteen); Commonwealth v. Davis, 396 Pa. 158, 150 A.2d 863 (1959); Commonwealth v. Green, 151 A.2d 241 (Pa. 1959) (defendant aged fifteen). In only one case (involving a sex murderer who was found mentally defective but neither legally nor medically insane) has he dissented (without opinion) from the affirmation of a death sentence. Commonwealth v. Graves, 394 Pa. 429, 147 A.2d 416 (1959).

25. Screws v. United States, 325 U.S. 91, 134 (1945).

31

motive for punishment by human agency has, of course, a sound theological basis; "for it is written, Vengeance *is* mine; I will repay, saith the Lord." [26] It can be argued that the citizens are happier if they believe that there is such a thing as abstract justice; it can also be argued that for most of them, for a long time to come at least, the concept of justice will include the notion that crimes which they regard as really reprehensible, or criminals whom they regard as really wicked, should not go unpunished—regardless of whether the punishment improves the criminal, or deters other potential criminals. So long as the citizen was convinced that the wicked man, though he seemed to be spreading himself like a green bay tree [27] and showed no sign whatsoever of a troubled conscience, would fry posthumously, that innate desire for justice—or vengeance—was satisfied. But, in the words of George Orwell, "the major problem of our time is the decay of the belief in personal immortality. . . ." [28] If that citizen begins to suspect that the malefactor may rest post-mortem quite as soundly as the rest of us, and maybe in a larger and more stylish mausoleum, it is perhaps pardonable for him to reconsider the merits of earthly vengeance—so long, of course, as the means of that vengeance do not diminish the citizens' happiness by brutalizing them or making the criminal a more dangerous criminal than he was before. Possibly all this is sophistry, but I do not think the rights and wrongs of punishment are quite so simple as the reader of *Star Wormwood* might be led to suppose.

At any rate it is undoubtedly true that punishment of the ordinary criminal, who (as Justice Bok rightly observes) [29] is

26. Romans 12:19. St. Paul's statement paraphrases Moses. Deuteronomy 32:35.

27. Psalms 37:35.

28. ORWELL, *Looking Back on the Spanish War*, in ENGLAND YOUR ENGLAND AND OTHER ESSAYS 151, 174 (1953); see HOLLIS, A STUDY OF GEORGE ORWELL 43 (1956).

29. P. 190.

much more likely to be poor and ignorant than wicked in any meaningful sense of that word, can at best be a disagreeable necessity to a decent man. Such a man tries at least to purge it of its connotation of vengeance, and he searches for alternative methods of preventing crime. Thus, Plato, who was not a lawyer,

> was not content with deterring from theft a man who still continued to be a thief at heart, with restraining a son who hated his mother from beating his mother. The only obedience on which he set much value was the obedience which an enlightened understanding yields to reason, and which a virtuous disposition yields to precepts of virtue. He really seems to have believed that, by prefixing to every law an eloquent and pathetic exhortation, he should, to a great extent, render penal enactments superfluous.[30]

Justice Bok, being a lawyer and having the advantage over Plato of some twenty-three additional centuries of penological experience, presumably takes little stock in eloquent and pathetic exhortations, at least when addressed to the criminals themselves; his preferred alternative is the currently more fashionable and probably much more rational one of substituting therapeutic treatment for punishment of the criminal. But the facts that the infliction of punishment (except in hot anger) is unpleasant, and that punishment may not be the only way of dealing with all criminals, should not blind us to its possible value as a deterrent. In the absence of statistics more convincing than any which now exist, we cannot be sure how great that value is, or even whether it exists at all, but it seems intrinsically likely that fear of punishment exerts a ponderable restraining influence on at least one very

30. MACAULAY, *Essay on Lord Bacon*, in BIOGRAPHICAL ESSAYS 118 (1886).

important class of criminals, about whom Justice Bok has little or nothing to say [31]—those who commit crimes for money, as a business. The delegates to the recent Apalachin convention exemplify this class; so do securities swindlers. Such men are not usually mentally ill in any normal sense of that term; even their greed and egocentricity probably do not pass whatever limit is set by our society. They are characteristically quite rational, and if they believe that the risk of punishment for a particular crime outweighs its financial rewards, they commonly eschew that crime. It is, for example, widely believed among cops, journalists, and lawyers that such criminals are rather careful to avoid violations of federal law, because they believe the federal police to be more efficient, and federal prosecutors and courts less amenable to political influence, than those in some other jurisdictions. Securities swindling, though by no means extinct, is rarer, pettier, and less blatant than it used to be; a large part of this improvement is almost certainly due to the development of a healthy fear of the Securities and Exchange Commission among those whose criminous proclivities tend in that direction. Income-tax evaders are another class on whom the fear of punishment probably has a powerful deterrent effect. The main trouble with punishment as a deterrent seems to be— as Justice Bok recognizes [32]—our defective system of law enforcement, which makes punishment most uncertain. Perhaps, before we heave punishment for deterrent purposes out

31. He lists five causes of crime: failure by the police and courts to solve more than one crime in five; liquor; bad home environment; "social weakness," such as poverty, and mass media like motion pictures and television which portray crime and violence; and "special reasons," such as the need of money for food, rent, and doctors. Pp. 187–88. None of these, except the first, seems an adequate explanation of the likes of Al Capone or Joey Fay. There seems to be room for at least a sixth major cause—simple desire to make a lot of money and be a big shot without having to engage in tedious work.

32. Pp. 208, 217. He thinks that in this country less than one crime in five is punished. Pp. 191, 208.

34

of the penological pharmacopœia, we ought to give it a better try—not by making punishments more savage (indeed, there is good reason to believe that there would be more convictions for some offenses if the statutory penalty were more consonant with juries' views of the seriousness of the offense) but by trying to make them more certain, even if that entails spending more money on law enforcement.

Limits of space prevent further dilation on Justice Bok's major theme, punishment. But some of his collateral theses deserve comment. In particular, I have profound doubts about the proposition that the adversary trial is part of the obsolete system of vengeance and punishment and ought to be replaced by "impartial inquiry." Justice Bok appears to believe that if in the future burglars are sent to a correctional institution which is more like a college or vocational school than a jail,[33] a man accused of burglary will not mind very much if he is convicted; "the same energy he now exerts in trial he would exert, under a new system, in improving himself and shortening his period of detention." [34] Justice Bok is plainly a good man and a man of parts; I believe him to be far superior to the common herd of judges. Therefore, I write with pain my best critical judgment on this proposition, which is that it is pernicious tripe. If I am accused of rape or larceny or barratry, I care not that the state pen may have been transformed into the likeness of The Homestead at Hot Springs, with golf, tennis, and psychiatry; I am going to holler that I didn't do it, and so are most other men in such a situation. Moreover, I am going to want the benefit, such as it is, of the presumption of innocence, counsel of my own choice, the right to cross-examine and to call witnesses, the right to appeal, and all the rest of the paraphernalia of our familiar adversary trial, possibly even including a jury of

33. P. 219.   34. P. 146.

my peers. I know of no lawyer who thinks of the adversary system as perfect, and I know of none who is sure he knows a better way to find the truth. I want to know a great deal more about Justice Bok's "impartial inquiry," especially who is to conduct it, before I start agitating for abolition of the adversary trial in criminal cases.

I view with suspicion almost as profound the idea that "the new form of sentence should include a short and flexible minimum, a long maximum, and an intermediate period, fixed by a diagnostic or parole board, of psychiatric, medical, and sociological procedures of an increasingly educative nature," [35] though I know the concept is no novelty to the law. The plain and short meaning of this is that an offender may be locked up until a panel of psychiatrists and sociologists decide that they like his attitude. That is not very far from locking him up in the first place for having wrong attitudes; and if *that* concept is adopted into our penal system, we are ready for totalitarian penology, complete with educative labor camps (the term *concentration camp* comes later) for social misfits—which, of course, is very far from Justice Bok's intent. *"Arbeit macht frei,"* read the huge sign over the gate of Dachau.[36] Until I acquire a great deal more confidence than I now have in the infallibility of psychiatrists and social workers, I prefer to leave price tags on crimes—and to retain the rest of due process of law. Says Justice Bok, "We think highly of due process because we want to keep inviolate our right to take an eye for an eye: revenge protected by rules of

35. P. 149.
36. U.S. OSS SECTION, SEVENTH ARMY, REPORT ON DACHAU 20 (1945). This was amplified, and the ghastly caricature of Justice Bok's "sociological procedures of an increasingly educative nature" pointed up, by a sign painted in large white letters on one of the buildings: *"Es gibt einen Weg zur Freiheit. Seine Meilensteine heissen: Gehorsam, Sauberkeit, Nüchternheit, Fleiss."* (There is a road to freedom. Its milestones are called: Obedience, Cleanliness, Temperance, Industry.) See *id.* at 19.

36

fair play amounts to holy war." [37] Comment on that one is, I hope, superfluous.

Finally, Justice Bok supports his views on capital punishment with some purely theological arguments. In the first place, there are powerful arguments against (and for) capital punishment without need of recourse to revealed religion; in the second place, I find Justice Bok's theological arguments theologically unconvincing. The Sixth Commandment, he informs us, "does not read: 'Thou shalt not kill except by due process of law.' " [38] True enough, but precisely that construction has been given it since its promulgation; moreover, it seems to have been the understanding of the Draughtsman.[39] For that matter, the literal wording of the Commandment does not exclude beef cattle, rats, mosquitoes, or pneumococci. Perhaps anticipating some such objections, Justice Bok invokes the New Testament, citing the Pericope Adulterae, the story of the woman taken in adultery.[40] But the thrust of those supremely moving verses is surely not a mere denunciation of capital punishment as distinct from other penalties. I do not pretend to know what Jesus thought about capital punishment. But when Justice Bok tells me that one "will look far before he finds in the life of Jesus the authority to take a life for a life," [41] I find that I need look no farther than the very first of the Synoptic Gospels,[42] and

37. P. 150.
38. P. 102. This statement actually appears in the closing speech of defense counsel, but it is fair to attribute to an author the sentiments he puts in the mouth of his Good Guy. He says practically the same thing *in propria persona*. P. 196.
39. See, *e.g.*, Genesis 9:6; Exodus 21:12, 22:18, 31: 14, 35:2; Leviticus 20:2, 21:9; *cf.* I Kings 21:10.
40. John 8:3–11. Justice Bok's reference is at 196. Many modern scholars suspect the story to be a late addition to the Gospel. See MENCKEN, TREATISE ON THE GODS 185, 186 (2d ed. 1946); STREETER, THE FOUR GOSPELS: A STUDY OF ORIGINS 36, 89, 123–24 (rev. 1930).
41. P. 111.
42. Then came to Jesus scribes and Pharisees, which were of Jerusalem, saying,

to the oldest of them,[43] to find such authority for taking a life for an offense which seems to us less heinous than murder. And when he says to me that not merely the taking but the *giving* of life is "God's right alone," [44] I begin to wonder whether he means to espouse the zany doctrine that the hellish works of modern medicine ought to be rejected by Christians as impudent interference with Providence. Probably not; I suspect that the reference to giving life is a mere rhetorical flourish, for not only is Justice Bok a Quaker (a sect which is, to the best of my knowledge, quite free of such ideas), but his obvious respect for the psychiatric branch of the medical profession makes it unlikely that he rejects the rest of it.

I suspect, indeed, that a fondness for lush, orotund, and, if the truth must be told, somewhat flatulent preaching has led Justice Bok into more than one statement which he would be too sensible to put into an opinion delivered from the bench. I pass by such sentences as "Freud has set a great wind blowing in man's mind, and the dark flowers that grow there are swaying before it, needing to be gathered and understood"; [45] at least it seems to mean *something*. But what are we to make of such passages as "Justice should be the little side chapel where the mysteries and the miracles of the

---

2. Why do thy disciples transgress the tradition of the elders? for they wash not their hands when they eat bread.
3. But he answered and said unto them, Why do ye also transgress the commandment of God by your tradition?
4. For God commanded, saying, Honour thy father and mother: and, He that curseth father or mother, let him die the death.
5. But ye say, Whosoever shall say to *his* father or *his* mother, It is a gift, by whatsoever thou mightest be profited by me;
6. And honour not his father or his mother, *he shall be free.* Thus have ye made the commandment of God of none effect by your tradition.

Matthew 15:1–6.
43. Mark 7:1–13.
44. P. 111.
45. P. 58.

38

stolid law take place"? [46] After weeks of meditation, interspersed with periodic rereadings of that sentence, in the hope that a night's sleep would bring sudden and blinding comprehension, I give up; for me, it is as devoid of meaning as the average extract from *Science and Health with Key to the Scriptures*. There are a great many similar sentences, paragraphs, and pages. They are particularly depressing when they come from a man who can write the honest and excellent prose which, for example, is found in the description of a courtroom at pages 63 to 65, or the description of a state penitentiary and its death cells at pages 152 to 157.

There is also, as I have tried to indicate, a good deal of sense in *Star Wormwood*. It is certainly true, for example, that men of the first ability ought to be encouraged to practice criminal law and to serve as trial judges.[47] It is probably true that the concept of treating the criminal rather than punishing the crime will and should play an ever larger role in our penology. There are many other sound and shrewd observations,[48] though it will take a discriminating reader to cull them out.

Having said all this, I conclude nonetheless that *Star Wormwood* is worth reading, if it is not gulped down uncritically. It has indeed (if the reader is not hypnotized into agreement by the mellifluous roll of Justice Bok's prose) one of the highest virtues possible to a book: it provokes thought.

———

The problems of penology are certainly no nearer solution today than they were when Justice Bok unburdened himself. Indeed, the science is probably in worse shape now than it

46. *Ibid.*   47. P. 151.
48. *E.g.*, pp. 138, 189, 194.

was then. We seem to have more criminals than any civilization ever heard of and less agreement on what to do about them. I claim no expertise. Lawyers could do more than they have done to make swifter and fairer the trials of those who are actually apprehended, but their ideas on the treatment of convicted criminals are entitled to no more weight than those of reporters, sociologists, cops, politicians, clergymen, or criminals.

I accept, because it seems obvious sense, the proposition that the only really effective way to reduce the incidence of crime (or at any rate violent crime) is to reduce the incidence of ignorance and poverty. The descendants of the Irish, Italians, Poles, Jews,* and so-called native Americans who used to staff the slum gangs of New York and Chicago are all hot for Law and Order today. But ignorance and poverty, even if we were to devote to them far more time, effort, and money than we have yet been willing to expend, are stubborn and intractable. Even if we reduced them to whatever minimum would exist in an ideal polity, there would still be an ample supply of crime. A Utopia in which 100 percent of a large population shared the same ethics, and voluntarily obeyed the same code of conduct, is unimaginable to me, for I cannot wholly dismiss original sin, or natural viciousness, as a cause of crime. Many prosperous, educated people commit crimes, and most poor, ignorant people do not.

Our ancestors, who troubled their heads very little about

* The Jews are justly proud of the fact that they got out of the slums faster than most of the other poor immigrants who swarmed into America's big cities before World War I. But even they contributed their share of notable thugs—e.g., Monk Eastman, Big Jack Zelig, Gyp the Blood, Whitey Lewis, Dopey Benny Fein, Chowderhead Cohen, and many others. The Chinese, although among the most law-abiding of the immigrants to the New World, produced hatchetmen of singular ferocity in the days when the On Leong and Hip Sing Tongs were struggling for control of the profits from gambling, dope, and prostitution. See generally ASBURY, THE GANGS OF NEW YORK (1928).

the socio-economic causes of crime, or whether it was to be blamed on the criminal or society at large, had penological principles which were at least simple and generally accepted, however inhumane. Moreover, such evidence as there is suggests that in most times and places they kept crime down to levels which were tolerable to the community, and without great expense. The Romans, for example, relied heavily on corporal punishment. If the offender was able-bodied, he might be condemned to the mines, the galleys, or some other form of productive labor so hard, disagreeable, and dangerous (in a technologically backward economy) that its manpower requirements could not be satisfied either by free workers or valuable slaves. If there seemed to be no utility in preserving the criminal, the Caesars had, of course, no scruples about capital punishment—generally in some form calculated to increase the popular enjoyment of a Roman holiday. Medieval penology was not essentially different. Until well into the nineteenth century, capital and corporal punishment, the gallows, the stocks, or the cat, plus sentences to the galleys, the treadmill, or such tasks as picking oakum, were standard cures for criminality.

For better or worse (better, I think), few existing governments are so ruthless; even Russian penology seems to have become comparatively humane (at least for non-political offenders) since Stalin's death. Although the death penalty remains on the books in most jurisdictions, in practice we limit ourselves to imprisonment under theoretically humane conditions. As preventers of crime our penitentiaries and reformatories have on the whole been dismal failures. They do in all probability serve some deterrent purpose: confinement in many prisons is in practice a more scarifying experience than corporal punishment. How many young robbers, given a free choice between the cat-o'-nine-tails and two years at the Happy Meadows Study and Treatment Center for Boys (or whatever euphonious and charming name is given the

41

reform school), would choose the latter? But it is notorious that they almost never succeed in what is ostensibly their principal goal, which is to reform the criminal and turn him into a useful and contented member of society. It is a truism that the ordinary convict (especially if he be young) emerges from the pen a meaner, more embittered and incorrigible criminal than he was when he entered.

We cling to imprisonment as our principal therapy for crime from force of habit; because the prisoner's sufferings, being out of sight and not (as a rule) deliberately inflicted, do not affront our sensibilities; and because it undoubtedly serves the useful purpose of removing a pest from circulation for a longer or shorter period. But it is enormously expensive and typically produces nothing except mailbags or license plates of inconsiderable value.

We are not likely to return to the rough old remedies. I cannot imagine even the least civilized elements of a modern population crowding Shea Stadium on Sunday afternoon to watch burglars battling with bears, lions, and each other. But better methods of deterrence and even reform are at least imaginable. Rare, exceptional correctional institutions really do seem to succeed in educating and otherwise reshaping some of their inmates; at least their graduates have a rate of recidivism which is appreciably lower than the average. More could be done with rewards and incentives. Perhaps we should not reject out of hand the idea that corporal punishment might do some criminals more good (or at least less harm) than the treatments now in vogue. As Justice Bok obliquely recognized, there is probably nothing to do with some criminals except to remove them permanently from society by incarcerating or (maybe more humanely) hanging them. Penologists have plenty of ideas, and some of them deserve a better try than they have had. Justice Bok, at bottom, was not wrong-headed, but only muddle-headed.

Pricing Death and Mutilation:
The Trouble with Torts

YALE LAW JOURNAL, 1960

MELVIN BELLI, author of *Modern Damages*, blushingly styles himself The King of Torts, and so he is—or at least of the great province of that noble discipline which is concerned with sudden death and maiming, "of most disastrous chances, of moving accidents by flood and field."[1] Not for him such quaint, esoteric torts as the wanton, reckless, and willful promulgation of an *Accounting Research Bulletin* on declining-balance depreciation.[2] But within the field of personal injury, which probably accounts for the bulk of tort litigation, Mr. Belli can fairly claim to be the reigning monarch. His verdicts are the highest, and so, presumably, are his fees; his publications are the most voluminous; and, it may be added, his publicity is the most flamboyant, in a

1. *Othello*, act I, scene 3.
2. See Appalachian Power Co. v. American Institute of Certified Public Accountants, 177 F. Supp. 345 (S.D.N.Y.), *aff'd per curiam*, 268 F.2d 844 (2d Cir. 1959). This pioneering effort to push back the frontier of the law of torts got short shrift from an unimaginative judiciary.

field whose leading practitioners are rarely shrinking violets.

Moreover, that field is a most important one. In addition to its enormous social and economic significance, it is probably, along with criminal law, the part of the law which impinges most directly on the consciousness of the average citizen and by which that citizen tends to form his judgment of law and lawyers. The problem of compensation for personal injury suffered at another's hands is certainly among the oldest in jurisprudence; *Homo Neanderthalensis* probably exercised his far from backward brain upon it (for we know he had a well-developed theology, which implies ideas on ethics), and there is today no tribe of savages so primitive as to lack definite ideas on the subject—and those ideas are often disconcertingly close to the ones still prevalent in the most progressive and high-toned jurisdictions. The one thing, in fact, on which there is nearly complete agreement among plaintiffs' lawyers (including Mr. Belli), defendants' lawyers, and professors is that our present system of compensation is antiquated, clumsy, expensive, and frequently unjust in its operation.[3] The defects in our system of determining appropriate damages for personal injury (leaving to one side, as outside the scope of *Modern Damages* and therefore of this review, the problems incident to adjudicating liability in the first place) are numerous and obvious; only the most salient need be mentioned.

1. Generally speaking, damages must be awarded once for all and in a lump; the plaintiff must, within a comparatively short time after the accident occurs, recover for *all* of his loss of earnings, medical expense, and pain and suffering —including those which he has yet to suffer and may never

3. See, *e.g.*, James, *The Columbia Study of Compensation for Automobile Accidents: An Unanswered Challenge*, 59 COLUM. L. REV. 408 (1959); Jones, *Evaluation and Settlement of a Personal Injury Damage Claim*, 1959 INS. L.J. 559.

suffer.[4] In many cases, of course, it is exceedingly difficult for doctors, let alone jurors, to make such a forecast with even a semblance of accuracy, and the difficulty is raised to the order of impossibility when it is required that this conjectural decrease in income and increase in outgo be capitalized in contemporary dollars. Moreover, while the purpose of the award is, of course, to put the victim in the same economic situation in which he would have been if the accident had never occurred (with appropriate lagniappe for his pain and suffering), the state of mind of the gratified recipient of a sudden and substantial (or even stupendous) bundle of cash is often and regrettably much less like that of a man who has traded future earnings for investment cash than like that of a man who has just won the Irish Sweepstakes.[5]

2. The evaluation of damages is at best inexact and at worst capricious. How can a jury or a judge calculate the effect of a broken nose on a spinster plaintiff's chance of making a profitable marriage? What is the cash value of a four-year-old to his parents? Of an amputated finger to an ambitious but maybe untalented student of the violin? Should a widow who is an overpowering cutie with a wide choice of rich second husbands receive lesser damages for the wrongful death of a husband than a relict who is painfully plain? It is hardly a matter for wonder that lay and judicial assessors

4. Fetter v. Beale, 1 Raym. 339, 91 Eng. Rep. 1122 (K.B. 1699), *aff'd sub nom.* Ferrer v. Beale, 1 Raym. 602, 91 Eng. Rep. 1361 (K.B. 1702). The plaintiff collected £11 for the defendant's tortious battery upon his skull. Thereafter, he developed alarming sequelae—"part of his skull by reason of the said battery came out of his head"—and sought additional damages. The defendant successfully pleaded in bar the original recovery, Chief Justice Holt remarking that when the case was originally tried before him, "the plaintiff and defendant appeared to be both in drink, and the jury did not well know which of them was in fault, and therefore they gave the less damages." One wonders whether this important principle of the common law would be the same if Fetter (or Ferrer) had been sober when his cranium was cracked.

5. See James, *supra* note 3, at 412; Jones, *supra* note 3, at 565–66.

wandering in such a maze too frequently give weight to such extraneous but tangible factors as the personality of the plaintiff or the picturesqueness of his injuries.

3. If it is possible to calculate medical expenses with some approach to exactness and to make guesses at loss of earnings which are at least educated, the intrinsic impossibility of pricing pain is such as to cause some commentators simply to throw up their hands and propose that this element of damages be abolished.[6] The one yardstick which naturally suggests itself to the juror—"what would I charge to suffer this pain myself?"—is also, as Mr. Belli points out,[7] the one which the court firmly instructs him to ignore. Yet damages for pain are often the largest component of an award.[8]

4. As noted above, the sum handed a successful plaintiff in theory is supposed to put him in the financial position he would have occupied if he had suffered no injury. In fact, as Mr. Belli frankly recognizes, a third or a half will normally go to pay his lawyer's contingent fee.[9] Courts, of course, shelter juries from such information as sternly as Victorian parents sheltered children from sex. Fortunately, the juries (like the children) usually know it anyhow and often take care of this item by inflating the rest of the damages; it has been suggested that in practice "pain and suffering" is frequently a term of art meaning "counsel fees."[10] I intend no pharisaical reprobation of the practice of charging such a substantial contingent fee. Given the present system of awarding compensation, it seems to be about the only way to assure competent representation of an impecunious plaintiff; "it can

6. E.g., GREEN, TRAFFIC VICTIMS—TORT LAW AND INSURANCE 88 (1958).
7. Pp. 18–19.
8. See Morris, *Liability for Pain and Suffering*, 59 COLUM. L. REV. 476, 479–80 (1959).
9. P. 29.
10. See Morris, *supra* note 8, at 477–78.

hardly be said as a general proposition that counsel who conscientiously satisfies himself of the merits before taking on an indigent plaintiff's case on a contingent basis is necessarily any less ethical than counsel who vigorously defends a clearly meritorious case because for so doing he is in receipt of a fat fee from a wealthy defendant." [11] Whether a system of compensation which entails such costs can and ought to be radically changed is, of course, quite another question.

5. The upshot is that an award which fairly compensates a claimant for his injuries, which is neither inadequate nor excessive, is so rare as to be practically unheard of. The layman, morosely perusing the insurance-company propaganda which accompanies the annual notice that his liability-insurance premium has been raised again, develops a stereotype of an imbecile jury, mesmerized by the baroque rhetoric of a wily ambulance chaser, lifting a plausible malingerer to sudden affluence. There is some truth in the picture, but probably not much. Mr. Belli, the Apostle of the Adequate Award, makes out a persuasive case for the proposition that, at least in cases of serious injury or death, the average award in most jurisdictions tends to be far too low. More, he makes the surprising, but apparently accurate, assertion that juries are habitually more niggardly than judges in making awards.[12] On the other hand, the undoubted rise in recent years in the cost of settling personal-injury claims (a rise which is too large to be accounted for merely by inflation) [13] may in large measure be attributable to the fact that the comparatively trivial injury is often grossly overcompensated—

11. Angoff v. Goldfine, 270 F.2d 185, 191 (1st Cir. 1959).
12. E.g., pp. 27, 33. Mr. Belli picks up somewhat unexpected support from a veteran member of the defendants' bar, who estimates on the basis of the experience of one large insurance company in the year 1958 that juries on the average give the plaintiff rather less than a fourth of the sum he is demanding. See Jones, *supra* note 3, at 559–60.
13. See James, *supra* note 3, at 411.

not so much by judges or juries as by the insurance companies themselves, who, penny wise and pound foolish, think to save litigation costs by compromising such claims without regard to merit.[14]

The subject matter of *Modern Damages* is therefore of vast importance, and few men are better qualified by experience to discuss that subject than is Mr. Belli. The more, then, is the pity that he has stuffed his opening chapters with claptrap and composed much of them in a style which makes it exceedingly hard to take his really valuable collection of data on damages as seriously as it deserves to be taken.

Of the three chapters of the present volume, chapter I, "Modern Damages in Perspective," is a disorganized editorial devoted to the general proposition that damages for personal injuries ought to be higher than they are. Here and there a nugget of worthwhile information gleams in the heap of dross—for example, the report that some insurance companies now deal with the problem of the future effects of plaintiff's injuries by handing him, along with damages for what he has already suffered, a paid-up insurance policy payable in the event that serious consequences actually develop.[15] But no real attempt is made to discuss or even to describe alternatives to the present system—possibly because Mr. Belli is personally very well satisfied with the essentials of that system, provided only that something is done to increase the size of awards. Specifically, Mr. Belli makes virtually no mention of the principal suggestion for reforming the law of personal injury where it most needs reform—the institution of some sort of Automobile Compensation Plan, analogous to workmen's compensation.[16] Chapter II, "History of the

14. See Jones, *supra* note 3, at 563–64.
15. Pp. 32–33.
16. Mr. Belli's superficial allusion to the problem is at 26–27. For a concise but informative treatment, see GREGORY & KALVEN, TORTS 743–83 (1959). Interest in such reforms is not limited to professors.

Law of Damages," is an ill-advised effort to give the humble
Claimants' Compensation Attorney (as he likes to call himself, in the manner of the Morticians, Realtors, Beauticians,
etc., etc.) the illusion that he practices a profession which is
not merely useful but full of book learning, by presenting, in
somewhat the style of a Hearst Sunday supplement, a history
and comparison of the law of torts in different times and
places. Leading off with a sonorous misquotation from
Shakespeare,[17] Mr. Belli pays his respects, *inter alia*, to Ham-
murabi, Moses, Confucius, Ulpian, Justinian, Mohammed,
and the fathers of the Common Law. It is probably impossible adequately to summarize this mass of jurisprudence in
eighty-three pages; certainly Mr. Belli has not done so.[18]
Moreover, granted that Mr. Belli is a busy man, with no time
for such pedantries as proofreading or the employment of a
dictionary, I cannot feel that the status of law as a learned
profession is enhanced by such astonishing phrases as "appellate judicial circumcision of awards." [19]

The State of Maine, which is not noted for rash sociological experi-
mentation, is seriously considering the creation of a state-administered
motor vehicle accident indemnity fund. See Opinion of the Justices, 155
Me. 125, 152 A.2d 494 (1959).

17. Mr. Belli's version, which he attributes simply to an inscription
"which appears above the entrance to the Archives Building in Washington," is "The past is but a prologue to the future." P. 64. The actual text is "What is past is prologue," *The Tempest*, act II, scene 1,
and it is in fact correctly quoted on the pedestal of one of the heroic
sculptures which adorn the National Archives Building—all of which
Mr. Belli might have learned by the simple expedient of consulting Bart-
lett. These errors, which of course are unimportant in themselves, are
symptomatic of Mr. Belli's slapdash approach to legal writing.

18. *Cf., e.g.*, the statement that "The Roman Legal System . . .
disappeared in about 650 A.D." P. 94. This is assuredly one of the most
summary dismissals ever accorded the Byzantine Empire. In particular,
it seems most unfair to the memory of Basil I, the Macedonian, who,
when not preoccupied with war or theology, turned his forceful personality and considerable talents to the modernization and revivification
of Justinian's Code. See 1 VASILIEV, HISTORY OF THE BYZANTINE EM-
PIRE 339–43 (2d ed. 1958).

19. P. 30. I learn from my own dictionary and the King James version that the word "circumcise," in addition to its primary meaning,

Chapter III, however, redeems the work. It is simply a state-by-state tabulation of significantly high awards, many of them unreported elsewhere, for wrongful death and various types of personal injury, accompanied both by shrewd practical comments and by figures on judicial salaries and average lawyers' incomes in the particular jurisdiction (although not, unfortunately, the fees of counsel in the individual cases reported). As might be expected, California (Belli's home ground) and New York set targets for the rest of the nation to shoot at when it comes to adequacy of awards for personal injury—for example, a California verdict of $85,000 for two broken legs and a broken cheekbone.[20] The states of the late Confederacy lag badly, particularly if the plaintiff is a Negro,[21] but show signs of improvement. In some jurisdictions at least, there seems to be an instructive correlation between the size of awards and the size of judicial salaries. These are, of course, merely examples; hundreds and maybe thousands of interesting conclusions can be extracted or deduced from Mr. Belli's figures.

At the very least, his chapter III ought to be a Golconda of information, comparable to Bowditch's *Practical Navigator*, for the lawyer who wants to know what his client ought to settle for, for the student or teacher of torts, and for those who, like myself, merely find facts fascinating.[22]

---

has a secondary meaning, to purify spiritually. *E.g.*, Colossians 2:11. I doubt, however, that Mr. Belli had in mind this somewhat uncommon usage, for his dislike of remittitur makes it unlikely that he would regard such circumscription of the jury's discretion as "spiritual purification."

20. P. 264.
21. P. 148.
22. I appreciate with peculiar keenness the practical value of *Modern Damages*, for, as it happens, I was once myself a personal-injury claimant and would have greatly benefited from Mr. Belli's *vade mecum* if I had had it. A massive marble table, negligently installed by a landlord, lit on my great toe, with excruciating results. I was at the time associated with a corporation-law firm which frequently handled private placements for insurance companies, and the consensus of my colleagues

Mr. Belli's collection of cases—which Professor Harper's introduction justly terms "a monumental piece of research" [23]—is, so far as I know, unique. It goes far toward meeting one of the major prerequisites to intelligent study and solution of the problem of compensation for wrongful death or injury, in that it brings up to date, and amplifies, some of the principal findings of the famous Columbia *Study of Compensation for Automobile Accidents* of 1932.[24] We can look forward with keen interest to the publication of Volume 2, which will contain further tabulations.

A word or so ought to be said about the album of LP records which accompanies the volume and which preserves for posterity a selection of Mr. Belli's more successful arguments to juries. On the strength of the first two chapters of *Modern Damages,* I expected to hear some pretty perfervid oratory— something along the line of the late Ol' Gene Talmadge rousing a rabble. I was completely wrong. Mr. Belli is an exponent of the soft sell, and he does it brilliantly. His statements were reasonable, lucid, and factual, and they thoroughly persuaded me; only on a replaying did I pick up here and there a subtle insertion of some fact not legally germane but likely to affect the jurors, such as incidental mention, in describing the background of a tragedy, of decedent's membership in a large fraternal organization with which some of the jurors probably had a connection. His voice was soft and pleasing, but not soapily so; he cooed no more than he bel-

---

was, roughly speaking, that I'd be lucky if I collected fifty dollars; the most senior of the lot seemed to think that if I didn't antagonize the landlord's insurer with the extortionate demand that it pay my medical expenses, it might be willing to overlook the damage to the table and the disturbance caused the landlord by my unseemly squawks of agony. Had Mr. Belli's work then been published, I might have learned (p. 780) that in the jurisdiction in question $4,000, exclusive of loss of earnings, is regarded as "adequate" for an identical injury.

23. P. vi.

24. See James, *supra* note 3, at 412.

lowed. The whole tone was that of a highly competent teacher elucidating facts to a reasonably bright class. It was an impressive performance, and the records might well be a useful adjunct in teaching the art of advocacy.

─────────

The defects of the traditional common-law system of compensating tort victims (mostly, of course, people injured by automobiles) have finally become so obtrusive that they are visible not merely to law professors but to legislators and even insurance companies. Some people who are injured in automobile accidents are grossly overcompensated; most get only a fraction of their real economic loss or nothing at all. The resolution of the complex issues involved in determining who was at fault and the cash value of the plaintiff's injuries clogs court calendars—delays of two years in reaching trial are common and six years not extraordinary—and makes the compensation of accident victims inordinately expensive. It costs, in fact, about $2.20 in insurance premiums to get a dollar to the actual sufferer. There has thus been great discussion of plans for automatic compensation, without regard to fault, for the actual economic loss (principally medical bills and lost wages) of the inevitable victims of automobile technology. The best-known such plan is that devised by a couple of law professors, Robert Keeton of Harvard and Jeffrey O'Connell of Indiana, but it is significant that some big insurers are promoting a similar plan—thus lending credibility to the industry's loud complaints that not even the enormous premiums now charged are sufficient to make the business profitable.

The huge tribe of lawyers who are the only undoubted beneficiaries of the present system are, of course, strongly opposed to any such breaking of their rice bowls; they argue that it is impractical, unconstitutional, and contrary to natural law. Despite their doughty efforts (which managed to defeat one such bill in Massachusetts), Massachusetts has now enacted a limited version of no-fault compensation, and New York and several other states seem on the verge of adopting some such scheme.

Juries: Drama and Justice

YALE LAW JOURNAL, 1963

I UNDERTOOK TO REVIEW *My Life in Court*, by Louis Nizer, about a year ago, and I have regretted it, and put the job off, ever since. It is not that it makes difficult or tedious reading; far from it. *My Life in Court* deserves its place at the top of the nonfiction best-sellers, for Mr. Nizer really has played a major role in some of the most diverting litigation of our times; he seems to have almost total recall (and, no doubt, excellent files); and the good stories lose nothing in his telling of them. As bedside reading for lawyers and laymen, he is hard to beat.

Part of the inordinate delay is attributable to the mere length of the book; no legal career below the level of Marshall's or Holmes's really deserves what must be well over a quarter million words. But most of my procrastination was because I found it prudent, even essential, to take Mr. Nizer's memoirs in small, well-spaced doses. Hero worship tends to cloy, and hero worship, amounting to uncritical adulation, is what Mr. Nizer plainly feels for the subject of his autobiography. Some such weakness was probably unavoidable; had he suffered from modesty or shyness, his career would never have furnished the raw material for a book like this one. A first-rate trial lawyer who hated himself would be a *lusus naturae* as astounding and improbable as a diffident, shrinking actor. But the art of self-praise is one whose extreme difficulty is insufficiently appreciated by most of its numerous practitioners. It is true, as Samuel Butler astutely remarked, that "the advantage of doing one's praising for oneself is that one can lay it on so thick, and exactly in the right places." Great as is this advantage, however, the compensating risk is even greater. To avoid overdoing it, or to achieve the *coup de maître* of letting one's light shine freely while seeming modestly to place it under a bushel, requires skill of a superlatively high order—a skill denied even to such consummate masters of self-laudation as Marcus Cicero and Bernard Shaw. Indeed, the only example which comes readily to mind of self-glorification which does not fatigue the reader, because it is done with a masterly appearance of objectivity and impartiality, is Julius Caesar. Mr. Nizer is not among the select company of subtle masters of the art and mystery of the higher egotism. The tone of the work is set by the dust jacket and end papers, which feature no less than six different pictures of the author in various forensic poses, every one of them dignified, intellectual, and impressive. The "I" count is also very high: on a couple of pages selected by opening the book at random,[1] I find no less than twenty-four first-person pronouns. I assume that Mr. Nizer *must* have lost a case at some time since he took to the law; it is even possible that he has been outfoxed by an opponent. But no hint of any such contretemps appears in these pages. By the same token, I assume that he did not fight every battle alone; but I cannot recall any place in which he mentions the name of a partner or associate.

Nevertheless, Mr. Nizer's chapters are highly enjoyable and in places instructive, for he is one of those uncommon fellows who is in cold fact, and as the record shows, almost

1. Pp. 182–83.

as good as he thinks he is. As an office lawyer—by which I mean one whose practice consists largely of divining the law and applying it to his clients' problems—he appears to be reasonably competent. But his talents in this end of the business are by no means as spectacular as a lay reader might suppose after perusing, for example, his stream-of-consciousness account of his own legal reasoning on matters of corporation law in the course of the great battle for control of Loew's.[2] It is notorious that great advocates are not necessarily, and perhaps not even usually, great lawyers—Lord Erskine is one demonstration of that proposition, and Sir Edward Marshall Hall another.[3] It is safe to say that there are at least a thousand lawyers on Manhattan Island, and not a few students in this and other law schools, who could have done as well or better on these not very difficult questions of corporation law.[4] But there are not a dozen who could have matched Nizer's performance, chronicled in the first chapter, in persuading a jury to award Quentin Reynolds punitive damages of monstrous size in his libel suit against Westbrook Pegler and the Hearst Corporations.[5] That chapter makes superb reading, in part, of course, because it is al-

2. See, *e.g.*, pp. 466–69, 490–92.

3. See Lord Birkett's article, on Erskine in *The Listener*, June 29, 1961, p. 1128; MARJORIBANKS, LIFE OF SIR EDWARD MARSHALL HALL, K. C. (1929).

4. Mr. Nizer seems to lack that precision and attention to detail which usually are regarded as helpful, if not essential, in the practice of corporation law. For example, he states that "The By-laws of the corporation provided for cumulative voting." Actually the provision was located in Loew's certificate of incorporation, as, under Delaware law, it had to be. DEL. CODE. Tit. 8, § 214 (1953); see Campbell v. Loew's, Inc., 134 A.2d 852 (Del. Ch. 1957).

5. The difference between Louis Nizer as a courtroom lawyer and Louis Nizer as an office lawyer is further exemplified by a statement on page 151. "What Reynolds had not known was that compensatory damages are substitution for lost income and are taxable. Punitive damages are not." We may hope and assume that Mr. Reynolds' tax returns are prepared by somebody else, for Mr. Nizer's proposition is not known to tax lawyers either. See C. A. Hawkins, 6 B.T.A. 1023 (1927); Rev. Rul. 54–418, 1958–2 CUM. BULL. 18.

ways pleasant to see the likes of Pegler get their comeup-
pance, but largely because of the virtuosity of Mr. Nizer's
handling of the witnesses and jury. That virtuosity is demonstrated again and again and in many contexts in the succeeding chapters, for Mr. Nizer is a specialist only in the sense
that he specializes in litigation. As a litigator, he comes about
as close as a lawyer can to being a general practitioner, save
that he seems to have avoided criminal cases, or at any rate
includes none in these chronicles. Otherwise, as the present
volume shows, all is grist that comes to his mill—copyright,
personal injury, malpractice, domestic relations, savage corporate infighting, in and out of court.

Here, then, is a series of accounts of what are often termed,
especially by Mr. Nizer, courtroom dramas which are fascinating in their details and which constitute, moreover, excellent clinical studies in trial practice, step-by-step demon-
strations by an undoubted master of the conception and
execution of some of his principal masterpieces. It is generally interesting, and even exciting, to watch at work a
master of any art, craft, or skill, however humble, even yo-yo
twirling or golf. I well remember, for instance, spending a
long and blissful afternoon watching billiard balls, under the
command of the late Willy Hoppe, move through fantasti-
cally intricate evolutions with the snap and precision of
Kaiser Wilhelm's Prussian Guard. And yet Mr. Nizer's ex-
hibition of his skill, though dazzling, somehow failed to afford me that simple and strong pleasure. After some cogita-
tion, I have concluded that the trouble is that a very great
part of Mr. Nizer's art or craft is essentially meretricious.
This is not his fault, for he must work, and do the best he
can for his clients, within the system which exists. Nor can
he reasonably be expected to subject that system to critical
examination, any more than Mr. Vholes was likely to deplore
(even in his own mind) the Chancery practice of the time of
Bleak House, for he gets his bread and butter by it, with a

heavy coat of jam. Moreover, very few of us are objective enough to ask if what we do with great dexterity is really worth doing at all. Mr. Nizer, of course, is no Vholes, for every page of his book shows that he is one of those lawyers who wholeheartedly (and warmheartedly) make their client's cause their own; his jubilation in victory plainly reflects more than mere gratification at personal triumph. Nevertheless, the total impression with which I am left is that Mr. Nizer is a good man in a bad trade, or at least a trade which ought to be a great deal better than it is.

The depressing fact is that *My Life in Court* seems to me to raise anew, however unintentionally and even against interest, a suspicion that has been gnawing at my vitals for years: to wit, that our ancient system of trial by jury is in some contexts not merely ancient but antiquated, and that it stands in need of some fundamental re-examination and maybe revision. I do not suggest, of course, that the jury be abolished. Indeed, I think that in some types of litigation— for instance, the ordinary personal-injury action and many or most criminal cases—the jury, though far from perfect, is still in all probability the best available device for securing substantial justice. Moreover, I am well aware that to a very numerous class of judges, lawyers, professors, politicians, and plain citizens the jury is still a totem figure comparable to Mother or Dwight D. Eisenhower. The orthodox appraisal of the jury system is still probably represented by the famous dictum of Blackstone, recently endorsed by Mr. Justice Black,[6] that "the trial by jury ever has been, and I trust ever will be, looked upon as the glory of the English law. And if it has so great an advantage over others in regulating civil property, how much must that advantage be heightened

6. See Reid v. Covert, 354 U. S. 1, 26–31 (1957). Mr. Justice Black's opinion, in which the Chief Justice and Justices Douglas and Brennan concurred, quotes or cites a number of other tributes to the jury system by eminent authorities, none of which (except his own opinion in Toth v. Quarles, 350 U. S. 11 [1955]) is very recent.

when it is applied to criminal cases! . . . [I]t is the most transcendent privilege which any subject can enjoy, or wish for, that he cannot be affected either in his property, his liberty, or his person, but by the unanimous consent of twelve of his neighbors and equals." [7] In our time and place, this majestic rhetoric requires qualification in certain important areas. Try reading Blackstone to a Negro charged with raping a white woman in Yahoo County, Mississippi, and see if he breaks into cheers. Blackstone, of course, wrote in the light of the history he knew, and that history gave some ground for the assumption, implicit in his encomium, that brave, honest, and intelligent jurors might well interpose themselves between a subject and a tyrannical sovereign —at least where the tyrant's prejudices ran counter to those of the mass of his subjects. He had in mind, no doubt, such instances as the acquittal of the seven bishops whom James II had caused to be tried for publishing a seditious libel.[8] But Blackstone and Black might have recalled some defendants in the long and not always glorious history of the common law up to Blackstone's own day who perhaps would not have thought so very transcendent the privilege of entrusting their lives to twelve of their neighbors and equals— for an obvious instance, the Roman Catholics whom juries sent to the gallows on the evidence of Titus Oates and his coadjutors in the invention of the Popish Plot.[9]

But whatever the truth of Blackstone's statement in the

7. 3 BLACKSTONE, COMMENTARIES 379 (1829).
8. See 2 MACAULAY, HISTORY OF ENGLAND, ch. VIII, pp. 289–99 (1856). But the currents of prejudice ran somewhat crooked even in that case, for one of the panel was Michael Arnold, brewer to the court, who is supposed to have said, "Whatever I do, I am sure to be half ruined. If I say Not Guilty, I shall brew no more for the King; and if I say Guilty, I shall brew no more for anybody else." He very nearly succeeded in hanging the jury. *Id.* at 292, 298.
9. See 1 MACAULAY, HISTORY OF ENGLAND, ch. II, pp. 181–85. "The juries partook of the feelings then common throughout the nation, and were encouraged by the bench to indulge those feelings without restraint."

eighteenth century, there are not many immutables in the common law, and it does not by any means follow that because it was then true, or mainly true, that it ought to be accepted unquestioningly and in all circumstances today. In fact, of course, it is not unanimously accepted; perceptive judges and lawyers have long been afflicted with a cankerous suspicion that the jury system, as presently constituted, may not be particularly well calculated to produce justice in *every* case between man and man or man and sovereign— that it is sometimes, in short, a sort of vermiform appendix in the body politic, like segregation or the Congressional seniority system, whose malfunctioning may be the cause of appalling bellyaches. Probably the most acute and reasoned criticism is that of Jerome Frank,[10] but the most quotable is Mr. Dooley's: "Whin the case is all over, the jury'll pitch th' tistimony out iv the window, an' consider three questions: 'Did Lootgert look as though he'd kill his wife? Did his wife look as though she ought to be kilt? Isn't it time we wint to supper?' "[11] Without attempting to recapitulate Judge Frank's detailed analysis, it is obvious that there are some cases (antitrust litigation, for instance) in which it is virtually impossible to find twelve laymen who, with the best will in the world, can understand what the incredibly complicated and voluminous evidence is all about, and others (civil-rights cases, for example, in some of the states of the late Confederacy) in which it is virtually impossible to find twelve jurors who will let their verdict be influenced either by the evidence or the law. And there are still other cases in which there is only too much reason to suspect embracery.[12]

10. See, *e.g.*, FRANK, COURTS ON TRIAL *passim* and especially ch. VIII (1949).
11. Dunne, *Mr. Dooley on Expert Testimony*, in MR. DOOLEY IN WAR AND PEACE (1898).
12. For an entertaining, if unedifying, account of the jury trial and acquittal of a defendant with almost unlimited wealth, see the account

Even in run-of-the-mill cases, it is common knowledge that jurors often find it easier to follow their prejudices than the evidence. It is instructive to listen to an experienced trial lawyer dispense his ripe wisdom on the subject of picking a jury. I once heard a very eminent criminal lawyer, since turned hanging judge, discourse on his technique. What he wanted in a juror, of course, was warmheartedness and sympathy, and so, since he happened to be a Jew, he recommended Jewish jurors, though he also had a good word for Italians. An equally eminent Irish lawyer spoke warmly in favor of Irishmen. If he had been a Turk or a Cambodian he would have counseled the selection of Turks or Cambodians.[13] The point is that few or none of them are interested in picking a juror who will do even-handed justice, and all of them assume that it is possible and desirable to pick jurors who will be suitably prejudiced. It is nearly axiomatic that a lawyer who is sure his client is right on the facts will do his best to get a trial before a judge, while a lawyer who knows his client's evidence is weak will demand a jury. In the criminal area, it is hard to say whether more harm is done by unjust convictions or unjust acquittals. Perhaps the latter, for an appellate court can weed out the unjust convictions, and there is a fair to good chance that it actually will do so. There is not much in the argument that juries stand between the public and undue enforcement of harsh or unpopular laws. Aside from the orthodox rejoinder (which, it must be admitted, has more theoretical than practical force) that the best way to get rid of such a statute is to enforce it strictly, there is the highly practical consideration that most District Attorneys are hopeful politicians,

of the trial of Harry Sinclair in WEINER AND STARR, TEAPOT DOME, chs. 9 and 11 (1959).

13. It is a fact that I have yet to hear any criminal lawyer, even a Yankee criminal lawyer, recommend that the jury be loaded with Yankees. Personally, I regard Yankees as a very softhearted lot.

and few of them see much advantage in zealous enforcement of a statute which runs counter to the mores of any considerable section of the electorate.

The principal alternative to trial by jury is trial by a judge, and it must, of course, be conceded that judges are but men and not invariably very good men. Since 1688, in the English-speaking countries at least, we have seen no such monstrous and terrible judge as Baron Jeffreys, but in very recent times there have certainly been a few who in their small way were no roses. The late junior Senator from Wisconsin, Joseph R. McCarthy, got his political start as a trial judge, and a marvelously bad one at that.[14] The successful Ku Klux Klandidate for governor of Alabama, the honorable George C. Wallace, is another example of a trial judge who seems a trifle lacking in what is usually regarded as the judicial temperament.[15] I could probably think of other such specimens, but not very many. Such judges are sufficiently rare so that their antics attract attention, most of it unfavorable, which they would attract in no other trade. Taking one day with another, the average judge has the intelligence, experience, and ability needed to weigh the evidence in any case which is likely to come before him, and almost always, however cantankerous he may be, he can be counted on to make a sincere and generally successful effort to put aside his own prejudices. Moreover, his decision can almost never be bought for money, and usually (particularly in the case of federal judges) it cannot be influenced by political pressure. In short, while the superiority of judges to juries is far from clear-cut, and is probably nonexistent in many kinds of

14. See State *ex rel.* Dep't of Agriculture v. McCarthy, 238 Wis. 258, 299 N.W. 258 (1941); *The Judge on Trial*, The Progressive, April, 1954, pp. 6–8.

15. He recently denounced the entire federal judiciary, en masse and without exception, as "lousy and irresponsible." See *Time*, June 8, 1962, p. 25.

trial, my own belief is that, in some situations, it might be useful to reconsider the appropriateness of the popular assumption that jury trial should always be available.

These skeptical (but not cynical) reflections are reinforced by perusing Mr. Nizer's account of how to win cases and ingratiate oneself with juries. I hasten to say that he does nothing in the least improper, nothing that his duty to his client does not—under the present system—require him to do. According to the law books, Mr. Nizer's job in the *Reynolds* case was to persuade the jury by a preponderance of the evidence that the defendants had falsely, and without a privilege to do so, published matter defamatory to the plaintiff.[16] In reality, what Mr. Nizer had to do was persuade the jurors that Reynolds was one of nature's noblemen and Pegler a five-star stinker. The latter hardly required a legal Hercules; it might have been done by a lawyer of quite ordinary talents, although Mr. Nizer's pulverization of Pegler was certainly extraordinarily thorough and satisfactory. But a great part of the strategy of counsel was devoted to problems which should not have mattered at all, and probably would not have mattered if the case had been tried to a judge. For example—and it is only one example—some of the jurors were Catholics, and it is obvious that Mr. Nizer assumed that they might well vote for the side which most gratified their religious sensibilities and against the side so unlucky or inept as to offend those sensibilities.[17] Pegler was a Catholic, but so was Reynolds, and if "no one would have compared [Reynolds'] worldliness with the holy dedication of priesthood," [18] Pegler was also lacking in some of the attributes of saintliness. So far, a draw, although apparently Mr. Nizer would have despaired of justice had Reynolds

16. See RESTATEMENT, TORTS §§ 558, 569 (1939).
17. Pp. 123–25.
18. P. 123.

been, say, a Seventh Day Adventist. But Pegler's counsel
calls a priest, one Father Braun, as a witness; Mr. Nizer is
"disturbed by such a display of clerical garb in front of the
jury box." He agonizes over the question whether to trump
Pegler's priest with Bishop Sheen—then only a Monsignor
but already pretty well known—and finally decides not to;
neither does he cross-examine Father Braun, for that might
mean "attacking him and perhaps offending the sensitivity
of some jurors." [19] In fact, neither Father Braun nor Monsignor Sheen had any evidence of importance, and if the
trier of the fact had been a judge, of whatever religious persuasion, it is very unlikely that either side would have gone
through any such charade. There are other similar examples.[20]

Not surprisingly, Mr. Nizer greatly prefers juries to judges.
I probably would too, if I were he. Not only does his trade,
which is persuading juries that his clients ought to win, keep
him in considerable style, but it is obvious that he hugely
enjoys playing a succession of starring roles in courtroom
dramas. He says:

> Although jurors are extraordinarily right in their con-
> clusion, it is usually based on common sense "instincts"
> about right and wrong, and not on sophisticated evalu-
> ations of complicated testimony. . . . Because judges,
> sometimes, consciously reject this layman's approach
> of who is right or wrong and restrict themselves to the
> precise legal weights, they come out wrong more often
> than juries.[21]

This is a polite way to put it, and appealing too; but, *mutatis
mutandis*, it comes to pretty much the same thing as the

19. P. 125.
20. E.g., pp. 393–95. This one involved Lutheran pastors, testifying
to the value of an advertising man negligently killed by the Long Island
Railroad.
21. P. 313.

64

dicta of Mr. Dooley and Jerome Frank.[22] It certainly does
not justify every jury trial. I suggest that the reader try applying Mr. Nizer's reference to the jury's "common sense
'instincts' about right and wrong" to the Mississippi Negro
charged with rape of a white woman or the Mississippi Ku
Kluxer charged with lynching that Negro, and see how it
sounds.

You can't blame a bartender, however, for not joining the
Anti-Saloon League, and the foregoing querulous comments are not just criticisms of Mr. Nizer's book. Our jury
system is with us, and probably will be for some time to
come—and one virtue it certainly has. It often produces
wonderful reading matter. When lawyers are arguing to a
court, the record, as the learned readers of this *Journal* well
know, usually makes dry and indigestible reading. And that
is a charge which neither judge nor jury would ever sustain
against *My Life in Court*.

———

*Mr. Nizer, undaunted by this review, has since produced
another volume of his reminiscences, which sold nearly as
well as the first. But to a generation accustomed to the courtroom histrionics of William Kunstler and his disciples,
Nizer must seem staid, unobtrusive, and retiring—almost
bashful, in fact.*

*My doubts about the jury system have not been dissipated.
An unjust conviction—if it is affirmed on appeal—means
that the accused has been denied the protection of the law.*

22. "The jury are more brutally direct. They determine that they
want Jones to collect $5,000 from the railroad company, or that they
don't want pretty Nellie Brown to go to jail for killing her husband;
and they bring in their general verdict accordingly. Often, to all practical intents and purposes, the judge's statement of the legal rules might
just as well never have been expressed." FRANK, *op. cit. supra* note
10, at 111.

This problem has, of course, been endlessly canvassed. An unjust acquittal, which cannot be reviewed, means that the victims of some crimes and criminals are denied the protection of the law. This problem has received far less attention from liberals. In the late Fifties and early Sixties more than a hundred Negroes and white civil-rights workers were murdered in the deep South. Although in most of these cases the federal government had convincing evidence of the perpetrators' identity, only four went to prison, none for longer than ten years. But the deep South no longer has a monopoly on racial and "political" violence. Neither is the unjust acquittal any longer a Southern phenomenon. When the Black Panthers insist that a jury of their peers means a jury of other Panthers, they are asking for the immunity long accorded to the white analogue of their organization in Mississippi. But they need not go so far. It takes twelve to convict. A black man who votes to convict a Panther in Connecticut will have to be as honest and brave as a white man who votes to convict a Ku Kluxer in Alabama—and I doubt that those qualities are any commoner in the one race than they are in the other.

The plain fact is that a jury drawn from a particular community, and reflecting the political prejudices prevalent in that community, is not a body which is well designed to do justice to one accused of murder or arson or any other crime committed for "political" reasons, whether he is a Ku Kluxer, a Weatherman, or a Black Panther. In theory, members of the panel who are prejudiced for or against the accused can be challenged and excluded from the jury. In practice, as every trial lawyer knows, the voir dire is not a very efficient mechanism for the exclusion of bias from the jury box. In a good many states the defendant in a criminal case can demand that he be tried by judges, which probably reduces the likelihood of an unjust conviction if the de-

66

fendant is so unpopular that almost all prospective jurors would be in favor of hanging him. But the defendants in "political" cases in such jurisdictions have not exercised this right—perhaps because they really believe that the judges, being creatures of the Establishment, are even less likely than jurors to treat them fairly, but more probably because they calculate that the laws of statistical probability will produce at least one juror whose sympathies or fears will lead him to vote Not Guilty without regard to the evidence or the law.

The Sixth Amendment, of course, denies any such option to the prosecution. At present the only possible Constitutional alternative to jury trial of "political" defendants who do not waive that right is trial by a military commission, in an emergency so extreme that the civil courts cannot function properly and martial law—or some degree of it—must be invoked. Abraham Lincoln, who was among other things the best lawyer who ever sat in the White House, resorted to military trials of Copperheads. His justification of his action in the case of Clement Vallandigham is worth quoting: "Nothing is better known to history than that Courts of Justice are utterly incompetent to try such cases. Civil courts are organized chiefly for trials of individuals or, at most, a few individuals acting in concert, and this in quiet times, and on charges of crimes well defined in the law. . . . Again, a jury too frequently has at least one member more ready to hang the panel than to hang the traitor."

But martial law is strong and dangerous medicine; politicians without Lincoln's genius are all too likely to administer an overdose, as was demonstrated immediately after his assassination. Political scientists, politicians, lawyers, and plain citizens ought to start considering whether better remedies are imaginable.

Thurman Arnold: A
Major Master of
a Minor Art

VILLANOVA LAW REVIEW, 1966

This was the last of the string of book reviews I wrote for the Yale Law Journal. In fact, it didn't appear in Yale. That year's editor, a pudgy youth of a political priggishness remarkable even among the Eagle Scouts of the New Left, refused to print it unless I deleted the paragraphs dealing with Chairman Mao, Dr. Castro, et. al., which he said were in poor taste. So it went to another law review, whose editor happened to be prowling Yale's corridors in search of contributions.

Arnold's best book was probably The Folklore of Capitalism, *which broke a lot of icons sacred to the corporate bar of the 1930's. He spent the latter part of his life representing, with enormous success, the big businesses he had bedeviled in earlier years. He died in 1969—a great loss to the people who have to attend law-school alumni dinners, and perhaps to wider sections of the public as well.*

THURMAN WESLEY ARNOLD has had, over the last half century (and a bit more), a varied, successful, and eminently useful career at the bar. He has been an elected official,[1] a practicing lawyer, a professor of law, a high official of the Department of Justice, a federal appellate judge, and again a practicing lawyer. His *cursus honorum* thus includes, as is no longer very common among American lawyers, most of the jobs in which a lawyer can advantageously employ his legal education. In each of them he has distinguished himself above the common, but in none could it fairly be said that he has stood in the very first rank. Were this all, his *Fair Fights and Foul: A Dissenting Lawyer's Life,* a combination of autobiography and chrestomathy, would be of interest only to sedulous graduate students delving into the minutiae of the Age of Roosevelt. But it is not all. In one art Arnold stands without a master or a peer: he is the ablest living teller of funny stories, many of them his own,[2] and, what is still more remarkable, most of them printable. What Boswell is among biographers, what Newton is among mathematicians, what Shakespeare is among playwrights, Thurman Arnold is among after-dinner speakers. Nor is this praise intended as a sneer; the splendid practitioner of a humble art is far rarer and far more deserving of public esteem than is the converse.

1. Member of the Wyoming House of Representatives, Mayor of Laramie.
2. But not all. His story about the banker who wouldn't extend another loan to a large borrower ("My client replied, 'John, have you ever been in the sheep business?' 'No,' replied the banker. 'Well, you're in it now.' "), which appears on page 34, has been current for at least a century in New York, usually being set in the underwear business. No doubt its application to wine, pickled olives, salt fish, or amphorae raised guffaws in Periclean Athens.

The history of post-prandial and other occasional oratory
deserves more scholarly attention than it has received, for it
must account for a high percentage of the sum of human
misery, and a very much smaller fraction of the total of human joy, since Neolithic times. The Greeks, although partial
to political oratory, as we all learn from Thucydides, seem
to have discouraged monologues in other circumstances.
The Romans, however, must have suffered abominably, for
not only were they buffeted by gales of political and forensic
oratory, but also every hopeful literatus compelled his
friends, freedmen, and clients to listen for hours and even
days to public recitation of his tragedies, comedies, histories
and epics.[3] The Roman after-dinner speaker, if he was not
talented, was at least wealthy, and his audience was commonly consoled and sedated by several courses of sow's
udder, dormice stewed in honey, peacocks' brains, and
other classical delicatessen, washed down by a sound selection of Chian and Falernian vintages. No such Lucullan
compensation is available to American audiences, whose
agonies of boredom are more than likely to be compounded
by dyspepsia. More than once I have reflected in such circumstances that the number of recorded discourses which
a civilized man in his right mind might regret not having
heard live is two: The Sermon on the Mount and the Gettys-
burg Address. To these morose meditations Mr. Arnold is a
shining exception; I have heard him several times, and I
would do it again tomorrow night if I had the chance. Many
of Mr. Arnold's finest here[4] find a better preservative than
the memories of his audiences, which is a boon to posterity.

The quantity and quality of Mr. Arnold's wit is particu-

3. See CARCOPINO, DAILY LIFE IN ANCIENT ROME 195–201 (Yale
Paperbound ed. 1960); DILL, ROMAN SOCIETY FROM NERO TO MARCUS
AURELIUS 172–74 (Meridian ed. 1956).
4. E.g., pp. 28–34. I commend particularly the story about clockless
cuckoos.

larly astonishing and gratifying when one realizes that he is, after all, at bottom a reformer and even a bit of a revolutionary. As a general proposition, Mohammed and Marx, Lenin and Hitler, Malcolm X and Mary Baker Eddy are united by their total lack of humor. Not only do they lack humor themselves; they distrust and dislike it in other people. The fate of the genuine humorist (as distinct from the laborious hacks whose dreary and sometimes nauseating output passes for satire in such publications as *Der Stürmer* or *Krokodil*) is likely to be harsh under their regimes. Most of their movements soon develop a repellent cant, usually an imitation and exaggeration of the stylistic peculiarities of the Founder. Communist cant, for example, is full of phrases ("dialectical materialism," "inner contradictions," "historical necessity," etc., etc., etc.) derived from Marx's version of the German polemic style of his day, further debased and made more banal by Stalin.[5] The cant of the English Puritans, to select a rather different example, was (like that of many religious cranks of less note) a vulgarization of the language of the King James version—"comfortable scriptures," "sweet experiences," "unsavory discourse," "smite the Amalekites," etc., etc., etc.[6] I do not, of course, intend to carry very far the comparison between Cromwell's followers and modern Communists. It is none the less a fact that a reading of modern Communist homiletics and polemics leads to a better understanding of the unfeigned joy with which the population of England in 1660 exchanged the efficient and honest government of the Saints for the inefficient and corrupt regime of the Stuarts. The likes of Titus Oates or

5. The coarseness of the current Communist *Schimpflexikon* ("lackey," "running dog," "hyena" and so forth) seems to be specifically Russian; at least it is not characteristic of Marx, nor of Engels (who in fact wrote very elegantly).
6. See 1 MACAULAY, HISTORY OF ENGLAND 125–30 (1856) for an account of some of the peculiarities of the Saints.

the late Andrei Vishinsky become as fluent in such duck-speak as the true believers and rise high in the hierarchy of the elect. For a man like Thurman Arnold, such mimicry would be simply impossible.[7]

It could hardly be otherwise, for a world-saver with a sense of humor would be almost a contradiction in terms. The foundation of true humor is a correct appreciation of the speaker's place in the universe. The underdeveloped George Washingtons who have been saving such countries as Cuba and (until recently) Ghana and Indonesia from the dangers of imperialism, capitalism, neo-colonialism, and overeating are, if not fully divine, Messiahs to a man. Indeed, theophany and theocracy, which most people had supposed extinct since Diocletian's time or thereabouts, seem to be making a strong comeback, sometimes in previously civilized countries. Aside from Little League Mussolinis like Sukarno and Nasser, there is some reason to believe that the more sinister egomaniac who reigns as Son of Heaven and Chairman of the Chinese People's Political Consultative Conference may have begun to suspect that dogmatic atheism is one more error of the Russian *Untermenschen*, that there is a God, and that He is in fact incarnate in the somewhat tubby (but none the less imposing and even graceful) person of Mao Tse-tung. Is it possible that one whose Methods of Thinking permit even his dullest catechumens to arrive at Correct Conclusions, who holds the absolute power of life and death over six (or seven or eight) hundred million people, who

7. I must in fairness concede what is obvious: that Fascists, Communists and religious cranks are not the only people who talk cant. The Babbitry of the 1920's, for instance, had their own cant, though it was, on the whole, more ridiculous than sinister. See, *e.g.*, BARTON, THE MAN NOBODY KNOWS (1924), which contains, among many other choice specimens, an entire chapter (VI) devoted to the proposition that Jesus was "The Founder of Modern Business." Barton was a minister's son and full of *Reader's Digest* piety, but he must be classified as primarily an apostle of Babbitism rather than Christianity.

writes, moreover, poetry of transcendent and unearthly beauty—is it possible that such a one is merely one more specimen of *homo sapiens*, scarcely exalted above common politicians like the President of the United States? Plainly not. Therefore. . . .

It is obvious that such theomaniacs can neither make nor tolerate jokes; no tincture of humor can coexist with a persuasion that one is, if not God, at least one of His intimates and favorites. Certainly there is no record of the cracking of a joke by Hitler or Mao or even Nkrumah. Dr. Castro is only an apparent exception to the rule. Not many Latins are capable of the murderous seriousness of Himmler, Stalin or Mao, and I must in fairness concede that Castro (like the late Benito Mussolini, whom he resembles in a number of other respects) has demonstrated a talent of the highest order for political buffoonery. But it is instrinsically improbable that even his wildest antics, such as the discovery of a nefarious anti-Castro plot between the Chinese Dogmatists and the Yankee Imperialists, are intended to furnish amusement. No clown with the most rudimentary sense of timing would declaim for five or six hours at a stretch, as Castro does with dismal regularity. Similar comments apply to Colonel Nasser.[8]

All of these are, of course, unusual cases—reformers on a large and ruthless scale. But first-rate senses of humor are not common among even moderate and humane world-savers,

8. Another possible exception to the rule that theomaniacs do not have senses of humor is Gaius Caligula, who had occasional flashes of a sort of sanguinary wit—*e.g.*, when asked why he had burst out laughing at a dinner he gave for the consuls of the year, he explained that there had just flashed through his mind the thought that "at a single nod of mine, both of you could have your throats cut on the spot." I SUETONIUS, THE LIVES OF THE CAESARS 455–56 (Loeb ed. 1914). But Caligula, aside from the fact that his wit could not have furnished much amusement to its hearers, was not in any sense a reformer, and so differed fundamentally from the Redeemers discussed in the text.

perhaps because the humorist's view of man is likely, as in the case of Mark Twain, to lead to the conclusion that he and his lot are not really capable of improvement. When one does find an honest, warmhearted enemy of injustice who is at the same time a very funny man, he is worth hearing. Such a one is Mr. Arnold.

No one—least of all Mr. Arnold—would claim that *Fair Fights and Foul* is a heavyweight contribution to jurisprudence or history. Arnold is not by temperament or training a Profound Thinker. His devotion to the Sherman Act, for example, seems to be largely an outgrowth of old time Populism—a Westerner's fear and dislike of Eastern big business and big finance (*e.g.*, pp. 33–34, 50, ch. 14 *passim*)—what he terms "absentee corporate control over local industry by inexorable corporate empires" (p. 52), as if there were something intrinsically immoral about the corporate form of doing business. He is not at all troubled by the double think implicit in advocating simultaneously free competition and the protection of Little Business from the effects of that competition. He seems indeed to regard the restrictive practices of big business as responsible not only for the stockmarket crash of 1929, but also for World War II (p. 52)—a belief which does far less than justice to the Satanic genius of Adolph Hitler.[9]

There are other passages which strike me as oversimplifications of very complex questions. Is it so crystal clear that

9. On the other hand, I am glad to find that I have distinguished company in my total inability to follow the reasoning of United States v. Hutcheson, 312 U. S. 219 (1941), and the rest of the decisions of the Supreme Court exempting labor unions from the antitrust and antiracketeering statutes. Mr. Arnold's comment on United States v. Local 807 Teamsters Union, 315 U. S. 521 (1942), which held that holding up trucks at the New York end of the Holland tunnel and demanding pay for unnecessary services, at the point of a gun, was not racketeering, exactly describes my own state of mind: "The decision puzzled me then and, after mature reflection, it still puzzles me." P. 117.

"property" rights can readily be distinguished from "human" rights and that the latter are always to be preferred (see, *e.g.*, pp. 69, 72)? Communist polities seem to suggest that one set of rights is not worth much without the other. Historically, men have always been as strongly attached to their property as to their liberty, and sometimes more so; indeed, they have frequently been found ready to hazard their lives in defense of their property. It was not blind conservatism which caused the draftsmen of the Fifth Amendment to link life, liberty, and property. Similarly, has Mr. Arnold really reduced the conservative ethos to an absurdity (his favorite and most effective polemical tactic) when he speaks of "the former conservative belief that poverty is due to lack of initiative on the part of the poor" (p. 97)? [10] The fact is that the poor resemble the rich in this much: some people inherit poverty which they do not deserve; some achieve it by their own merit; most can thank a combination of the two causes. By the same token, there is considerable evidence, historical and contemporary, that the proposition that relief, unaccompanied by jobs, is harmful to the recipients (p. 54) may not be totally absurd. [11] Nor do I find wholly convincing Mr. Arnold's reduction to absurdity of the deterrent theory of punishment (p. 231). He adduces as authority to support his position the shopworn allegation that "when men were hanged for picking pockets in England, pickpockets were busy plying their trade among the crowd witnessing the hanging" (p. 231). Maybe. But how many pickpockets? Were there more thieves then than there are now? Neither Mr. Arnold nor I nor anyone else really knows. But I gladly concede that elsewhere Mr. Arnold's use of *reductio ad absurdum* shows that the master's hand has lost nothing

10. See also p. 275.
11. See, *e.g.*, ORWELL, THE ROAD TO WIGAN PIER 77–85 (Berkeley paperback ed. 1961).

75

of its skill [12]—although it hardly requires Mr. Arnold's finesse to reduce Eisenhower economics to absurdity.

It will be well for the industrious graduate student of the future to bear in mind that Mr. Arnold's autobiography is not intended as scholarly history, for some of his statements are excellent examples of the reason why lawyers are taught to check primary sources. Here is Mr. Arnold's version of the persecution of Theron Lamar Caudle, a former Assistant Attorney General in charge of the Tax Division of the Department of Justice:

> He prosecuted and convicted a well-known person for tax evasion. He resisted all the pressures put on him to drop the prosecution. One day he learned that a certain oil interest of trivial value had been transferred to him by the defendant he was investigating. He immediately wrote an indignant letter and repudiated the gift. Nevertheless, he found himself prosecuted and convicted and sent to prison, his entire career ruined, and his family impoverished. (P. 148).

It fairly made my blood boil. The trial of Joan of Arc was nothing by comparison. But, alas, a check conducted *ex abundantia cautelae* showed that the martyred Caudle's relations with taxpayers whose affairs were under investigation were not quite as Mr. Arnold recalls them. The uncontroverted testimony was that these taxpayers lent Mr. Caudle money which was not repaid; [13] that they furnished him a private plane for blithesome little trips to Florida [14] and paid for a longer European junket; [15] that they gave his wife the mink coat which was then *de rigueur* in such cases; [16] and

12. *E.g.*, chapter ten.
13. *New York Times*, Nov. 27, 1951, p. 1, col. 2.
14. *Id.*, Nov. 28, 1951, p. 1, col. 4.
15. *Id.*, Dec. 10, 1951, p. 1, col. 5.
16. *Id.*, Nov. 30, 1951, p. 1, col. 4.

that they paid him "commissions" totaling $6,000 for arranging the purchase of sundry oil interests and an airplane.[17]

In one respect, however, Mr. Arnold's contribution to history ought to be of the highest interest and value, for he has written a somewhat impressionistic but splendidly illuminating account of the Yale Law School in the Thirties (*e.g.*, pp. 35, 57–68, 135–36). It may be that not the least of Mr. Arnold's claims to a place in history is that he [18] was one of that little band of serious and frivolous thinkers who made the Yale Law School—not what it is today, but something perhaps even better, fuller of experiments still more preposterous (*e.g.*, pp. 62–63) and professors even nuttier (*e.g.*, p. 62) than those who distinguish and adorn it today. In those days going to the Yale Law School took more imagination and nerve than I [19] had, but the product, if it did not take to drink or legal philosophy, or otherwise fly off the trolley, was often truly superb.

Mr. Arnold, and Mr. Arnold's book, really deserve much more space than I can give them here and now. His shrewd observations far outnumber the inaccuracies and naïvetés, which I, being a book reviewer, have unfairly emphasized. In particular, his sixteenth chapter, "Why Government Service Is a Dubious Career," is a remarkably penetrating critique of the American bureaucracy, particularly "that essential supplement to Parkinson's Law commonly known as Arnold's Corollary, the principle of which is as follows: No new government activity can possibly be effectively carried out by any established government organization" (p. 155). Whosoever invests a modest $5.95 will learn a great many

17. *Ibid.*
18. A.B., Princeton, 1911; LL.B., Harvard, 1914. WHO's WHO also discloses a Yale M.A., but I suspect that this is one of the fictitious degrees which Yale confers *privatim* upon any full professor whose background is so deprived as not to include a genuine Yale degree.
19. LL.B., Harvard, 1940.

things, some old,[20] some new, about an intelligent, warm, generous, and, above all, witty man. As legal autobiography goes, it is very hard to beat.

20. Mr. Arnold has liberally availed himself of the opportunity to reprint articles, briefs and judicial opinions which he thinks—not always rightly—deserve more attention than they got when they first appeared. E.g., chapters 5, 18, 20.

Law, Liberty, and Psychiatry

HARVARD LAW REVIEW, 1965

‗‗‗‗‗‗

INSANITY HAS LONG BEEN generally recognized as a form of disease, in principle no different from measles or arthritis. But if the erstwhile lunatic is now considered "sick," yet his sickness remains a peculiar variety of disease; consciously or unconsciously, most people regard it as embarrassing or even disgraceful. It is a cliché of humor that the average man will readily regale his friends with an account of the adventures of his colon, liver or vermiform appendix, but it is a highly exceptional man who will favor them with an account of his last bout with paranoia.[1] The stigma that attaches to the disease is shown by the progressive euphemism which is so marked a feature of its lexicon: we have gone from "madness" to "insanity" to "mental illness" to "nervous disorder";

---

1. The clinical monologues, which in less sophisticated strata of society tend to focus on the speaker's tripes, are in more polished circles likely to revolve around his relations with his psychoanalyst. But it is notorious that such amateurs of psychoanalysis do not usually suffer from any mental defect more serious than silliness; rarely does their malady rise above the level of neurosis.

from "raving" to "violent" to "disturbed." Offhand, I can think of but one other instance in medicine in which there has been a concerted effort to soften the harsh name of a dreaded malady: that is the attempt to rechristen leprosy as "Hansen's Disease."

A number of explanations suggest themselves. Perhaps there lingers some remnant of the theory, at one time universally held, that the lunatic is possessed by a peculiarly disagreeable and tenacious devil or crowd of devils;[2] one is dealing not with afflicted fellow men, but with the legions of Hell. It may be more than coincidence that the etiology, diagnosis, and treatment of leprosy were for long similarly dominated by theological considerations. A more significant parallel between the two diseases is that in each case diagnosis commonly leads to loss of freedom and probably to confinement in an institution that might as well be called a prison as a hospital or sanitarium. In the case of insanity, the symptoms that land the sufferer in the asylum are very often superficially identical with those that land other people in penitentiaries. Indeed, it is only in comparatively recent times that there has been an effort to draw a clear line between criminality and insanity. In *Law, Liberty and Psychiatry*, Thomas S. Szasz develops at length the proposition that this line is still very far from clear and that it may in fact be in the process of becoming more blurred and meaningless than it was a hundred years ago.

As insanity is a peculiar malady, so is psychiatry a peculiar branch of medicine. For one thing, it remains among the most backward of the healing arts. If the prospect of cure

2. See, *e.g.*, Matthew 8:28-33; Mark 5:1-16; Luke 8:26-36. The diabolic contents of a single man—or two men, according to Saint Matthew—was enough to induce psychosis, accompanied by pronounced disturbance, in a large herd of swine, put at 2,000 by Saint Mark. But even a single devil could cause severe functional disorders. See Matthew 9:32-33.

in cases of insanity is somewhat better than that for the common cold or acne, it is certainly no better than for cancer. Only in very recent years, with the advent of various drug therapies, has there been a significant advance. The literature of the subject tends to be full of gaseous theory and strange, astounding jargon, more suitable to theological works than to books dealing with medicine or any other science. This is not surprising, for it is plain that the needs that psychiatry—and in particular psychoanalysis—satisfies are in very large part those that used to be satisfied by religion. Its catechumens tend to be drawn from the more educated and solvent sects, such as Episcopalians and Jews, who can no longer swallow the myths and dogmas of their ancestral faiths, but who still find intolerably bleak a life in which there is neither juju nor the delightful tremors, compounded half of fear and half of ecstasy, conveyed by the ministrations of witch doctors. Psychoanalysis, describing itself as a science, a branch of medicine, but trading heavily in charms and liturgy, meets their need a great deal better than the colorless rites of other decompression chambers for ex-believers, such as Unitarianism and Universalism. I confess some surprise at the failure of Bahaism, Rosicrucianism, Yoga, and similar exotics,[3] which certainly cannot be accused of drabness, to pick up greater shares of the market. It is probable that the flamboyance of both their doctrines and their disciples has tended to repel people who believe that they believe in the scientific method.

It follows that psychiatrists, though they are by definition doctors of medicine, are frequently highly idiosyncratic speci-

3. Christian Science, which of course is home grown, is a special case. Mark Twain considered Mrs. Eddy's brand of divinity so admirably calculated to meet the spiritual cravings of the average flathead that he expected it to become the national religion. See TWAIN, CHRISTIAN SCIENCE (1907). The error must be attributed to the extreme pessimism that overwhelmed that great man in his old age.

mens of that breed. Many or most of them are no doubt as hard-working, useful and inconspicuous, not to say humdrum, as so many pediatricians or oculists. But the popular image of the profession is dominated by the bands of Janizaries, drawn from the ranks of psychoanalysts consecrated unto Freud,[4] whose dissonant kettledrums, trumpets and cymbals, and uncouth war cries, leaps, and whirlings daily astound and terrify the public.[5] The holy name of Freud is embroidered on their banners, but actually he bears no more responsibility for them than Marx does for Stalin or Castro, or Jesus for Pius XII or the Reverend Billy James Hargis. Freud actually knew something about the scientific method,[6] as Marx actually knew something about economics (and Jesus, perhaps, knew something about God), and so would have been incapable of the flights of richly hued fancy embarked upon by his disciples and *their* disciples. Dr. Szasz is quite right in making and amply illustrating the point that in this branch of medicine it is often exceedingly hard to tell the physicians from the patients (pp. 21–22, 64–65, 210–11).[7]

4. I recognize, of course, that there are many balanced and reasonable men among even psychoanalysts. I myself actually *know* two or three such, but it would be invidious to name them.

5. Szasz has been fairly criticized for confounding psychiatry with psychoanalysis and ignoring every other therapy for diseases of the mind. See Stafford-Clark, Book Review, 74 YALE L. J. 392, 393 (1964). Szasz simply follows the popular stereotype, but of course he ought to know better.

6. Indeed, he carried it to preposterous lengths, as in his elaborate dissection of a number of fragile little jokes, with a view to preserving in formaldehyde, describing, and classifying the essential principle of humor. See FREUD, JOKES AND THEIR RELATION TO THE UNCONSCIOUS 16–27 (Norton ed. 1963). The better opinion seems to be that this celebrated opus of the Master was not itself intended as a joke. Apparently Freud had a sincere admiration for jokes and merely wished to discover how one was made, like an earnest child pulling apart a butterfly. I am reminded of Rudolf Virchow's statement that he had dissected 10,000 cadavers and never found a soul.

7. The phenomenon was noted by Edgar Allan Poe, a connoisseur of madness, more than a century ago and chronicled with his usual

No system of politics, economics, religion or health, however addled, can really do very much harm so long as the customers are free to accept or reject. In a free market, it will have to abandon its patent absurdities, however cherished by its founding fathers and present management, or see the trade go to rivals. Thus the Church of Rome, no longer able (and perhaps no longer inclined) to enforce orthodoxy by the free use of autos-da-fé, is demonstrating its unparalleled talent for survival by debriding itself of doctrinal growths that hamper that survival. It is plainly getting ready to heave overboard its ban on birth control, and it is not very risky to prophesy that sooner or later a like fate awaits its prohibition of divorce, which must have cost it millions of communicants. The Communists, of course, are still in that primitive stage of development in which it is imagined that thought can be prohibited and the Pure Faith imposed by force, forever and ever, world without end:

> Such as do build their faith upon
> The holy text of pike and gun . . .
> And prove their doctrine orthodox
> By apostolic blows and knocks.[8]

(I admit that I assert the wrongness of this basic Marxist tenet with a good deal more assurance than I actually feel. George Orwell's *1984* is a powerful argument for its correctness. On the other hand, it is impossible to achieve technical efficiency—which the Communists really seem to want, at least to the extent necessary to manufacture hydrogen bombs and military hardware—without creating a class that

---

macabre drollery. See *The System of Dr. Tarr and Professor Fether*, in THE COMPLETE TALES AND POEMS OF EDGAR ALLEN POE (Modern Library ed. 1938).

8. BUTLER, HUDIBRAS, Part I, Canto I, lines 195–96, 199–200 (Bell & Sons ed. 1907).

has at least a technical education. The question is whether any variety of education can be stopped short at the border of independent thought. Macaulay said that the Jesuits "appear to have discovered the precise point to which intellectual culture can be carried without risk of intellectual emancipation." [9] Whether there really is such a point, and whether it is really possible to strike it precisely, is not at all clear. As the guiding geniuses of the American Medical Association daily demonstrate, political enlightenment is not a necessary by-product of a scientific education.)

In the United States, it can be argued—Dr. Szasz does argue at considerable length—that only the psychiatrists can actually call in the police to enforce conformity to their views (pp. 59–61). If it is next to impossible to send a man to jail for religious heresy and difficult to imprison him for political crimethink, it is relatively easy, possibly too easy, to lock him up when he deviates noticeably from the psychiatrist's standards of mental normality—standards that are quite likely to include the particular psychiatrist's notion of sound political opinions (pp. 3–4, 247). Szasz probably exaggerates the prestige and public acceptance of psychiatry and particularly psychoanalysis. It is probable that most God-fearing people, particularly run-of-the-mill Roman Catholics, Whole Gospel Protestants, and other such non- or anti-intellectuals, regard it with indifference or suspicion. But its faithful, though relatively few in numbers, are commonly men of high intelligence and education, full of public spirit and philanthropy. They hold positions of power out of proportion to their numbers, particularly in the legal profession, and they tend to regard most of life's problems as soluble by the proper application of psychiatric principles. It is this marriage of psychiatry and law, and the resultant issue of what Dr. Szasz sees as new crimes, new punishments, and

9. 1 MACAULAY, HISTORY OF ENGLAND 542 (Dutton ed. 1953).

new tyranny, that is the major thesis of his book.

Szasz, of course, is still a psychoanalyst and by no means free of the stigmata of his order. He reminds one of those men of the sixteenth century—men of the breed of Matthias and Knipperdoling—who, having thrown off the spell of Rome, proceeded to conceive theological lunacies far more preposterous than any of the superstitions they had renounced. Like a good psychiatrist he commences with shock therapy, by administering horse doctor's doses of nonsense. There is no such thing as mental illness! (Alarm in the audience.) There should be no such thing as involuntary mental hospitalization! (Panic and general rush for the fire exits.) If these assertions are made *pour épater les bourgeois*, as is probably the case, they have succeeded admirably, at least among Dr. Szasz's more staid colleagues, many of whom affect to take his iconoclasm literally and tap their foreheads knowingly when he is mentioned.[10] But in fact, our author is by no means so crazy as he seems, for it shortly appears that he is merely playing with labels. Though "mental illness" is imaginary, Dr. Szasz admits the existence of "problems in living" which require remedies essentially similar to those applied to mental illness (pp. 13-17). After we have abolished "involuntary mental hospitalization," we shall still have "legal provisions for so-called psychiatric emergencies," such as a maniac with a bundle of dynamite (p. 226). My alarm abates.

Once having satisfied myself that Dr. Szasz is in fact far from *meshuggah*, I am ready to recognize that there is a core of sound good sense at the heart of his jeremiad. That core is contained in chapter 10, "Criminal Responsibility," which deals with legal definitions of insanity, particularly the *Durham* rule, and chapter 11, "Acquittal by Reason of Insanity," which considers the disposition of persons so ac-

10. See, *e.g.*, Stafford-Clark, Book Review, 74 Yale L.J. 392 (1964).

quitted. His major propositions can be stated pretty shortly. The expansion of the insanity defense against charges of crime has produced not greater protection for those who deviate from accepted mores, but less; not greater separation of the criminal from the lunatic, but greater homologization of the two. For the first time in this country we have developed a system of oubliettes and *lettres de cachet* worthy of Louis XI or J. V. Stalin. The tale is most instructive, and not well understood by most laymen or even by lawyers.[11]

It is probable that for most people the problem of abuse of the insanity defense is still conceived in its classic form: the unjustified acquittal and release of a criminal rich enough to hire lawyers and alienists to persuade a maudlin jury that he had been temporarily insane. Mark Twain saw the problem so almost a century ago: "[T]he prisoner had never been insane before the murder, and under the tranquilizing effect of the butchering had immediately regained his right mind. . . . Formerly, if you killed a man, it was possible that you were insane—but now, if you, having friends and money, kill a man, it is *evidence* that you are a lunatic." [12] The archetypical case, still unforgotten after sixty years, is that of Harry K. Thaw, an unprepossessing wastrel whose mother's bottomless purse kept him out of the electric chair when he murdered Stanford White, an architect of real eminence.[13] Such highly publicized cases, featuring reams of psychiatric testimony, of which nothing is comprehensible to the newspaper reader except that each squad of experts denounces as ignorant flapdoodle the opinions of the other, have natu-

11. For a pioneering and prescient description and analysis of the problem, see Goldstein & Katz, *Dangerousness and Mental Illness: Some Observations on the Decision to Release Persons Acquitted by Reason of Insanity*, 70 YALE L.J. 225 (1960).

12. TWAIN, A *New Crime*, in SKETCHES NEW AND OLD 220, 222, 225 (Harper ed. 1917).

13. See O'CONNOR, COURTROOM WARRIOR: THE COMBATIVE CAREER OF WILLIAM TRAVERS JEROME 171–242 (1963).

rally tended to give the insanity defense a public reputation that is at best dubious.

This jaundiced view of the defendant who claims to be insane fits well with one common American attitude toward criminals, which is that they ought to be given the shortest shrift compatible with a strict construction of the Bill of Rights. The hanging judge, the man whose short way with criminals is one of his main qualifications for the job, has always been rather popular with the laity and even with large sections of the bar.[14] But, as usual with us, ruthless Mr. Hyde and compassionate Dr. Jekyll coexist (not always peacefully), and Dr. Jekyll sees the criminal defendant in a very different light. The infliction of punishment is acutely painful to Dr. Jekyll, for he cannot really bring himself to believe that there is such a thing as a bad man, who deserves to be punished.[15] This second American attitude toward criminals is splendidly illustrated by Will Rogers' idiotic remark that he never knew a man he didn't like. If Dr. Jekyll, having this state of mind, finds himself upon the bench, he is obviously in an agonizing dilemma; if he inflicts punishment upon a "criminal," in whose existence he does not believe, such dreadful feelings of guilt oppress him as might have afflicted a seventeenth-century judge who did not believe in witches. He is thus ripe for the psychiatrist, ready to grasp eagerly the suggestion that the prescription of therapy for sick men is a wholly different thing from the punishment of

14. A splendid specimen of the breed was Recorder John W. Goff, of the old New York General Sessions Court, of whom an admiring cop once said, "Recorder Goff is a fine man, but he thinks everybody ought to go to jail at least once." Old-time reporters and policemen told many such tales of Goff, mostly with affection.

15. As Recorder Goff was a prize-winning specimen of the hanging judge, so the points of the other breed were strongly developed, perhaps even overdeveloped, in the late Justice Curtis Bok of Pennsylvania. I have heretofore commented on Justice Bok's *Weltanschauung* in my review of his book, *Star Wormwood*, 69 Yale L.J. 193 (1959). See pp. 25–42 above.

bad men and that virtually all criminals are really sick. Hence the *Durham* rule,[16] designed to transform as many criminals as possible into patients of psychiatrists.

Action, of course, begets reaction. *Durham* stimulated Mr. Hyde to convulsive activity. Hyde echoes Festus: "Hast thou appealed unto Caesar? unto Caesar shalt thou go." [17] If you claim the benefits of insanity, we will see that you get them, in full measure, pressed down and running over. The speedy result of *Durham* was the passage of an act of Congress making commitment to an insane asylum mandatory for persons acquitted by reason of insanity.[18] The net result is that, in jurisdictions with mandatory commitment statutes,[19] one who successfully establishes his innocence by reason of insanity is likely to be a good deal worse off than a genuine criminal, who is sent to jail. Dr. Szasz makes abundantly clear—and here he has plenty of corroboration—that if the mental hospital to which the blameless one is dispatched differs at all from a penitentiary, it differs for the worse (pp.

16. The rule denies criminal responsibility if the accused's unlawful act "was the product of mental disease or mental defect." Durham v. United States, 214 F.2d 862, 874–75 (D. C. Cir. 1954).

17. Acts 25:12.

18. D. C. CODE ANN. § 24–301(d) (1961); see Krash, *The Durham Rule and Judicial Administration of the Insanity Defense in the District of Columbia*, 70 YALE L. J. 905, 941 (1961). Dr. Szasz reminds us of a half-forgotten piece of history. The protagonist of M'Naghten's Case, 10 Cl. & F. 200, 8 Eng. Rep. 718 (H. L. 1843), which laid down the orthodox rule on the insanity defense, ended his days in Broadmoore, the English equivalent of Matteawan. In fact, as Dr. Szasz does not seem to realize, the practice of automatic commitment of persons acquitted by reason of insanity goes back at least to the beginning of the last century. Even before the original Act of Parliament (39 & 40 Geo. 3, c.94) English and American courts on their own initiative assumed power to order such disposition of insane defendants. See Lynch v. Overholser, 369 U. S. 705, 720, 724–25 (1962) (Clark, J., dissenting).

19. There are at least a dozen, including New York. See Lynch v. Overholser, *supra* note 19, at 709 n.4. Similar problems seem to exist in England. See Thomas, *Theories of Punishment in the Court of Criminal Appeal*, 27 MODERN L. REV. 546, 561–62 (1964).

Law, Liberty, and Psychiatry

83–84).[20] There is scarcely a pretense of therapy. No term
is set to his imprisonment. He may very well pay five or ten
years for a crime that a sane man could commit for a maximum price of eighteen months. Indeed, since there is no
psychiatric therapy for "sociopathic personality disturbance,
antisocial reaction," a piece of psychiatric cant meaning
criminal propensities, it is entirely possible that the psychiatrists in charge of the institution will *never* be willing to cer-
tify that he can be released without danger to the public.

Thus, the merciful *Durham* rule permits life imprisonment
for relatively minor offenses. Worst of all, the gates of the
Durham type of prison are far harder to push open by legal
means than are those of the ordinary pen. No matter how
indifferent or arbitrary the refusal of the prisoner-patient's
medical custodian to release him as sane, it is exceedingly
difficult even for an inmate who has friends and money—
and virtually impossible for the ordinary wretch—to obtain
meaningful judicial review. In theory, of course, the Great
Writ runs to the superintendent of a hospital as surely as
to the warden of a penitentiary. Practically, Dr. Szasz is right
in saying that habeas corpus is far from an adequate remedy
(pp. 66–70). Considering the fact that asylums, unlike prisons, do not usually have law libraries, the writ is sought by
surprising numbers of inmates (practically all of them on
the criminal side of the campus), but with minimal success.
The reasons for this monotony of result were candidly stated
by a majority of the court in *Ragsdale v. Overholser.*[21] The
court is naturally inclined to lay great weight on expert evi-

20. The Court of Appeals for the Second Circuit has found it unnecessary to decide whether Matteawan is a hospital or a jail, although
it exhibited a strong preference in favor of the jail classification. United
States *ex rel.* Carroll v. McNeill, 294 F.2d 117, 121 (2d Cir. 1961),
judgment vacated and case remanded with directions to dismiss as moot,
369 U.S. 149 (1962).
21. 281 F.2d 943 (D. C. Cir. 1960).

dence, which is almost always unanimously against an indigent petitioner; indeed many a judge may suspect that a petition in forma pauperis emanating from a mental institution is probably itself a symptom of paranoia. Even if the claimant to sanity (or at least harmlessness) is rich enough to hire his own psychiatrists, the expert testimony will be in sharp conflict—and the mandatory commitment statute has been construed to mean not only that the petitioner must bear the burden of showing that his release creates no potential danger to the public, but that he must do so *beyond a reasonable doubt*.[22] Even in the rare cases in which the psychiatrists are willing to take a chance, the courts are likely to throw up legal obstacles to freedom.[23] In short, the odds against the petitioner are today so crushing that only a lunatic would allow himself to be acquitted by reason of insanity.

The problem is beginning to be perceived, and limits are beginning to be set to the more or less benign despotism of the psychiatrists under the *Durham* rule and the anti-*Durham* statutes. The Supreme Court has limited the District of Columbia mandatory commitment statute, and presumably its congeners in other jurisdictions, to cases in which the defendant himself pleads the defense of insanity; the Court invoked the rough justice of the "appeal unto Caesar" argument.[24] The D. A.'s office can no longer, by itself raising the insanity defense, turn the *Durham* rule into a device for the indefinite incarceration of nuisances.[25] Moreover, there are other judicial intimations that some process is due even a putative madman. In the *Ragsdale* case itself, in which

22. *Id.* at 946–47.
23. *Cf.* Hough v. United States, 271 F.2d 485 (D. C. Cir. 1959); *In re* Golden, 341 Mass. 672, 171 N.E.2d 473 (1961).
24. Lynch v. Overholser, 369 U. S. 705, 715, (1962).
25. See Note, A *Logical Analysis of Criminal Responsibility and Mandatory Commitment*, 70 Yale L. J. 1354 (1961).

the majority of the court laid so much stress on the presumption against release, Judge Fahy, concurring, made the modest suggestion that "due process may well require . . . that within a reasonable time, which will vary from case to case, continued confinement be made dependent upon civil commitment proceedings, with their greater procedural safeguards. . . ." [26] The Court of Appeals for the Second Circuit has held unconstitutional, as denying the equal protection of the laws, a New York statute that permits the Commissioner of Mental Hygiene to transfer from an ordinary mental hospital to an institution for the criminally insane anyone who happens to be an ex-convict, if he "manifests criminal tendencies"—as by trying to escape—while in the noncriminal loony bin. Unfortunately the petitioner's death while the appeal was pending caused the Supreme Court to vacate the judgment as moot.[27]

Most important of all, there are many indications that the bar, or its more conscientious elements, has begun to realize that the person accused of mental illness has no less need of counsel than the person accused of crime.[28] The key to the problem appears to lie in the devising of fair procedures, not wholly dominated by psychiatrists, to review involuntary confinement for mental illness, and in making sure that counsel are available for those inmates who are capable of cooperating in their own hearings. Habeas corpus *can* be an adequate remedy, when even the indigent inmate has a lawyer and a chance to be examined by impartial doctors. This, of course, is far easier said than done, but the problem must

26. 281 F.2d at 951.
27. United States *ex rel.* Carroll v. McNeill, 294 F.2d 117 (2d Cir. 1961), *judgment vacated and case remanded with directions to dismiss as moot*, 369 U. S. 149 (1962).
28. See, *e.g.*, the October 1964 issue of THE LEGAL AID BRIEF CASE (Vol. 23, No. 1)—the organ of the National Legal Aid and Defender Association—which is largely devoted to "Legal Rights of the Mentally Ill."

be tackled if we are to avoid Dr. Szasz's peculiarly unpleasant version of Orwell's *1984.*

Dilation upon the criminal problem precludes adequate comment on some of Dr. Szasz's secondary philippics—notably his argument that simplicity is anything but a virtue in civil commitment procedures, since it is a synonym for the easy railroading of the unwanted and for the denial of due process (ch. 5); and his very shrewd analysis of the absurd and undignified role of the psychiatrist in probate proceedings, which is essentially to create "the impression that a scientific decision has been reached" (p. 76) by giving a scientifically impossible expert opinion on the sanity of a man on whom he never laid eyes. Szasz may be irreverent, he may even be guilty of some hyperbole, when he says that "questioning the testator's sanity serves to set aside a will that injures the community's sense of fair play in the inheritance game" (p. 75),[29] but he is uncomfortably close to the truth.

I cannot forbear mention of one fearsome problem that Dr. Szasz raises but (most uncharacteristically) leaves unresolved. That is the problem of the madman who is also a head of state. Szasz actually raises the problem in its least serious form, as exemplified by King Ludwig II of Bavaria (pp. 48–53). Ludwig, though dotty enough, resembled his equally dotty Roman prototype, the Emperor Elagabalus,[30] for he was dangerous to nothing except the Treasury. If he

29. But I cannot take literally his statement, on the same page, that the very fact that the will is contested shows that the testator had adequate contact with reality, because it demonstrates that he wanted to disinherit his natural heirs and knew the rules for doing so. An octogenarian's desire to leave his wealth to a cutie in white, who has fed him his gruel and pills and otherwise soothed his aches and pains, may denote contact with reality; as much can hardly be said when the principal beneficiary is a crank foundation.

30. See 1 GIBBON, DECLINE AND FALL OF THE ROMAN EMPIRE 282 (Milman ed. 1914).

had been a private citizen there would have been no reason to lock him up. But what are we to do when a Roman Caesar, *deus ac dominus,* or the Autocrat of all the Russias, or *der Führer,* or the First Secretary of the Communist Party, happens to be a homicidal maniac? We need not look backward to Caligula or Ivan the Terrible: Stalin's unending purges and Hitler's *Endlösung* of the Jewish question are still quite fresh in memory. The chances of popular revolt against such tyrants seem to be practically nil; they are, in fact, usually admired and even loved by the rabble. We are told that for long after Nero's death his tomb was regularly adorned with flowers,[31] presumably by humble citizens who admired his grandiose style, as the German *Spiessbürger* of thirty years ago admired Göring's. The only ways, other than natural death, to remove such monsters have been external conquest or palace conspiracy, usually the latter. In such polities the palace revolution, despite its obvious deficiencies, seems to be the best solution so far devised, and maybe the only imaginable one. Whether future Harmodiuses and Aristogeitons will consult their psychiatrists before resolving to remove the contemporary Hipparchuses remains to be seen.

This review is of inordinate length. That it is so is a tribute to Dr. Szasz's considerable ability to make challenging and provocative statements—and to the fact that he is rarely *totally* wrong.

———

Dr. Szasz still gets occasional headlines by laying down rolling barrages on his colleagues, but the surprise and shock

31. See 2 SUETONIUS, THE LIVES OF THE CAESARS 185 (Loeb ed. 1930).

effects have largely worn off. Psychoanalysis itself seems to be held in lower esteem, and to excite less interest and controversy, than was the case even five years ago. This is probably because there is growing realization that, however interesting and entertaining its theories, it is not an effective method of dealing with serious mental disorders, and also for the reason that the mullahs of the Old and New Lefts, who exert a powerful influence on the psychoanalysts' natural constituency (which approximately coincides with the bi-weekly circulation of the New York Review of Books), tolerate no orthodoxies other than their own. Yoga, whose failure to pick up more of the market caused me some surprise in 1965, does, to be sure, seem to be enjoying something of a revival; Maharishi Mahesh Yogi's brand of unreason competes with Jerry Rubin's on a number of campuses and probably does even better among the middle-aged and elderly. But the young seem to take very little interest in Freud, Jung, Adler, and their epigones.

My prediction that the Catholic Church was about to change its views on divorce and birth control was at least premature. Pope Paul VI clings to them long after they have ceased to be marketable, as Henry Ford I clung to the Model T. But he is getting more back talk from the faithful, and even the hierarchy, than any pope since Leo X and Clement VII, and I still think it probable that Holy Church will change her mind almost as soon as Paul is gathered to his fathers.

The law is still wrestling with the problem of the insanity defense and is likely to do so for decades to come. Perhaps the difference between the old McNaghten rule (a defendant is legally sane if he knows the nature and quality of his act and that it is wrongful) and the new Durham rule (he is legally insane if his act "was the product of mental disease or mental defect") has less practical importance than

94

has been thought; judges and juries are likely to reach the same result in a given case no matter which verbal formula is applied. The question of proper disposition of the criminally insane is far tougher and far more important. The Soviet government's recent free resort to the technique of getting rid of dissenters by incarcerating them in insane asylums shows the dimensions of the problem.

The "Warren Court"

THE NEW YORK TIMES MAGAZINE,
September 7, 1969

THE JUDGMENT OF HISTORY may well be that the Supreme
Court was the distinctive feature of the polity of the United
States, as extraordinary as the dual kingship of Sparta or the
Mameluke slave-sultans of Egypt. Since 1803, when the
Court decided *Marbury v. Madison,* it has been settled that
"a law repugnant to the Constitution is void." In practice
this means that five of nine lawyers (not all of them statesmen, or even politicians) have the power, in the name of
the Constitution, to nullify acts of the President, the Congress and the states and sometimes to compel them to do the
five Justices' will. Charles Evans Hughes (before he went on
the Court) phrased it with characteristic directness and
accuracy: "We are under a Constitution, but the Constitution is what the judges say it is." If the judges see in it things
not visible to the eyes of laymen, or even other lawyers, the
only recourse of those aggrieved is to persuade the Court to
overrule itself, which is difficult, or to amend the Constitution, which is still more difficult.

Whether this enormous power can fairly be deduced from

the language of the Constitution, and whether the framers of that instrument intended to confer it on the Justices, has been the subject of vast learned controversy, much of it highly polemical, still continuing and unlikely ever to be resolved. The proposition that a law repugnant to the Supreme Court is void is certainly not self-evident. Andrew Jackson and Abraham Lincoln strongly disputed it. Franklin Roosevelt not only accepted the Court's power with very ill grace but vigorously, though unsuccessfully, attempted to do something about it. Other countries with written constitutions have no such doctrine. In trying to explain it to Frenchmen and Germans, and even Englishmen, I have encountered difficulty resembling that which a higher mathematician would face if he tried to teach me that on the planets circling Alpha Centauri two plus two is sometimes three and sometimes five but only occasionally four.

No matter; the power exists—in large part because the Court has used it sparingly and generally prudently. John Marshall, indeed, first invoked it in order to extricate the Court from an embarrassing predicament, by holding that an act of Congress which gave the Court jurisdiction of a hot political potato was inconsistent with the Constitution and therefore void. Rarely have the Justices pushed their prerogative so far as to remind Congressmen that under Article III of the Constitution the Court has appellate jurisdiction "with such Exceptions, and under such Regulations as the Congress shall make." The Court's most clearly disastrous interpretation of the Constitution, in Dred Scott's case, was overruled at Appomattox.

There have been, of course, long periods when the Court did nothing in particular and generated correspondingly little interest and controversy among the nonlawyer part of the American public. But there have also been periods of galvanic activity when it played a major role—perhaps *the*

97

major role—in the governmental process. One such was John Marshall's tenure as Chief Justice. Another was the Hughes Court of the 1930's. The decisions of those Courts were epochal, but it is doubtful that either of them was half so well known to its contemporaries, or excited half so much public enthusiasm and detestation, as the Court over which Earl Warren presided from 1953 until June of 1969. It would be hard to find many ordinary people who know what the Supreme Court held in *Marbury v. Madison* or even *Schechter Poultry Corporation v. United States* (which shot down the blue eagle of F. D. R.'s National Recovery Administration). But most literate Americans know, and probably have strong opinions about, the decisions of the Warren Court in the school desegregation case (*Brown v. Board of Education*), the reapportionment case (*Baker v. Carr*) and the right-to-counsel cases (notably *Gideon v. Wainwright* and *Miranda v. Arizona*).

The Court's friends think it has rejuvenated the Constitution, turned its guarantees into something more than Fourth-of-July rhetoric and extended them to people to whom the Bill of Rights had never before been of much use. The school of opinion whose views crystallized in vociferous demands for Earl Warren's impeachment saw the Court as a gang of elderly hippies in judicial robes, persecuting religion and encouraging license on a scale unheard of since Nero's time. It had abandoned the Republic to the depredations of anarchists, atheists, black revolutionaries, pornographers and muggers; nothing could save us but prompt impeachment of the Chief Justice and restoration of the Constitution to its original condition.

Although I use the term myself as a convenient bit of shorthand, it should be stressed at the outset that it is inaccurate to label the Supreme Court of 1953–1969 as "the Warren Court." Seventeen Justices sat on the Court during

98

these years, most of them men of strong intellect, strong personality and strong convictions. When the Chief Justice, former Governor of California and aspirant to the Republican nomination for President, came to the Court, he joined five of Franklin Roosevelt's appointees (Black, Reed, Frankfurter, Douglas and Jackson) and three of Harry Truman's (Clark, Burton and Minton). Only the Chief himself and the durable Justices Black and Douglas sat during the entire sixteen years. The others were succeeded by four men of generally liberal persuasion (Brennan, Goldberg, Fortas and Marshall), two who cannot even roughly be classified as conservative or liberal (Stewart and White) and only two who could with approximate fairness be described as conservatives (Harlan and Whitaker).

President Eisenhower is reported to have called Warren's appointment "the biggest damfool mistake I ever made," which is saying a good deal. If it was a mistake, it was not all that big, for it is unlikely that the Court's decisions would have been greatly different if Warren had turned out to be precisely what Eisenhower supposed him to be. The Chief Justice has one vote out of nine. He is raised a little above his brethren in that he is paid $62,500 a year instead of $60,000. He rates a limousine and an additional law clerk, but is entitled to no extra ruching on his robe. He does preside over oral arguments and the conferences at which decisions are reached; if he is one of the majority, he determines who shall write the opinion of the Court.

These levers of power, such as they are, may contribute something to the dominance of a strong Chief Justice, such as Hughes. But there is no evidence that Warren exercised any such commanding influence over his brethren. The theory that his persuasiveness produced an unusual harmony among the Justices during his tenure is simply not borne out by the facts; there were actually *more* dissents than usual during those years. The unanimity of the Court's opinion in the original school desegregation case has sometimes been credited to his statesmanship, but I think it far more probable that the cause of that unanimity is to be found in the merits of the question.

Regardless of whether the Court of 1953–1969 is called the Warren Court, or the Black-Douglas Court, or the Brennan Court (from Eisenhower's standpoint, Brennan was probably a worse blunder than Warren, for he is at least as "liberal" and "activist" and fifteen years younger), or simply the Goddamn Supreme Court, there is little doubt that it was the object of more heartfelt execration by conservatives than any other Supreme Court in our history— vials of wrath even fuller than those which liberals poured out on the Court of 1935. Some of the indignation might have been averted or at least mitigated without any sacrifice of principle, for the opinions of the Justices sometimes displayed an unfortunate and undiplomatic tendency to preach, to throw in arguments and authorities which were as unnecessary to the result as they were calculated to infuriate conservatives and irritate moderates.

Brown v. Board of Education could well have rested on the single, simple and straightforward ground that "separate educational facilities are inherently unequal," without adducing the "modern authority" of assorted psychologists and sociologists, most of them (with the oustanding exceptions of Kenneth Clark and Gunnar Myrdal) fairly obscure in 1954 and equally so today, to show that segregation retarded the mental development of Negro children. The holding of *Miranda v. Arizona,* that a man being questioned by the police is entitled to be told that he can remain silent and that he can have a lawyer, would surely have upset the cops and their friends much less if the Chief Justice had forgone a lengthy, lurid and probably somewhat overdrawn essay on

the physical and psychological "brutality" of police inter-
rogators. At the same time he managed to annoy the down-
with-the-Cossacks faction of liberals by holding up the F. B. I.
as an exemplar of fairness. (And from the rather special
standpoint of connoisseurs of classic murders, there was a
certain irony in the Court's heavy reliance on *Bram v. United
States*, which reversed the conviction of a man who had
butchered three harmless people with an ax.)

Some of the Court's unhappy public relations must be
blamed on sheer bad luck. It was not the Justices' fault that
Danny Escobedo, whose case laid down the not very startling
rule that a man who is being questioned by the police is entitled to a lawyer when he asks for one, happened to be the
sort who was pretty sure to get himself in further serious
trouble with the criminal law almost as soon as he was
sprung from the Illinois pen. Even worse luck was the
Fortas debacle. The rest of the Court, of course, had nothing
to do with either the rise or fall of Mr. Justice Fortas, and
indeed seems to have given him scant sympathy. Nonetheless
he was, on and off Capitol Hill, a highly visible and vulnerable symbol of the "Warren Court." As Dickens proved in
what may be the greatest scene in *Pickwick*, when the Reverend Mr. Stiggins appears at the monthly meeting of the
Temperance Association far gone in rum-and-water, nothing
gladdens the public heart so much as the fall from grace of
the excessively righteous—and Mr. Justice Fortas had treated
the public to some of the most righteous homilies ever delivered from the highest bench. When the news was told in
Gath and published in the mass media of Askelon, the liberals did not openly join in the rejoicings of the Philistines, but
neither did they look particularly downcast.

All this said, I concede that no sugar coating could have
been thick enough to make some of the Court's major decisions—notably in the sensitive areas of electoral equality,

race relations and criminal procedure—palatable to large segments of the population, including a great many highly vocal politicians. But in these areas it is my judgment (which I readily admit to be only that of an ordinary citizen, for I am not by trade a Supreme Court watcher and handicapper) that (1) the Court was right and (2) most people know it was right.

Earl Warren's own judgment was that the single most important decision of the sixteen years was *Baker v. Carr*. Most political scientists and politicians would agree with him. By 1962, when the Court at long last decided that it had the right and duty to hear a voter's complaint that his vote was unconstitutionally debased by an antiquated Tennessee statute's allotment of members of the legislature among the state's counties, legislative malapportionment had become a scandal and an affront to democracy. In Tennessee, a vote in Moore County was worth nineteen in Hamilton County—and Tennessee was not a particularly horrible example. There were several states in which a rural vote weighed a hundred times as much as an urban or suburban one. Congressional districts were somewhat less bad, but there were half a dozen states in which some members of the House represented three times as many voters as other Congressmen.

Felix Frankfurter was, of course, right when he called the situation a "political thicket," but he was wrong when he warned the Court not to enter it. The plain fact was that if the Court would not treat the disease, it would go untreated and maybe kill the patient, for the rustic politicians whose dominance of state legislatures malapportionment had made possible could hardly be expected to pass reform legislation which would abolish their power and themselves. As Mr. Justice Clark said, "I would not consider intervention by this Court into so delicate a field if there were any other relief available to the people of Tennessee."

In fact, although the Court shortly extended to Congressional districts and local governments the requirement that "a State make an honest and good faith effort to construct districts, in both Houses of its legislature, as nearly of equal population as is practicable," the Justices' ventures into what Frankfurter and Harlan called "a massive repudiation of the experience of our whole past" and also an assertion of "destructively novel judicial power" has not proved a catastrophe. The inferior Federal judges, who bear the brunt of enforcing the one-man-one-vote rule, have, of course, had to grapple with ferocious geographic and demographic problems, complicated by the introduction of computers and such peculiar concepts as election districts in the shapes of doughnuts and dumbbells. They have nonetheless managed greatly to reduce the incidence of rotten boroughs without much actual resort to such drastic remedies as ordering elections at large.

The change in the quality of state legislatures has naturally been startling and alarming to conservatives: Many of the states are actively considering, for example, reforms of their laws on divorce and abortion which would have been unthinkable a few years ago. The earnest efforts of Ev Dirksen and like-minded politicians to overrule *Baker* and its progeny by amending the Constitution are unlikely to succeed, for the simple reason that the people who benefited from reapportionment greatly outnumber those who lost by it. Indeed, the Court's intervention has been so successful that it may be encouraged to do something about another time-honored and cherished political racket, the gerrymander. (But the outstanding example of over- and under-representation, the United States Senate, is beyond the Court's reach, for the provisions which give two Senators to New York and California and two also to Alaska and Nevada are entrenched in the Constitution itself, as part of the original bargain, and cannot be changed without the consent of the very states which are so magnificently over-represented.)

Brown v. Board of Education and the rest of the desegregation cases, although they marked a new era, cannot really be regarded as innovations of the Warren Court. By 1954 *Plessy v. Ferguson,* the original "separate-but-equal" case, was plainly on its last legs. It could not have survived reconsideration by even a conservative Court. Overt resentment of *Brown,* like its impact, has been largely confined to the states of the old Confederacy and is by no means universal even in them. Not many modern Americans would defend segregation by law; it is doubtful that even those brothers under the skin, George Wallace and Stokely Carmichael, would *openly* argue that it ought to be illegal for black and white to intermarry or use the same swimming pool.

In any case, judicial efforts to frustrate the stalling tactics employed to preserve legal segregation (and those efforts have often been marked by more deliberation than speed) cannot cure the greater ill, which is *de facto* segregation. The courts cannot, for example, do much to keep middle-class parents from escaping to unbusable suburbs or expensive private schools. They can do even less to abolish slums, segregated or integrated.

I take a very skeptical view of Justice Douglas's recent dictum that it is racial discrimination in the sale or rental of housing which "herds men into ghettos." The real-estate business is undoubtedly full of such discrimination, but no imaginable reform in the attitudes and practices of real-estate dealers, assuming that the courts could bring it about, would translate black slum dwellers (or white ones) into hygienic and more or less educated neighborhoods. That will require radical social and economic change, which only the executive and legislative branches have the means to accomplish. In the long run, the importance of *Brown* and the other desegregation cases may be seen to lie in their having put the law behind the Negro's claim to equality and reminded Congress of its constitutional power to outlaw private discrimination and do something to make the poor less poor.

The ordinary man's bitterest complaints about the Warren Court are based far less on the desegregation or reapportionment cases than on his notions of its attitude toward criminals. He sees it as a little clique of merciful asses, brimful of what Learned Hand once called the "watery sentiment that obstructs, delays and defeats the prosecution of crime." Not content with ordering a general jail delivery, it has instigated a carnival of crime by making it virtually impossible for the police to obtain a conviction or even make an arrest. The criminals in "Dick Tracy" prate incessantly and arrogantly about their constitutional rights; even Dick is able to obtain convictions only by paralyzing them with moon rays and photographing them *flagrante delicto*. Sometimes he can protect the public only by shooting the criminal himself. The picture is frightening, but not entirely accurate.

If we actually look at the Court's best known decisions on due process in criminal cases, we find that *Gideon v. Wainwright* gave indigent defendants in all state felony trials what they already had in Federal courts and the courts of most of the states, a right to a free lawyer; *Escobedo v. Illinois* held that police interrogating a suspect in their custody must honor his request to consult with his lawyer; and *Miranda v. Arizona* added to this that prior to interrogation a person in police custody must be told that he is not required to say anything, that anything he does say may be used against him, and that he is entitled to a lawyer (free if he is broke) if he wants one—warnings reminiscent of the Judges' Rules which have long been in force in England and are familiar to all readers of detective stories.

None of these decisions seems revolutionary. In essence, they gave to poor, unskilled criminals what Mafiosi and the likes of Louis Wolfson had had all along—the means to exercise their constitutional rights to keep silent and talk to a lawyer. They took some of the sting out of Mr. Dooley's remark that "a poor man has a chanst in coort. . . . He has th' same chanst there that he has outside. He has a splendid poor man's chanst." Whatever merit there may be in the argument that society needs more protection and criminals less, there can be none in the proposition that rich, sophisticated criminals deserve a better chance than poor, ignorant criminals.

Moreover, such studies as have been made seem to suggest that Congress's attempt in the Crime Control Act of 1968 to overrule *Miranda* and similar cases is not only unconstitutional but unnecessary. Diligent students of the Yale Law School, manning around-the-clock shifts in New Haven police stations during the summer of 1966, concluded that *Miranda* had made very little difference to law enforcement in our fairly typical city—in part because the police rarely arrest suspects without substantial evidence and thus do not rely heavily on interrogation, and partly because compliance with *Miranda's* requirements does not seem to increase suspects' reluctance to answer questions. The decision's main visible effect was a certain sapping of police morale, resulting from its perfectly gratuitous strictures on police practice.

In short, the popular view that the Court has coddled criminals is simply not supported by the facts. Its holdings have not been revolutionary, and they have not crippled law enforcement. Some of them in fact, such as those which upheld the policeman's right to stop and frisk in circumstances which would not justify an arrest, or to conceal the identity of informers before trial, are regarded by some emotional liberals as evidences of a cop mentality. These decisions have received far less publicity than *Gideon* and *Miranda*—perhaps because they do not fit the Court's image.

There is no more rational basis for the opinion that the Court is determined to bulldoze down the Temples of the Gods and generally to eradicate religion from American life. *Engel v. Vitale*, which was widely mistaken for a holding that it is illegal for children to pray, held only that the use of public school time and teachers in the recitation of a blandly undenominational little prayer (addressed to "Almighty God" and seeking special favor for children, teachers, parents and the country at large) was an unconstitutional "establishment" of religion. Justice Black, who wrote the Court's opinion, did his best to soothe the sensibilities of the pious by inserting a little sermon in favor of both religion and prayer. He might have added that the effect of the decision on the quantity of genuine religion in the United States would be approximately nil; children (as I can testify from personal experience) do not become devout by gabbling twenty-two words once a day. The children and the teachers were left with perfect freedom to pray as much as they liked and in any form that appealed to them, at home or in church or, for that matter, in school. The real mystery is why the plaintiffs, the defendants, or the twenty-two state attorneys general who filed briefs *amici curiae* urging that the prayer be upheld cared enough to litigate the case.

Similar observations may be made about *School District v. Schempp*, which came to the same conclusion about Bible reading in the public schools. I have long been made unhappy by the rising generation's almost total ignorance of the majestic literature of the Old and New Testaments, but I doubt very much that they would be better off for being exposed to a few verses at the beginning of the school day.

In areas of greater practical importance, the Court treated

organized religion very kindly indeed. It held, for example, that the states could constitutionally supply textbooks to parochial schools; moreover, it did so by reasoning which has suggested to many state legislators that grants of public money to religious schools might also be constitutional. It held that a state cannot deny unemployment compensation to a Seventh Day Adventist who turns down a job which requires work on Saturday. And it refused to review state court decisions that property used for religious purposes could constitutionally be exempted from taxation. *That* enormous question will arise to plague the Burger Court.

In one treacherous area nearly everybody seems to agree that the Court has gone wrong, although there is no agreement among the Justices or anyone else as to the course it should have taken. I refer, of course, to the question of the extent to which the constitutional guarantee of freedom of speech stands as a shield between the police and "obscenity," whatever that word may mean. In half a dozen major cases the Court (and the individual Justices, for most of them filed separate and lengthy opinions) struggled with the monster, and in each one elaborated and augmented the confusion created by its predecessors.

The opinions are rich in touchstones by which censors and lower courts may tell "obscenity," which is not protected by the First and Fourteenth Amendments, from unconventional art and literature, which are. A book is obscene if "to the average person, applying contemporary community standards, the dominant theme of the material taken as a whole appeals to prurient interest." Fearing that this lucid explanation might be open to misunderstanding, the Court added that even material which did appeal to prurient interest and was, moreover, "patently offensive" could not be suppressed unless it was "*utterly* without redeeming social value." The lower courts, alas, continued to show signs of bewilderment. So the Court added yet another test: Does the publisher's advertising demonstrate an intent to "pander" to his customers' "erotic interest"? Peering through all this verbal murk, I sympathize, though I do not agree, with Justice Stewart, who equated obscenity with "hard-core pornography" and added that, although he would not and perhaps could not define that phrase, "I know it when I see it."

"Obscenity" remains triumphantly undefined. The upshot is that nine middle-aged or elderly (and, with one or two exceptions, sedate) lawyers have spent an inordinate amount of time reading books and watching movies which would bring a blush to the cheek of a mule or even of an editor of the Grove Press. The lower courts have wasted still more time in such pursuits. (This is, by the way, more than the sellers of dirty books have to do, for the Court mercifully held unconstitutional an ordinance which imposed strict criminal liability on a bookseller regardless of whether he had any knowledge of the book's contents.)

Oscar Wilde said, "There is no such thing as an immoral book. Books are well written or badly written." For some reason, pornography is with few exceptions badly written. It may be that the only alternative to the agonies of judicial boredom implicit in the present rule (if it can be called such) on obscenity is the straightforward and simple view of Justices Black and Douglas that *all* varieties of expression, "obscene" or no, are protected by the Constitution. Justice Douglas, indeed, cast a solitary vote in favor of reviewing the case of a couple of young ladies from Southern California who claimed that the Bill of Rights included a right to express themselves by wearing topless costumes. But the rest of the court, including Justice Black, had apparently had enough.

This summary of the Court and its doings in sixteen turbulent years includes, of course, only those decisions on which the public image of the Court was based, and not all of them. Much could be, has been and will be written, for example, about the Court's antitrust decisions, remarkable chiefly for the violence of the arguments among lawyers and economists as to their meaning and the fact that from 1953 to 1967 the Government won forty-two out of the forty-five cases in which it was the plaintiff.

Something might be said about the nettles which the Court chose *not* to grasp—notably the question of the constitutionality of exempting from conscription people who object to war on religious grounds but not those who have philosophical reservations about it, and the problem of the President's power, without a declaration of war, to send the armed forces of the United States into combat overseas. These questions may—but probably will not—be tackled by the Burger Court, if it comes to be called that.

Despite the ritual garment-rending of the more excitable liberals, that Court is unlikely to reverse course and head back into the dark ages. True, Warren and Fortas, both mainstays of the "liberal" or "activist" wing of the Court, have already been replaced by Burger and Blackmun, both of them lawyers with conservative (although not reactionary) leanings; Justices Black, Douglas and Harlan, all of them born in the 19th century, may well die or retire in the next four (or eight) years. A Court composed of five Nixon appointees, plus Stewart and White, with only Brennan and Marshall left to fly the old flag, would certainly be more inclined than the Warren Court to proceed slowly and with circumspection—in any direction.

It is likely that the sort of lawyer who inspires confidence in Mr. Nixon will be temperamentally cautious and responsive to the mood of the "forgotten Americans" who feel that criminals have received far too much solicitude and protection and their victims far too little. Both Burger and

Blackmun seem to fit that description. A Nixon Court could in strict theory undo everything the Warren Court has done since 1953, putting criminals, minorities and urban voters back where God and the Founding Fathers intended them to be. There is, of course, nothing but judicial etiquette to deter the Supreme Court from changing its mind and over-ruling its own earlier decisions; it has often done so, although usually only after a decent time had elapsed and circumstances and prevailing attitudes had changed. Indeed, many of the Warren Court's landmark decisions—*Brown v. Board of Education, Baker v. Carr* and *Gideon v. Wainwright,* for example—more or less frankly overruled earlier cases.

But this is very unlikely to happen. Few people today would want to kill *Brown, Baker* or *Gideon,* and in any event these cases have largely done their work. The vulnerable decisions are *Miranda* and the related cases on police interrogation, which are also the most unpopular among rank-and-file voters.

I do not think that even a Court with a law-and-order majority would overrule *Miranda.* There are, however, several ways in which it could narrowly circumscribe whatever effect the case might have if left in full vigor. It could, for instance, take a very strict view of what constitutes police "custody" and a very liberal view of what constitutes "waiver" by a suspect of his right to counsel. Congress has tried to dilute the *Miranda* rule by providing in the Crime Control and Safe Streets Act of 1968 that voluntary confessions shall be admissible in Federal trials and that a confession may be found voluntary despite the failure of the police to inform the suspect of his rights to remain silent and talk to a lawyer. By the same token, the provision of that act which requires the admission of eyewitness testimony seems to be intended to kill *United States v. Wade,* which extended the *Miranda* rule by holding that evidence of identification in a police lineup could be barred unless the suspect was represented by counsel. A Court so minded could retreat from *Miranda*, without actually overruling it, by holding (wrongly, in my opinion, but not altogether implausibly) that legislative approval and authorization (though unaccompanied by any legislative effort to insure that a suspect's constitutional rights are observed) confer on police practice a sufficient aura of legitimacy to make constitutional the admission of evidence so obtained. These provisions of the Crime Control Act apply only to Federal trials, but many state legislatures would not be hesitant about copying Congress.

At any rate, it is safe to predict that such a Court would not be quick to invent new protections for criminals, rich or poor. The right to a free lawyer would not be extended to persons accused of misdemeanor (though conviction of some misdemeanors can have serious consequences). When confronted with the argument that the death penalty, having become unusual, has thus become cruel as well, and so forbidden by the Eighth Amendment, a majority of such a Court might be swayed by the old-fashioned, perhaps reprehensible, but undoubtedly popular notion that in some criminals hanging effects a salutary improvement and ought to be more usual than it is—an attitude summed up in the well-known observation of a Scotch judge that the defendant "would be none the worse for a hanging."

Such a cautious Court would not borrow trouble. It would not, for example, go so far out of its way to kick Congress in the pants as did the Warren Court in the case of Adam Clayton Powell. (The Court was probably right in holding that the Constitution did not permit Congress to exclude— as distinct from expel—an elected representative who met its explicit requirements that he be twenty-five years of age, a citizen of the United States for seven years, and an inhabitant of the state in which he was elected; but the practical effect of that decision, like the Court's reason for making it, remains somewhat obscure.) It may likewise be surmised that such a Court would not be eager to wade deeper into the slough of obscenity; the lower courts would be left to make what they can of the existing ground rules.

But even if the Court comes to be dominated by Nixon appointees—which will not happen right away, if ever—it will not overrule the great decisions of the Warren Court, or even distinguish them out of existence. The Court has too much continuity for that. Moreover, as almost everyone knows, the records of its members before their appointment have rarely been reliable predictors of their conduct as Justices. After all, Earl Warren laid the foundation of his career as a tough prosecuting attorney.

━━━━━━━

My guesses about the post-Earl Warren course of the Supreme Court have not yet been falsified. Chief Justice Burger and Justice Blackmun, although they respect the Constitution, are not likely to try to improve it. Epater les bourgeois is not their style.

Since I wrote, in September, 1969, the Court has handed down a number of important decisions, but no blockbusters like Brown v. Board of Education or Baker v. Carr. Perhaps its most remarkable performance is Welsh v. United States, in which a plurality made up of the Old Guard (Black, Douglas, Brennan, and Marshall) sternly refused to face the question of the constitutionality of the provision of the Selective Service Act which exempts from the draft religious, but not philosophical or moral, objectors to war. Welsh himself honestly denied that his opposition to war had any

connection with religious training or belief, but the four
Justices knew better. Reversing the lower court for placing
"undue emphasis on the registrant's interpretation of his own
beliefs," they pointed out that "very few registrants are fully
aware of the broad scope of the word 'religious' as used in
§ 6(j) of the Act." Small wonder. Congressmen were equally
ignorant, until the Court explained to them that what they
really meant by "religious" was any belief, whether moral,
ethical, or religious, which is "held with the strength of
traditional religious conviction." (The four did not place
undue emphasis on the fact that Congress had explicitly
provided that "religious training and belief . . . does not
include essentially political, sociological, or philosophical
views or a merely personal moral code.") In all the Court's
long history there is no finer example of the art of dodging
an explosive constitutional-political issue by turning upside
down the perfectly plain, although probably unconstitutional, intent of Congress.

I I

Morality and Politics,
Old and New

The Rise and Fall of
Sancho Panza

YALE LAW JOURNAL, 1961

THE FIRST FEW PAGES and the last couple of chapters of Frank Gibney's welter-weight work *The Operators* raise a perennial and perplexing question and one of the highest importance: What accounts for the periodic rise and fall in the morality of human society in general and the United States in particular?

This timeless problem has, of course, been endlessly masticated by generations of philosophers, historians, and politicians, certainly since Sumerian and probably since Mousterian times, but it remains as tough as ever, for there are not many among the long, sometimes tedious and sometimes stimulating, parade of Jeremiahs, Marcus Catos,[1] Savonarolas and Barry Goldwaters who have been able to get very far from their own notions of morality or their preconceptions as to the causes of its decline. "The complaints of contemporary writers, who deplore the increase of luxury and depravation of manners, are commonly expressive of their peculiar

1. I have in mind both the eminent M. Porcius Catos—the elder, the great and disagreeable Censor, and his comic, pathetic and noble-minded great-grandson, Cato Uticensis.

temper and situation. There are few observers who possess a clear and comprehensive view of the revolutions of society, and who are capable of discovering the nice and secret springs of action which impel, in the same uniform direction, the blind and capricious passions of a multitude of individuals." [2] Most of them have attributed the particular gangrene which fretted them to one or more standard causes: (1) a falling away from the old-time religion, whatever it happened to be; or (2) "luxury"; or (3) the misleading of the populace by scoundrelly demagogues, usually of leftish persuasion. Mr. Gibney's situation is that of a long-time denizen, or inmate, of the Time-Life empire, but he seems on the whole innocent of the peculiar temper of that realm. He plugs no specific explanation or cure, though toward the end of the book I seem to detect a leaning in the direction of number (1), *supra*.[3] He is a competent reporter, and as befits a competent reporter, he reports. But a reader or reviewer can scarcely resist the temptation to speculate upon the etiology of the morbid phenomena which he describes. "Luxury" can probably be dismissed at once as a cause of moral (as distinct from physical or military) decay. For one thing, it usually proves on examination to mean that the critic's richer compatriots have been rubbing in the fact that their standard of living is more elegant than his own, or that those who used to be poorer have begun to emulate that standard, by indulging in the contemporary equivalents of Cadillacs, TV sets and fancy plumbing.[4] For another, to the extent that

2. 2 GIBBON, THE DECLINE AND FALL OF THE ROMAN EMPIRE c. XXVII, p. 45 (Modern Library ed.).

3. E.g., pp. 265–69.

4. Compare, for example, *Piers the Plowman*, whose fourteenth-century author thwacked peer and peasant with notable impartiality. E.g.,

Laborers that have no lande to live on but their handes,
Deyned not to dyne to-day on night-old worts.
May no penny-ale please them, nor no pece of bacoun,
But it be fresh flesh or fish, fried other bake,

high living really is an evil, it is a symptom rather than a cause. For a third, there is no evidence whatever that the inhabitants of "under-developed"—*i.e.*, poor—countries are much less prone to lying, hypocrisy or public and private thievery than are, for example, Swedes, Englishmen or Americans, though their opportunities may be less. As for the other two causes, it is notorious that the two most corrupt eras in American history (leaving aside for the moment the one with which Mr. Gibney is concerned), those of Grant and Harding-Coolidge, were marked by the political dominance of sound, conservative statesmen and the prevalence of at least the sort of piety which expresses itself in regular devotions and ostentatious reverence for clergymen.

The patent fact is that nearly every man is part hog and part hero, though the proportion in which these ingredients are mixed varies enormously among individuals, and also in the same individual from one time to another. Were it not so, the species would likely have long since joined the stegosaur and the saber-toothed tiger. Thus, it is well within the bounds of possibility that the "reputable executive," whose hoggish and larcenous day, spent largely in theft, embezzlement, bribery and general cheating of his employer and his government, Mr. Gibney entertainingly chronicles in Chapter I, spent a good part of World War II enduring (though probably not uncomplainingly) discomfort and danger which would have struck a Spartan [5] as severe. As usual, George Orwell has put it better than any other modern:

And that *chaude* or *plus chaud* for the chill of their mawe.
But he be highly hired, else will he chyde, . . .

LANGLAND, PIERS THE PLOWMAN, Passus VI, lines 309–14, pp. 77–78. (10th Skeat ed. 1932). I have slightly modernized the spelling.

5. The modern stereotype of the hardy and ascetic Spartan may be somewhat exaggerated, though the Greeks themselves seem to have regarded them as retaining a greater measure of antique virtue than any other Hellenes. But it is a somewhat disconcerting fact that each and every Spartan hoplite was accompanied to Plataea by a squad of seven Helot batmen, to shine his armor, lug his baggage, do kitchen police and generally relieve the Spartan of menial fatigues—a circumstance

119

Evidently it corresponds to something enduring in our civilization, not in the sense that either character is to be found in a "pure" state in real life, but in the sense that the two principles, noble folly and base wisdom, exist side by side in nearly every human being. If you look into your own mind, which are you, Don Quixote or Sancho Panza? Almost certainly you are both. There is one part of you that wishes to be a hero or a saint, but another part of you is a little fat man who sees very clearly the advantages of staying alive with a whole skin. He is your unofficial self, the voice of the belly protesting against the soul. His tastes lie towards safety, soft beds, no work, pots of beer and women with "voluptuous" figures. He it is who punctures your fine attitudes and urges you to look after Number One, to be unfaithful to your wife, to bilk your debts, and so on and so forth. . . .

Codes of law and morals, or religious systems, never have much room in them for a humorous view of life. . . . Society has always to demand a little more from human beings than it will get in practice. It has to demand faultless discipline and self-sacrifice, it must expect its subjects to work hard, pay their taxes and be faithful to their wives, it must assume that men think it glorious to die on the battlefield and women want to wear themselves out with child-bearing. The whole of what one may call official literature is founded on such assumptions. . . .[6]

This is undoubtedly true; and it is a step, but only a step, toward understanding. It does not tell us why in this country

---

which so impressed Herodotus that he mentions it no less than four times. See HERODOTUS, PERSIAN WARS, Bk. IX, chs. 28–29 (Rawlinson transl., Modern Library ed. 1942).

6. Orwell, *The Art of Donald McGill*, in A COLLECTION OF ESSAYS 111, 120–21 (1954).

Sancho Panza was so alert and aggressive, and Don Quixote so subdued, not to say comatose, in the years of Grant, or Harding-Coolidge, or Eisenhower. It is quite unfair to blame it on the eponymous statesmen of these eras. All of them, of course, believed in soft-pedaling the demands of the state on the citizen, and all of them stood for a cheerful, determined, and probably quite genuine ignorance of gathering thunderheads, but they did not by eloquent demagogy persuade the people to adopt such ideas. None of them, indeed, had taste or talent for that kind of demagogy (which, after all, is only a *schimpfwort* for the knack of arousing the people); none had at his command anything approaching eloquence or even lucid English; [7] and in any case none had any ideas which could have been made to appear important or exciting by any rhetorical frescoing less coruscating than that of Marcus Cicero or William Jennings Bryan.[8] On the contrary, they were elected, with cheers and enormous popular majorities, precisely because their ideas or lack of ideas perfectly expressed the prevailing temper of the electorate. We are left still wondering *why* the electorate felt that way at these particular times.

For these American examples of precipitate decline in national virtue there is at least one very obvious explanation; it is surely more than coincidence that each of them followed hard upon the heels of a major and correspondingly disagreeable war. Sancho Panza, having been suppressed, ignored, and snubbed for several years, simply burst from his cell with a hell of a yell and thoroughly indulged his long pent-up libido. Probably this explanation is too simple to be wholly

7. A partial exception must be made in favor of Grant, whose autobiography is straightforwardly and admirably written. But here he dealt with matters about which he actually knew something.

8. Again a partial exception must be made for Grant, who undoubtedly had in his great days significant ideas on how to win wars. But this ability proved, as everyone knows, incapable of transfer to the chores of the presidency. It seems intrinsically likely that its successful functioning depended on the presence of a Lincoln in the background.

accurate, and it is certainly not exclusive. For one thing, the Civil War and both world wars were, like most wars, periods of rapid technical development, so that at the close of each there was a huge reservoir of industrial progress and production to fill the equally huge demand for consumer goods; the appetite for gravy grows with what it feeds upon.

The problem for lawyers and politicians in such eras is the extent to which their art and science can arrest the progress of the disease—I will not say cure—and contribute to the patient's convalescence. Mr. Gibney seems in two minds about this. At one point he places a large part of the blame on "due process of law," [9] by which I hope he means not the injunctions of the Fifth and Fourteenth Amendments but the unnecessarily slow, cumbrous, feeble, and archaic enforcement machinery, very little of which is required by the Constitution, which converts so much of our criminal law into the likeness of a monkey, especially if the criminal is a well-heeled operator. Elsewhere the author refers to the "futility of mere legal correctives" unaccompanied by "some strong self-governing help from the men who live under those laws," [10] which is a sound observation, if not original. Equally valid, and not as common as it ought to be, is his perception of the fact that one of the principal roadblocks in the way of catching up with those Operators who actually violate the criminal law is "the federal system of government." [11] There is generally some place in which the crookedest operator can operate, if not legally, at least with confidence that the local law enforcers will not molest him and that the holy principle of states' rights will hamper and maybe block altogether the efforts of the feds to get at him. "Every effective operator is a strong states' rights man," says Mr. Gibney.[12] There are dark days when it seems to me that I can detect any kind of

9. P. 16.
10. Pp. 256–57.
11. P. 16.
12. *Ibid.*

rascal (whether downright felonious or merely anxious to preserve the integrity of some political or economic device whereby A can bully or swindle B out of his rights) by the loudness and fervor with which he chants his litany to states' rights.[13]

Nevertheless, I think the law, if intelligently drafted and enforced, could do a good deal more than it does to discourage at least the more pernicious and outrageous symptoms of hoggishness, of the sort to which Mr. Gibney devotes the bulk of his book. There is certainly, for example, plenty of room for improvement in the Internal Revenue Code and the laws dealing with advertising and securities, and still more room for improvement in the enforcement of those laws, even in their present inadequate state. Some of my youth was spent in the courts in enthusiastic and sometimes successful efforts to break up or avenge various crude and refined schemes to bilk the government and the public. In those days I was convinced that the moral tone of the citizenry could be raised to a dizzy height if only Congress would enact a few more statutes, raise my pay and hire a lot more of my contemporaries. These beliefs have followed my hair—going but not gone, and in spots putting up what the French Army's communiqués used to call *"une résistance opiniâtre."* I still think that tougher laws and tougher enforcement could accomplish a good deal in at least some of

13. Here, lest I be accused of wanton and aggravated assault upon a cow sacred to many diverse castes, some of them perfectly honest, I go on record to the effect that my deep suspicion of most of the people who talk too much about states' rights does not necessarily mean that I favor their abolition. There was a good deal of practical truth (though very few liberals admitted it) in the observation of the late Frank Hague that "When I hear a man talking about his Constitutional rights, I say to myself, 'That man's a Communist, that man's a red' "; but no rational man sees in the fact that rascals regularly invoke the first ten Amendments a reason for repealing them. I doubt that Mayor Hague himself had such ideas.

the Operators' favorite areas, though I recognize that the validity of this idea is to some extent predicated on the supposition, which is unsupported by the available evidence, that the ethics of legislators are appreciably higher than those of their constituents.

Certainly no legal therapy affords a sure-fire cure for the malady. Neither, alas, does any effort, theological or philosophical, to persuade individuals voluntarily to behave more decently. It has been tried, of course, in all times and places, and on a few occasions the results have been impressive and lasting. But not even such gigantic reformers as Christ or Buddha managed to reform the species, or even their followers, completely and permanently, though the world's stock of decency would surely be far less without them. It wasn't long after their departure that their successors had to resort to threats of hell-fire and sanctions still less spiritual, as they still do. The most that can be said—it is much—is that penalties and exhortation between them can greatly aid the natural forces of the body politic. Fortunately, the disease seems to be self-limiting. Very rarely, if ever,[14] does it actually kill the patient; usually, for whatever reason, the society gets well, or, at least, the more alarming symptoms abate. Something happens, perhaps a war or a depression, perhaps simply a revulsion against fleshpots and the mentality that goes with them; Don Quixote wakes again, and most people behave more decently for a while.

At any rate, most of Mr. Gibney's chapters are devoted not to such inconclusive speculations but to an entertaining classification and description of the various frauds and cheats who proliferate on the contemporary scene. His facts are largely drawn from the archives of the Federal Trade Com-

14. Perhaps it did in such cases as the Roman and Byzantine empires, though historical pathologists in these cases are by no means in agreement on the results of the autopsies.

mission, the Department of Justice, the Post Office, the Federal Bureau of Investigation, the Securities and Exchange Commission, the Better Business Bureau and the Internal Revenue Service. Roughly speaking, his principal categories of Operator are consumer fraud specialists; patent nostrum peddlers; securities swindlers; confidence men, large and small; embezzlers and takers of bribes and kickbacks; expense-account artists; and tax evaders. It is readable stuff, and even instructive in places, but it adds very little to the sum of knowledge. Essentially it is no more than an up-to-date Bestiary of Operators, a Newgate Calendar of white-collar crime. It convinced this reader not so much that we live in an era of unprecedented depravity as that after all we get off pretty easy, for all of Mr. Gibney's horrible examples, save a couple (such as TV repair frauds) which are intrinsically modern, are old stuff. Most of them indeed are but tame and pallid reflections of the gaudy and gargantuan frauds who made life interesting for our ancestors. True, the TV commercials for cathartics, reducing pills, cures for headaches, anxiety, tension and insomnia, stimulators of golden liver bile and all the rest are ineffably vulgar and tedious, and no doubt as dishonest as the proprietors dare, but it is not probable that they actually kill many of their customers. Compared to the Homeric quack salvers of two or three centuries ago,[15] or the cures for cancer, syphilis and tuberculosis which lined the shelves of every enterprising drugstore sixty years ago, or even to the almost modern Doctor Goat-glands Brinkley, their contributions to the limitation of the half-wit population are pitifully small. My own guess is that far more of this good work is accomplished by the huge tribe of Christian Science practitioners

15. See, *e.g.*, HAGGARD, DEVILS, DRUGS AND DOCTORS, chs. XIII, XIV (1929.)

and other faith healers—a category of frauds [16] which Mr.
Gibney fails to include in his encyclopedia, perhaps because
he shares the prevailing American view that good manners, if
not the First Amendment, prohibit public criticism of any
religious group having more than 10,000 adherents and not
preaching cannibalism, ritual murder, or un-American activities.

Or take Mr. Gibney's Chapter IV, devoted to boiler-room
operators and other securities swindlers. No doubt they are
pests, and no doubt they fleece the unwary to the tune of
several hundred millions a year, but they are to the giants of
the past as the Alexandrine poets are to Pindar and Sappho.
Where among them is the peer of Jay Gould or Jim Fisk, or
even the minor masters of that superb school of swindlers? [17]
Or Howard Hopson, the nobly gifted inventor of the collapsible debenture? [18] We shall not soon look upon their like
again, for which the Lord be praised. Tax dodgers, to be sure,
probably bilk the government on a scale previously unknown
to history, simply because their opportunities are so much
greater; honest men are taxed at rates unheard of since the
times of Diocletian and Louis XIV, and the humane mores
of our government preclude recourse to the strong-arm collection methods of those monarchs' tax-gatherers. Taxpayers are

16. Another caveat must be inserted here, for numbers of them undoubtedly believe in their own magic and so, strictly speaking, are not
fraudulent, though not many are in business for their health. Moreover,
their therapy is often highly effective (as the orthodox faculty freely
concedes) in those cases, which are of course very numerous, where the
patient's troubles can be cured or alleviated by an improvement in his
state of mind. But the same argument could be made for the old patent
medicines, especially those which contained a stiff lashing of alcohol.

17. See ADAMS, C. F. AND H., CHAPTERS OF ERIE (Great Seal Books
ed. 1956); JOSEPHSON, THE ROBBER BARONS *passim* (1934).

18. A collapsible debenture was convertible into common stock at
the option not of the holder but of the issuing corporation. For an account of some of Hopson's choicer skulduggery, see *In re* Associated
Gas and Electric Co., 61 F. Supp. 11 (S. D. N. Y. 1944), *aff'd*, 149
F.2d 996 (2d Cir. 1945).

no more dishonest than they were in the Grant administration; the *ur* income tax of that day was enthusiastically evaded, and by devices at least as brazen as those in vogue today.[19] In short, about all that Mr. Gibney's opus establishes is that more Operators cheat more victims out of more money than was possible in similar eras of the past, for obvious reasons. It is an elementary law of biology that the fox and rabbit populations increase *pari passu*. The foxes are not less principled, or the rabbits more defenseless, than in the Grant and Harding-Coolidge eras; there are merely more rabbits, and they have more lettuce.

So also with respect to Mr. Gibney's chapter [20] on Graft and Government; no contemporary scandals can rival Teapot Dome, or the Tweed Ring, or the Crédit Mobilier or, fading back a couple of thousand years, the governmental corruption which was almost routine in classic antiquity.[21] Mr. Gibney, like many another moralist before him, harks back at one point to the civic virtue of the *Senatus Populusque Romanus* in republican times, "before the Emperors inaugurated statism, bread and circuses." [22] That civism is, however, largely imaginary, for the Senatorial oligarchs of the republic's last couple of centuries were corrupt on a scale which far surpassed anything seen after the reform administrations of Julius Caesar and Augustus had introduced a modicum of honesty into the Roman polity, and probably anything seen since. Mommsen's critical judgment was that King Jugurtha (who was in a position to know) "spoke no more than the simple truth when he remarked, on the occasion of his leav-

19. See, *e.g.*, Twain, A *Mysterious Visit*, in Sketches New and Old 384 (1875).
20. Ch. IX.
21. See, *e.g.*, Herodotus, Persian Wars, Bk. VIII, chs. 4–5 (Rawlinson Transl., Modern Library ed. 1942); Josephus, Antiquities of the Jews XIV, 9:3–5, XIV, 12:2 (Meridian ed. 1960).
22. P. 262.

ing Rome, that if he had only had enough money, he could easily have bought the city itself." [23]

From the standpoint of money honesty, the Eisenhower administration, if not quite as pearly as the celebrated hound's tooth, was not below the American average. Some of its members, of course, were on the take, but most of these operated at relatively low levels. Nevertheless, *The Operators* contains one really remarkable insight: to wit, that that administration had its own form of non-economic moral rottenness. "A public trust can be betrayed by cowardice, inaction or verbal misrepresentation as surely as it can be betrayed by graft," says Mr. Gibney,[24] and cites a number of examples, notably the President's astounding series of post-Sputnik statements, all designed to persuade the public that there was nothing to worry about, that the United States was comfortably ahead, or anyhow rapidly catching up, in the space and missile race. "One would hesitate to accuse President Eisenhower of the same conscious misrepresentation used by some members of his administration. . . . But it is hard to hold back the word 'misrepresentation' from excuses like the foregoing, made about a matter of the most vital national security. Suppose an official of a manufacturing company had made similar public statements about the value of a product, over a period of years. The verdict of the market place, I fear, would have been unmistakable." [25]

Now this, considering that it was written in 1960, is both perceptive and courageous. Hardly any among the small number of journalists and political experts who managed to stay immune to the Eisenhower charm went beyond cautious intimations that the President's intelligence, informa-

23. 2 MOMMSEN, RÖMISCHE GESCHICHTE 156 (9th ed. 1903). The bread and circuses, of course, long antedated the empire.
24. P. 245.
25. P. 250.

tion, and industry were not of the first order. A few, sourer and bolder than the rest, went so far as to suggest that his outlook might be usefully broadened if he were now and then to advise and consult with someone other than the board chairmen, oil millionaires, successful speculators and Chamber of Commerce presidents whose company he found soothing and edifying and whose political opinions, centering mostly on the Sound Dollar and No More Government Meddling, he all too plainly regarded as statesmanship of a high and superior order. But almost to a man these gentle critics prefaced or concluded their adverse comments, however mild, with touching tributes to the Little Father's benevolence and sincerity. An ineffectual and even bewildered President he might be, one whose trusting disposition and faith in the goodness of human nature were too often betrayed by scoundrels unworthy of his ideals; but nonetheless a Matterhorn of moral grandeur, a sort of Edward the Confessor. Mr. Gibney deserves high credit for being one of the very first to see and say that the beatified Ike was in fact an astute and not very scrupulous politician; he differed from his less successful protégé, Mr. Nixon, mainly in that, while neither allowed any finicky considerations of pedantic fact to get in the way of successful vote-catching, Ike managed to do it with a marvelous appearance of virtuous detachment from partisan politics. For this passage, if nothing else, *The Operators* will deserve a footnote in the histories of the age of Eisenhower.

For this and a number of other reasons, including its entertainment value, the book is well worth whatever it costs to rent it from the nearest circulating library. The evils its author describes and deplores really *are* evils, and dangerous ones at that; they call for neither tolerance nor complacency. That they are ancient evils, like smallpox or tuberculosis, is no reason for Mr. Gibney or you or me to shrug his shoulders. Mr. Gibney at least goes after them horse, foot, and guns, in a way which admirably exemplifies a fine old American tradition:

> . . . . we're wan iv th' gr-reatest people in th' wurruld to clean house, an' th' way we like best to clean the house is to burn it down. We come home at night an find that th' dure has been left open an' a few mosquitoes or life-insurance prisidints have got in, an' we say: "This is turr'ble. We must get rid iv these here pests." An' we take an axe to thim. We desthroy a lot iv furniture an kill th' canary bird, th' cat, th' cuckoo clock, an' a lot of other harmless insects, but we'll fin'lly land th' mosquitoes. If an Englishman found mosquitoes in his house he'd first thry to kill thim, an' whin he didn't succeed, he'd say: "What pleasant little humming-bur-rds they ar-re. Life wud be very lonesome without thim," an' he'd domesticate thim, larn thim to sing "Gawd Save th' King," an' call his house Mosquito Lodge.[26]

There is much to be said for the American reaction. It is about time for it to develop.

———

The reaction which I predicted in the last sentence did develop. The country is full of Don Quixotes tilting at the windbags of the Establishment and barefoot friars calling on the middle class for instant repentance and the donation of their worldly goods to the Black Panthers. The hippies, to be sure, are in the true line of Sancho Panza, porci ex grege Epicuri, but the practitioners of the New Politics hold them

26. Dunne, *National Housecleaning*, in MR. DOOLEY: NOW AND FOREVER 246–47 (1954).

in even lower esteem than does the bourgeoisie. A pall of Morality hangs over the campuses like smog over Los Angeles. A middle-aged professor *afflicted* with the tenets of traditional liberalism and cynicism feels like the only agnostic in the county during one of those nineteenth-century religious revivals. I almost yearn for Eisenhower.

The recrudescence of morality among the young is sometimes overlooked by those who judge morals largely in terms of sexual morality and who suppose that unbridled license is the rule among people under thirty. But I suspect that the sexual mores of the young are not as emancipated as they are let on to be. The lowly hippies, I admit, do seem as casual as cats in their couplings, although well below the feline standard of responsibility for the resulting offspring. But this is one of the areas in which their difference from the elite New Leftists is most pronounced. Few of the young ladies of the New Left or the Women's Liberation Movement would object on principle to fornication, but equally few seem to have the temperament for amorous dalliance. Some of them, indeed, seem far better qualified to sit at the foot of the guillotine, knitting—if someone could be found to teach them to knit. Madame Defarge in a miniskirt is still Madame Defarge. Others live grimly in sin, but I suspect that most of these liaisons are in reality trial marriages, of the sort advocated by Judge Ben Lindsey in the 1920's, with the lady making the decision as to the success of the trial. The male partner may think the love is free, but is likely to learn better.

Through the Bamboo Curtain with Staughton and Tom

HARPER'S, 1967

━━━━━━

This review of The Other Side *by Staughton Lynd and Thomas Hayden was actually devoted to criticism of the book itself rather than to my own ideas on its subject matter. The fact is that I stand almost alone among professors (of law or anything else) in laying no claim to "perfect under-standing of all things from the very first" (Luke 1:3) about the Vietnam mess. There are only two things about it of which I am fairly certain: First, in the light of hindsight, it was a wrong place for the United States to play the role of international policeman; second, the American states-men who got us into it, from John F. Kennedy down, were motivated more by morality than by self-interest (their own or that of the United States) or prudence. The Vietcong and North Vietnam were attempting a rape—but the victim was not of unblemished virtue, and the neighborhood was not one where it is advisable for a passerby to rush up a* dark alley whenever he hears a scream for help.

By the time I had finished The Other Side I was also convinced that, wherever the truth was, it was not in Messrs. Lynd and Hayden. Unlike the classic propagandists, such as Dr. Goebbels, they are not liars, for neither of them appears to be capable of distinguishing a lie from the truth. For them, indeed, there is really no such thing as objective truth, not even as an abstract concept like the fourth dimension. They were and are museum specimens of the New Left polemicist. The differences between them and the Old Left seemed to me less than has been claimed by the evangels of the new dispensation: Lynd and Hayden got on very amicably with Aptheker, an Old Leftist of unimpugned orthodoxy. But there are differences. The Old Left knew that Soviet Russia was the home of the Good, the True, the Beautiful. Thus, Old Leftists all said the same thing at the same time, thereby achieving a sort of consistency, although, depending on the erratic course of Russian foreign policy, what they all said this week might be quite opposed to what they had all said last week. The New Left has no Pope. It tends to treat Soviet Russia and its rulers with studied indifference, neither praising nor condemning: The invasion of Czechoslovakia, for example, was almost completely ignored by student radicals. It was not defended, but neither were there excited meetings and inflammatory posters denouncing it.

For some New Leftists, such as Lynd and Hayden, Chairman Mao is the Lord's anointed, with almost Stalin's infallibility. Some bow down before Castro, Guevara, Eldridge Cleaver, and many, many others—a pantheon as diverse and outlandish as the Hindu. At least their orgiastic drumming and chanting, their wild gyrations, prostrations, and genuflections, make them a better show than the Old Left ever was.

Lynd left Yale, threatening to sue the university for

denying him tenure, and has since devoted himself to the radicalization of the American Historical Association, with indifferent success. Hayden went on to glory as one of the defendants in the Chicago conspiracy trial of 1969, but his performance there was overshadowed by those of William Kunstler, Jerry Rubin, and Judge Hoffman. The first freshness of his youth is past, and I fear that he may have seen his best days.

———

STAUGHTON, Herbert, and Tom one night sailed off in a wooden shoe. . . . They sailed and sailed until they came to The Other Side, and this is the story of what they were told and what they were shown and what (in a manner of speaking) they thought after they got there. *The Other Side* is written in the third person, and only first names are used, for the boys are Great Chums. Herbert is Herbert Aptheker, by trade "a leading theoretician of the American Communist Party"; Staughton, of course, is Staughton Lynd, an Assistant Professor of History at Yale and a mighty paladin of the allegedly New Left; Thomas Hayden, a founding father of Students for a Democratic Society, while temperamentally incapable of playing Sancho Panza, is at least Robin to Staughton's Batman—for Staughton and Tom are fearless fighters for Good and against Evil and, luckily, never have any trouble in telling one from the other. Herbert did not help Staughton and Tom write the book, perhaps for fear that someone might question its objectivity. Fortunately, Staughton and Tom, though the terms of North Vietnam's invitation to Herbert specified that his fellow travelers must be "non-Communist," turned out to be virtuosi in their way. They must hold all American and world records for swallowing propaganda releases.

They give, indeed, every sign of relishing propaganda, of savoring it voluptuously, as a cat savors catnip. After listening to a harangue by a representative of the Vietcong, composed of clichés of Communist polemics, phrased in the commonplaces of the Maoist *Schimpflexikon,* and requiring a good hour to deliver, they describe the doubleplusgood duckspeaker who recited it as "this quiet man." A very large part of the book is, in fact, no more than direct quotation or paraphrase of standard Communist propaganda of the Chinese and North Vietnamese subspecies, connected by occasional paragraphs of gloss, usually of the "How true!" variety. Even such handouts may be to an uncertain extent adulterated with truth. But the book presents no new facts, nor even any new falsehoods; as an elucidation of a complex, tangled, obscure tragedy it is useless. Worse, it makes very hard reading.

Staughton and Tom were told and apparently believed, to select a very few gems from their collection, that Chinese eleven-year-olds have decided to "absolutely support the people in Vietnam," on the basis of meetings and school discussions, "as free and wholesome as any we know in America"; that food is the same for everyone in China (somehow, Chairman Mao doesn't look it); that Chinese factory workers design electric clocks better than foreign models by relying on Mao's *On Practice*; that criticism flourishes in China, unless, of course, it becomes "obstruction." They believe that Peking is "stunning"—not because of such relics of the deplorable past as the Winter and Summer Palaces, but because of the new state offices overlooking "grounds where thousands upon thousands can gather for rallies." (It may be noted in passing that such words as "stunning" and "wholesome" are characteristic of the Staughton-Tom style, which has a curiously Sunday-school, ladies'-page flavor.) They believe that the United States is ruled by monopolists;

that these monopolists invaded South Vietnam in order to add it to the other American colonies; and that the American standard of living is maintained by exploiting these colonies. They believe that a North Vietnamese soldier who throws himself on a mine (grenade?) to save his comrades does so because of superior morale and political education. If they knew that soldiers of the United States have done the same thing, they would presumably attribute it to fanatical zeal to maximize the profits of General Motors.

Messrs. Lynd and Hayden are not wholly devoid of the critical faculty. They are not quite such fools, for example, as to ignore totally the considerable body of evidence that the Ho government carried out in North Vietnam an "elimination" first of landlords, then of "rich" peasants, then of ordinary peasant proprietors, which was quite on the Stalin scale. They notice that "First Amendment liberties [do not] thrive in North Vietnam." Neither do they ignore the evidence that the Vietcong has systematically and deliberately killed civilians who opposed them and frequently the families of such misguided persons as well. They have dealt with these unpleasant facts partly by minimizing them, but also by writing an apology for violence (when employed by Communists) which is acute, closely reasoned, and often persuasive. They fail to remark that many of their arguments also justify the use of counterviolence by anti-Communists.

When the authors view their own country, however, their critical sense evaporates. If they see clearly many things which really are wrong with the United States, they see many more that are not. The peculiar nature of their criticism is illustrated by the flat pronouncement that "freedom is lacking" in this country. ("Freedom Is Slavery," ran the slogan over the Ministry of Truth.) "Freedom," as I understand the word, means that considerable luxury, Staughton Lynd. What he and Hayden think it means, apparently, is obedience to the law of God, as revealed to His servants and friends, Staughton and Thomas. It is not a novel concept.

The Other Side, in sum, is of no help whatever in understanding the facts—let alone the rights and wrongs—of the confused and bloody tragedy with which it purports to deal. It cannot for a moment be compared with Bernard Fall's books or Susan Sheehan's recent *Ten Vietnamese.* Its real interest lies in the light which it throws on its authors. They are highly educated and probably intelligent men. They are surely good men, full of yearning to improve humanity by making it more like themselves. What their book shows is the facility of the descent to their particular Avernus: how easily idealism fades into crankiness, generous hatred of injustice into smug sanctimoniousness, independence of spirit into the slightly ridiculous.

Dr. Spock, the Reverend
Mr. Coffin, and the
ACLU—Especially
Mr. Coffin

HARPER'S, 1968

ON JANUARY 5, 1968, a federal grand jury indicted Dr. Benjamin Spock, author of the Bible's only real competition as an all-time best-seller, and the Reverend William Sloane Coffin, Jr., University Chaplain and Pastor of the Church of Christ in Yale University. These two, along with three smaller fry, were charged with conspiracy to counsel evasion and violation of the Universal Military Training and Service Act. The government's decision to confer the honor of martyrdom on the alleged conspirators naturally ignited an ammunition dump of political and legal problems. It also set off some of the most ferocious hairpulling, scratching, gouging, and kneeing in the clinches ever heard of within the American Civil Liberties Union. The Union has a rather uncharacteristic policy [1] against public reference to "any differences which arise within the Union's organization," but since some of the parties to the row were ignorant of the dirty-linen rule, and others too outraged to pay any attention to it, the warring factions filled the press with denunciations and counter-denunciations. As the Union's harassed Executive Director, John de J. Pemberton, gamely phrased it, "The fact that so many stories have highlighted the differences between the national position and the affiliates on *Spock* is an excellent example of our commitment to free speech and the right and value of dissent." It is all of that.

Pemberton, a Quaker lawyer from North Carolina via Minnesota, obviously does not enjoy the brawl. He is a good organizer and fund raiser who deserves much of the credit for the Union's phenomenal recent growth, but he seems not to be as rugged and tough a character as his predecessor, Roger Baldwin, who founded the ACLU almost fifty years ago. Like most executive secretaries, his instinct when caught in a crossfire seems to be to appease whichever side looks the more intransigent. He reminds one of U Thant during the events leading up to the Arab-Israeli conflict.

Part of Mr. Pemberton's troubles are implicit in the structure of the ACLU, which is loose even by the standards of liberal organizations. In theory, at least, the Union's constitution vests control in its National Board of Directors, a more or less self-perpetuating body whose members are nominated by a Nominating Committee, whose members are appointed by the Union's Chairman, who is elected by the National Board of Directors—a process generally similar to that by which the management of General Motors selects it-

1. This and other policies referred to in this article are taken from the Union's *Policy Guide*, published in 1966 in recognition of the rapid proliferation of the organization's local affiliates and chapters, many of them of highly independent and volatile temper, and the resultant need of "unity and consistency of policy."

self. But there the resemblance to General Motors and its subsidiaries ends. The Union has some forty-three state affiliates and several times that number of local chapters, many of them operated by individualists about as amenable to order and discipline as so many jackrabbits. In theory the affiliates and chapters march to the beat of the National's drum: The constitution provides that the affiliates "shall act in accordance with the policies of the Union, with the understanding that the purpose of this requirement is to obtain general unity rather than absolute uniformity." This is reinforced by policy-book statements forbidding affiliates and chapters to take positions on national legislation or issues except in accord with the national organization's position, and forbidding them to file pleadings in the Supreme Court without consulting the national office. Moreover, an affiliate can be suspended or expelled by a two-thirds vote of the National Board. Despite all these pious declarations, the Union has never been noted for "general unity." The National Board has never disciplined an affiliate and, despite considerable provocation, is very unlikely to do so in the present case. In fact, the affiliates on this occasion appear to have compelled the National to jump through their hoop.

The present controversy is merely the most recent manifestation of a schism which has plagued the Union since its birth. On the one side are the zealots, who believe that the Union's mission is to throw its considerable weight into the total defense of virtue in distress—i.e., to uphold the right, because it is right, and to do so by any legal or polemical means at hand, including in this instance contentions that the Selective Service Act is unconstitutional, that the war in Vietnam is not only unconstitutional but illegal and immoral, and that Lyndon B. Johnson and his myrmidons are war criminals unrivaled in atrocity since the demise of Adolf Hitler and the SS. They dominate most of the big affiliates—

for instance, those of New York, under the direction of
Aryeh Neier, and New Jersey, under the presidency of Emil
Oxfeld. They are vigorously represented by such key members of the National Executive Staff as Melvin Wulf, its
Legal Director. They showed their strength on March 2,
when they forced the National Board to reverse the stand
which it had taken on February 1. Then the National had
voted to limit its aid to Spock, Coffin, *et al.* to the defense of
their constitutional rights, by the filing of briefs as *amicus
curiae*, not as counsel to the accused. A month later a majority (twenty-six to twenty) voted to furnish money and
counsel to the accused. The distinction is no mere legal
technicality. Counsel for the defense do not represent the
Union, as do the counsel who prepare a brief for it in the
role of friend of the court. They represent the accused, and
it is their obligation to raise any available defense, whether
or not that defense has anything to do with the Bill of
Rights. This may well mean participation in efforts to con-
vert the proceeding into a propaganda trial of the Johnson
Administration. It is true that the minority managed to secure an amendment to the effect that the Union itself takes
no position on the legality or morality of the war in Vietnam, and it is also true that the lawyers furnished by the
Union will speak for their clients and not for the ACLU.
These subtleties are pretty certain to be lost on the public,
which will take the Union's action as an endorsement of the
political merits of the Spock-Coffin crusade—which is what
its sponsors intended.

The other school, represented by the minority of the National Board, clings to the old-fogyish notion that the
Union's duty is to see that the defendants' constitutional
rights are observed and treats as irrelevant the rightness or
wrongness of their political views. The zealots very naturally
regard the constitutionalists as "narrowminded and back-

ward-looking," at best Laodiceans, neither cold nor hot, and at worst "supporters of the war." The quoted phrases were fired off by the above-mentioned Emil Oxfeld and reported by *The New York Times* when the story broke three weeks later. An even better example of the heat of the debate is an article in *The Village Voice*, written *in propria persona* by the *Times* reporter who wrote the original story. Characterizing Mr. Oxfeld's language as "carefully chosen," he himself described the then majority of the National Board as "old-guard" and "reactionary" and their action as "the American Civil Liberties Union's latest cop-out." Their opponents, of course, are "open-minded" and "liberal."

While the controversy between the Union's two wings is constantly simmering, no ordinary cause could have brought it to such a rolling boil. It did not publicly erupt when, for example, in 1967 Charles Morgan, the Director of the Union's Southern Regional Office, acted as defense counsel in the court-martial of Captain Howard Levy. Levy, a medical officer, was charged with refusing to obey a lawful order of a superior officer to establish and operate a dermatology training program for Army Special Forces medical corpsmen destined for Vietnam. Morgan based the defense in large part on the argument that since the students would use their expertise in the cure of jungle itch to perpetrate crimes against humanity, the orders were not lawful—a defense whose connection with the captain's constitutional liberties was not very obvious to the traditional civil libertarians on the National Board. But not even the imaginative Mr. Morgan could make a really inspirational martyr out of poor Captain Levy, who had no more charisma than the average dermatologist. In the present imbroglio, much of the bitterness within the Union is due to the personalities of the accused.

Of good Dr. Spock there is not much to be said that is not

already known to anyone who has had an infant (or, in the last couple of years, a T.V set) in the house. He has about him something of the Henry Wallace of 1948, with perhaps a touch of Dr. Pangloss. He is evidence (if any evidence besides the American Medical Association were needed) that political sophistication is not a necessary concomitant of medical education and experience. But the Reverend William Sloane Coffin, Jr., is rather more interesting and, through no fault of his own, rather less familiar to the public outside the Ivy League.

Coffin is handsome, articulate, charming, humane, sincere, and courageous. His only weakness of character seems to be a certain appetite for publicity, a relish for press conferences, headlines, and appearances on television—a weakness which he shares with at least 90 percent of the sacerdotal caste. The same innocent and even amiable vanity prompts him to habitual use of all three of his names, in the manner of Henry Ward Beecher, Harry Emerson Fosdick, Norman Vincent Peale, and many another eminent Protestant divine.

Coffin is also the bluest of Old Blues. His family tree is full of Yale graduates, including at least one Presbyterian clergyman of flag rank. He is himself a product of furniture-store money, Andover, Yale (B.A. and B.D.), and even Skull and Bones, the world's best-publicized secret society. This impeccable background does not, of course, keep other Old Blues from filling the columns of the *Yale Alumni Magazine* with infuriated letters demanding that he be fired *instanter*. (He probably *could* be fired, if the president and fellows were so inclined, for he does not teach and so lacks academic tenure. But President Brewster has thus far shown himself to be far too astute a politician—and too good a believer in academic freedom—to do anything so foolish.)

Except for a stretch in the World War II Army, and an-

other with the CIA in the early 1950's, Coffin has spent all
his working life in the academic-chaplain business—first at
Andover, then at Williams, the last ten years at Yale. He is
thus by experience, as well as aptitude and inclination, magnificently equipped to activate the consciences of youth, particularly the Ivy League variety, and to administer to their
moral natures stimulants of the highest potency. He rouses
his clientele as Billy Sunday roused his. The more febrile
among them are the political equivalents of an old-time revival audience; their eyes roll, they develop the gift of
tongues, chant slogans, struggle with devils, and blockade
the recruiters of the Dow Chemical Company. (It should,
however, be emphasized that to the best of my knowledge
Coffin himself has not advocated violent interference with
Dow recruiters or anyone else.)

William Sloane Coffin shares with most of his brethren in
holy orders (and with most of his brethren in the human
race) another trait, having nothing to do with character: By
inclination and training he is averse to hard, complicated
thinking about hard, complicated problems, and, as a corollary, he instinctively rejects the tiresome concept that most
human institutions and activities come not in black and
white, but in lighter and darker shades of gray. Faced with a
problem, he is pretty sure to find a simple, forthright, readily
comprehensible solution of the Yea or Nay variety, based
not on painful analysis but on an efficacious substitute which
he calls conscience (twenty-one times in one two-and-one-
half-page sermon). The Newspeak of 1984 called it bellyfeel.
Does the government of the United States pursue a policy
which is pronounced by his conscience to be wrong? Then
the government's authority ceases *ipso facto* to be legitimate,
and he is privileged and indeed obliged to disobey its laws—
"confront" it, in the cant of the movement. (Here, lest all
my ideas be dismissed as those of a purblind reactionary, I

144

must explain that I believe American policy in Vietnam to be mistaken, although not immoral. Indeed, my objection to it is precisely that it has been based more on moral than on practical considerations. It is a conscientious, though imprudent, effort, devised by people whose ideas on international policy were set like concrete by the violent traumas of Munich and Korea, to keep the Communists from imposing a repressive regime by force on people who might well, if they had any choice in the matter, prefer even the present government of South Vietnam. My disagreement with the Spock-Coffin position is *not* based on belief that the United States' crusade in Vietnam is a good idea.)

It is often difficult to determine the details—even very important details—of Coffin's positions, for his conscience is likely to reach those positions in one soaring bound, without wasting time on their implications. One of his most brilliant headline catchers was his offer of Yale's Battell Chapel as a sanctuary, in the medieval manner, for violators of the draft law. Only a pedant would object to his failure to dig out the considerable disabilities which the common law of the Middle Ages attached to assertion of the right of sanctuary. (The fugitive had, among other things, to take an oath of abjuration of the realm—i.e., to leave the country and stay out—to forfeit all his goods and to suffer attainder and corruption of blood. This last, while less horrid than it sounds, was still fairly unpleasant; the person so attainted became incapable of holding or inheriting land or of transmitting a title by descent.) But it is not mere pedantry to remark that he forgot that the chapel was not his. By the same token, he omitted to consult its deacons, in whose dovecote there was, you may be sure, a fine fluttering—which offended him greatly and which he seems to have attributed to personal prejudice against him. It is not probable that he deliberately slighted the deacons; the point simply did not occur to him.

Nor, when he quite sincerely renounced the role of Pied Piper and began his successful campaign to get himself indicted, did it occur to him that there would be available to him defenses (which he has decided to utilize) which would not be available to young men who refused to report for induction. His unqualified denunciations of American policy in Vietnam have not been accompanied either by analysis and refutation of the government's reasons, or by suggestion of alternative policies. His most illuminating statement to date reads, *in haec verba:* "I am in favor of America staging very carefully negotiated withdrawal. The implementation can be very carefully phased and deliberate, but intent must be very clear." Personally, I shouldn't want to be the negotiator who was handed such terms of reference.

Total reliance on conscience is by no means a new method of arriving at a position, especially among the reverend clergy. One famous historical instance is the attitude of the nonjuring clergy in the time of William and Mary. Their consciences told the nonjurors that James II was King of England by divine right, that the authority given William by Parliament was therefore illegitimate, and that the subject was under no duty to obey his laws. One of the most talented and moral of them, Jeremy Collier, pronounced it no sin to plot the assassination of King William. (A grand jury indicted Collier for high treason, but the British government of 1696, wiser in its generation than the American government of 1968, never brought him to trial.) Another, more modern, example is the mental process which fifty years ago converted most of the men of God into red-hot Prohibitionists. One had only to look around to see miserable victims of the Demon Rum, wasted lives, broken families, neglected children. Therefore, booze was evil. From this premise only one conclusion was possible; booze must go. *Deus vult.* The same predilection for the simple, clear solution made them

146

sturdy anti-evolutionists; Genesis is clear and simple, easy to understand and to preach. Darwin and Mendel are not.

Coffin is in truth a best-in-show specimen of the New Breed of Clergy. Though a minority, and probably a fairly small minority, of the American clergy, the New Breed's congregations tend to be the richest and best educated, and its publicity is greater than that of the rest of the servants of God put together. It has very little interest in religion in the ordinary sense. Coffin makes frequent and generally favorable references to God, but his God strikes me as an amorphous and elusive fellow, more like the Third Person of the Trinity than the First. I suspect that Yale's Chaplain, though nominally a Calvinist, would be hard put to it to expound offhand more than one or two of the five basic principles of Calvinism. He might get as far as predestination and even total depravity (with the thought of Lyndon Johnson to help him), but would probably stumble on limited atonement, irresistibility of grace, and perseverance of the saints. This lack of interest on the part of the Pastor of the Church of Christ in Yale University may result from the fact that his very literate flock has lost the capacity (and perhaps the need) for belief in a glorious hereafter and that hereafter's proprietor, the old personal, sparrow-watching God.

But, of course, the priesthood has a second bow string. Though deprived of their magical functions—i.e., of their franchise to ingratiate the communicant with the Deity and get him past the celestial Immigration Service—the New Clergy can still hold themselves out as *ex officio* first among the guardians of morality, in all its forms. They say, in effect, what God would say if He understood the situation as well as they do. For all its self-confidence, however, it is very doubtful that the New Breed numbers in its ranks any Wolseys, Richelieus, or Mazarins. The painful truth seems to be that the ministry, lacking its nimbus of supernatural power,

no longer attracts intellects of the first order. It is impossible
to imagine in a modern pulpit an Aquinas, a Maimonides, a
Calvin, a Pascal, even a Jonathan Edwards or a Cotton
Mather. Such men are found today in the law school, in the
medical school, in the natural sciences. To find one in the
divinity school would be as startling as to find him studying
embalming.

The New Clergy intersects the New Left, which is viewed
with a very tolerant and even affectionate eye, like spoiled
but favorite children, by a type of civil libertarian particularly numerous in some of the Union's affiliates, such as
those of Southern California, New York, and New Jersey,
and also among the younger members of its staff. It would
be unjust to describe Coffin as a New Leftist; although he
was one of the sponsors of the 1967 New Politics Convention in Chicago, he seems to have been bewildered and ulti-
mately repelled by the brainlessness and brutality there displayed. But Dr. Spock is a tribal hero of the New Left, and
its members are as united as they ever are in supporting the
Spock-Coffin position.

The New Left is, of course, an enormously diverse group,
ranging from slightly disguised representatives of the Old
Left to political fauna so bizarre as to defy classification. Its
ideas and goals range from the eminently reasonable, or at
least defensible, to notions unmatched in the annals of lu-
nacy since the sixteenth-century Anabaptists converted Mün-
ster in Westphalia (an unlikely spot) into the City of God.
But the New Leftists have in common certain traits which
seem to justify their being described as the latest manifestation of classic American Puritanism. Not many of them, to
be sure, share the old Puritan's views on sex, work, religion,
and personal hygiene; they might place cleanliness next to
godliness, but not because they thought of either as a virtue.
What they do share with him are certain habits of mind

148

which are still more fundamental aspects of the quintessential Puritan: in Mencken's words, "his unmatchable intolerance of opposition, his unbreakable belief in his own bleak and narrow views, his savage cruelty of attack, his lust for relentless and barbarous persecution." The type has always been prominent in American politics. In 1918, if you were against American participation in the war in Europe, you were in favor of raping nuns, spitting babies on bayonets, and crucifying prisoners of war. In 1968, if you doubt that Lyndon B. Johnson is a Fascist aggressor and Stokely Carmichael a thoughtful reformer, you are not merely wrong, you are *immoral*, a murderer of little children, in intention if not in fact, and you ought to be suppressed. Since the government is itself the fount of evil, it is the duty of the enlightened to suppress the government. The New Left, of course, has never been numerous enough to suppress anyone; but the bloodthirsty fulminations of many of its charter members (e.g., the astounding platform produced by the New Politics Convention), their readiness to silence dissenters by slogan chanting, locked-arm picketing, car rocking, and similar debating tactics, and their morbid infatuation with the "burn, baby, burn" school of black statesmen are good indicia of what they would do if they had the chance.

Such Fifth Monarchy Men, no-compromise, root-and-branch eradicators of Evil, naturally invite persecution by the Establishment. Equally naturally they arouse the fiercest protective instincts of those civil libertarians who conceive of the Bill of Rights as intended to give virtue more protection than vice and tend to equate noble ends, sincerity, and "commitment" (i.e., zeal) with political virtue. Civil disobedience, they believe, when directed against the evil executors of evil (though constitutional) laws, is virtuous and moral; no other or better reason is needed to justify the Union's total defense of those who practice it. But the Union's National Board has so far taken a rather more cautious stand on civil disobedience, although the policy is now under attack. It defines civil disobedience in a pedantic, lawyerlike way as "willful, nonviolent, and public violation of valid laws, either because the violator deems them to be unjust or because their violation will focus public attention on other injustices in society to which such laws may or may not be related." No legal difficulty is presented when the violator, like Gandhi, freely concedes that the government is entitled to punish him. The problem arises when the Christian, though eager for the crown of martyrdom, demands that Nero be enjoined from throwing him to the lions. Only if he plausibly argues—as Spock and Coffin probably will— that the law under which he is charged is an invalid abridgement of his constitutional freedoms would the Union support his defense.

"For us," said a majority of the National Board in its 1967 statement on civil disobedience, "the single question is whether the act involved can reasonably be defended as an exercise of a constitutional right. If it can, then we will defend it; if not, we will not." The main constitutional question in the Spock-Coffin case seems in essence to be whether, in terms of Justice Holmes' famous test, "the words used are used in such circumstances and are of such a nature as to create a clear and present danger that they will bring about the substantive evils that Congress has a right to prevent"— whether, to adopt Holmes' still more famous illustration, they are equivalent to "falsely shouting fire in a theater, and causing a panic." This is not to be confused with the notion that somehow or other the First Amendment confers on every citizen a right to disobey any law whose purpose is not to his liking, if only he dislikes it so much that he can label the dislike a product of his conscience.

Until this March 2, the Union's position was that, if it believed that the defendants' advice to young men created no clear and present danger to the Republic, then it would argue—not as the lawyer for the accused, but as *amicus curiae*, a friend of the court—that to punish them for what they said would be to violate their First Amendment right to freedom of speech. It would not argue the merits of Spock's and Coffin's consciences or attempt to put the Administration on trial. Such a limited role in the defense was quite consistent with the Union's constitution, which states its object as "to maintain and advance civil liberties, including the freedoms of association, press, religion, and speech . . . wholly without political partisanship." But it produced yells of execration from those who believe that the Union's function is to defend Dr. Spock and the Reverend Mr. Coffin, not because they have a right to say what they think, but because what they think is right.

As I suggested a while ago, this difference of opinion has plagued the Union from its very beginning. It can explode, of course, when the Union defends Evil as well as when it is lukewarm in the defense of Good. Thus, Freda Kirchwey, for many years the presiding genius of *The Nation*, flounced out of the Union in World War II because it defended a few Fascists. It erupted more recently when the late George Lincoln Rockwell sought and got the Union's help. But the defense of Fascists has never been a serious problem, largely because most right-wing fanatics regard the Union as a Communist front and indignantly refuse to have anything to do with it. Although several of the Union's policies bracket Communists and Fascists for the sake of symmetry, only one of the more than two hundred policy statements is really addressed to the problem of the ultra-Right; that one explains, in an embarrassed way, the obvious fact that "in dealing with the problem of ultra-Right organizations the Union is confronted with the difficult dilemma of having to defend the civil liberties of groups whose activities do fundamental injury to civil liberties."

The ultra-Left, of course, presents ACLU with an identical problem. Moreover, it has done so very often, for, unlike the Nazi Bund, Silver Shirts, Ku Kluxers, and John Birchers, the Old and New Lefts have never minded identification with the Union. Prior to 1940, indeed, Communists were fairly prominent in its ranks. In that year (when, it will be recalled, Communists and Nazis were formally aligned in international politics) the Union announced its opposition to "police or single-party states, Communist or Fascist," and barred from its directing groups and staffs (both national and local) persons who are members of "any group under the control of any totalitarian government, Communist or Fascist." At least a dozen other policies wrestle in one way or another with the Communist problem.

Most of these policies, including the key one which excludes Communists from any role in the Union's direction, are now marked "Under Review" in boldface type, perhaps at the instigation of those who believe that the Cold War never existed—that it was merely a fiction invented by the Establishment as a cloak for neo-colonialism and imperialism.

The Union's preoccupation with the liberties of the far Left rather than those of the far Right is easy to understand. In modern times, at least, and in the United States, the assaults on the Bill of Rights have usually been mounted by conservatives and reactionaries. The members of the House Un-American Activities Committee are typical specimens. It is inaccurate and unfair to label HUAC's members "Fascists," but it is true that until recently they viewed Ku Kluxers very tolerantly, and even now they regard the ultra-Right as game much inferior to Communists. HUAC, it may be noted in passing, is almost an obsession with the Union, which tends to regard it as more dangerous than it really is. Though its proceedings are certainly calculated to bring representative democracy into disrepute, most of its recent victims have been as fraudulent and as eager for publicity as the Congressmen themselves. Stuffed Christians are being thrown to stuffed lions. But for the past half century, ever since the Union's birth, it has generally been superpatriots who have done violence to the civil rights of left-wing and even moderate dissenters.

It is also generally true in America that Communists have been far more attractive to intellectuals (a category which, in its broadest sense, includes most of the members of the ACLU) than Fascists or even ordinary conservatives. I cannot, after some effort, call to mind any American egghead who could fairly be called a Fascist, or even sympathetic to Fascism, with the solitary exception of Ezra Pound—and Pound, if not actually cracked, is at least exceedingly peculiar. There are very few who are even sympathetic to non-totalitarian right-wing politics—witness the pathetic failure of Barry Goldwater's (and even Dwight Eisenhower's) efforts to round up intellectual supporters, efforts which, to be sure, were neither energetic nor long-sustained. On the other hand, there are some Mandarins who are professing Communists of one sort or another and many more who can see no serious harm in Communism. A striking example of the scarcity of right-wing intelligentsia, and also of the intellectual's tendency to discriminate between the Fascist and Communist varieties of absolutism, is to be found in a recent essay by George Steiner on Louis-Ferdinand Céline, who was certainly a Fascist and possibly a major novelist. Steiner, searching for other exceptions to J.-P. Sartre's "confident identification of literature and freedom," finds exactly three: Yeats, T. S. Eliot, and Pound. To include Eliot and Yeats in a list of enemies of freedom is to stretch the facts, to say the least. He could easily have found more and better specimens by glancing to his left. Apparently the name of Bertolt Brecht, who composed panegyrics not only on J. V. Stalin but even on Walter Ulbricht, did not cross Mr. Steiner's mind in this context. For that matter, Sartre himself is not a very happy example of "libertarian commitment."

In part, no doubt, the intelligentsia's affinity for left-wing politics results from the fact that American conservatism is an intellectual wilderness, populated not by fascinating Proustian aristocrats and Medicean robber barons but by Babbitts and ex-plebeians who have acquired split-level ranch homes, hardtop convertibles, and color TV. It is also obvious that the ends of Communism are far more attractive to men of parts and good will than are those of Fascism. By the same token, American Communists have been infinitely more appealing human beings than the likes of George Lincoln Rockwell or the Imperial Wizard of the Ku Klux Klan, whatever his name is. Bar a few careerists, lusting for absolute power, limousines, and dachas, American Communists have been so transparently full of good intentions that it is nearly impossible to see them as sponsors of such peers of Himmler and Kaltenbrunner, such masters of organized terror, as Yagoda, Yezhov, and Beria.

Their weakness, of course, has always been that their wide eyes are too firmly fixed on the Delectable Mountains and the Celestial City to perceive the torture chambers of the Lubyanka or the Siberian death camps, let alone such minor blemishes as the total suppression of freedom of speech. Elizabeth Gurley Flynn, whose expulsion from the Union's National Board marked the decisive battle of the 1940 version of the present crisis, was assuredly as honest and philanthropic a fool as ever scraped the caked blood from J. V. Stalin's boots. It would be unjust to doubt the sincerity of her belief in civil liberties for Americans; the necessary doublethink would have been well within her capacity, or that of any other experienced American Communist.

Such considerations account for the view that the pure hearts of the Old and New Lefts make *their* civil liberties particularly precious. A handsome, blond, six-foot conscience like that of William Sloane Coffin seems to deserve a far more enthusiastic and less qualified defense than a deformed and ugly one, like that of the late Senator Joseph R. McCarthy. But Joe McCarthy asserted the rights of conscience quite as fervently as does William Sloane Coffin. For some reason the precedent has not been cited in the present controversy, but it is a fact that McCarthy in 1954 argued that a higher patriotism obligated government employees to disregard the law and turn over to him the loyalty and security files of other employees whom they thought subversive.

Thus, while the emotions of the Union's Massachusetts, New York, and New Jersey affiliates are very human and understandable, I find myself in accord with the mossback minority of the National Board. The fact is that the Divinity's built-in conduct regulator is sadly unreliable; even the best consciences do not all point in the same direction at the same time. Conscience is certainly a worse guide to conduct than the Constitution of the United States; it may be even worse than Congress. It is practically impossible to say that A, but not B, should have a right to be guided by his conscience and thus to practice civil disobedience whenever the conscience points in one direction and the law in another. What would the Union's Legal Director say if, for instance, President Johnson's conscience were to tell him to emulate Abraham Lincoln by suspending the writ of *habeas corpus*, throwing the leading opponents of the war in Vietnam into jail without trial, and disregarding the

Chief Justice's order to release them? The question is, of course, rhetorical.

The Bill of Rights (i.e., the first ten Amendments to the Constitution of the United States) is to this day the best solution ever devised to the dilemma expressed in Lincoln's famous question "whether any government, not too strong for the liberties of its people, can be strong enough to maintain its existence in great emergencies." It descends from the English Bill of Rights of 1689. That Bill of Rights followed a half century in which Puritans and Cavaliers, Whigs and Tories, had been killing each other, sometimes on the battlefield, sometimes (more barbarously) according to the forms of law. The old Puritans, like the new, recognized no law that went against what their hyperactive consciences told them was God's will. Bunyan put the seventeenth-century version of civil disobedience in words which William Sloane Coffin might well have borrowed had he been familiar with *The Pilgrim's Progress*: Faithful answered to the indictment brought against him in Lord Hategood's court in Vanity Fair, "That he had only set himself against that which had set itself against him that is higher than the highest. . . . And as to the King you talk of, since he is *Beelzebub*, the Enemy of our Lord, I defie him and all his Angels." It is impossible not to admire this, as it is impossible not to admire the Reverend Mr. Coffin's earnestness and courage; but it proved to be a hell of a way to run a country. After Judge Jeffreys' Bloody Assizes, even the stubbornest Dissenters were willing to concede some rights to Beelzebub in exchange for some rights for themselves.

The function of the Bill of Rights, which in the English-speaking countries ended the alternating persecutions of temporary minorities by temporary majorities, is to set bounds to the power of the majority to coerce the minority—and, as the price of this protection, to delimit the outer boundaries of the minority's freedom to disobey with impunity the majority's laws. I will defend the proposition that it is the best governor ever invented for the democratic engine and that, indeed, it is the principal reason why our democratic engine has lasted nearly two hundred years.

The balance between the security and survival of the democratic state and the liberties of its people is delicate. In this country, at least, the great dangers to that balance have not come from domestic Stalins and Hitlers. They come from what Justice Brandeis called "insidious encroachment by men of zeal, well-meaning but without understanding." The government is not the only habitat of those men of zeal.

The American Civil Liberties Union has been the most influential and effective protector of the citizen's freedoms under the Bill of Rights. Until March 2, it had by and large managed to do so without making moral or political judgments as to the rightness or wrongness of that citizen's ideas and without identifying itself with any political philosophy other than a devotion to personal freedom. The Union's stand had been (and may still be) that there is no privilege to disobey a *constitutional* law, no matter how unwise, or even immoral, that law may be, without paying whatever price is attached to that disobedience. I personally believe that Dr. Spock and the Reverend Mr. Coffin have not exceeded those freedoms which the First Amendment allows them. The Union could have argued that point with all vigor and authority—not as counsel to the defendants, but as a friend of the court and a friend of the Bill of Rights. To go farther, to endorse their political views (as it will surely be taken to have done), is to recast the saying of Voltaire, so that it reads, "I approve of what you say, and I will therefore defend to the death your right to say it." I know, of course, that not many men have ever really shared Voltaire's willingness to stand up for the right to express any idea, with a vigor which is unaffected by the defender's view of the merits of that idea. But it is peculiarly sad to see it abandoned by the American Civil Liberties Union.

───

This article had its genesis in a fortuitous and fortunate coincidence of interests. The editors of Harper's were interested in the convulsions then going on in the American Civil Liberties Union over its proper role in the Spock-Coffin trial; I was interested in the character of the Reverend William Sloane Coffin, Jr. The two dovetailed nicely, and the result elicited sacks of mail, about equally divided between hate and fan. The maddest correspondent was one of the three defendants whom I had lumped together, without much malicious intent, as "three smaller fry." This fellow, a previously obscure author, had been basking in a flood of bright, warm publicity (reporters friendly to the defense, as practically all of them were, usually referred to him not as "a writer" but as "the writer"), and my snub cut him to the quick.

Most of the hate mail, however, came from admirers of the sanctified Mr. Coffin. A majority of them assumed that I was working off some sort of personal grudge, that my comments arose out of what one of them called a "faculty feud." But in truth I had never met him and knew him by sight only because his imposing presence is impossible to ignore in a small community. He resembles nothing so much as a large, self-satisfied brahmin bull shouldering his way down the street of a Hindu village. The unbeliever's urge to boot that majestic behind is overpowering. I would have resisted the impulse had I thought he was in any serious danger of actually going to prison, but I judged (correctly) that there was small chance of any such outcome.

I do confess a long-standing dislike and distrust of clergymen who set themselves up as experts on public morals and sound politics. In my youth the holy men who took to politics were mostly pillars of conservatism or even reaction, but the divines of the Are-you-running-with-me-Jesus school, who predominate at the moment, inspire no more reverence in me than did Bishop Cannon or Father Coughlin. Their education, such as it is, is not conducive to thorough and dispassionate analysis of social, economic, and political questions. Thus, since few of them have much natural aptitude for this sort of mental exercise, they solve the most complex of such problems by generous use of conscience, intuition, and emotion. "The substance of things hoped for, the evidence of things not seen" (Hebrews 11:1) are good enough for the supernatural part of their business, where the results may not matter and in any case are not susceptible of evaluation, but they do not seem to me the best basis on which to decide what to do about Indo-China, the Middle East, the public schools, or terrorists.

Vietnam having lost steam as a political issue, Coffin has lately taken up the Black Panthers, particularly those who were on trial in New Haven for the kidnapping, torture, and murder of a suspected informer. He pronounced the trials to be "legally right but morally wrong." The logical corollary— though he did not see it—is that the kidnapping, torture, and murder (if the defendants were guilty, which is what the trials are about) were legally wrong but morally right. I had resolved to let Coffin alone, not because my needles were likely to penetrate far enough into his hide to wound him (if, indeed, he is aware of them at all), but because I was beginning to feel like Mr. Dick and also because I know that he is an honest, good-hearted man who really wants to make the world a better place. This latest gush of nonsense broke my good resolution. Unfortunately, he shows no sign of running dry; his reserves of such hogwash are conservatively estimated at two to three billion barrels. But, as in the case of the late Joe McCarthy, the fault is less with him than with the people who take him seriously.

The Civil Liberties Union's internal conflict is still unresolved. The "activists" seem to be in control at the moment. In the words of Justice Brandeis, they are "men of zeal, well-meaning but without understanding" of the fact that a storm trooper is no less a storm trooper because he decorates his armband with a peace symbol instead of a swastika and drowns out opposition by chanting "Power to the people" instead of "Deutschland erwache!" At least in the university community in which I live, the most dangerous enemies of freedom of speech in 1971 are not Birchers or Ku Kluxers, let alone the admirers of Vice President Agnew and Governor Reagan. It is not they who make it so difficult for speakers whose opinions they do not like to address campus audiences. It was not they who prevented Walt Rostow's return to M.I.T. Reactionary trustees bear little of the responsibility for the dreary conformity which afflicts so many faculties. A far more typical instance of the subtler pressures on free expression of opinion was the recent action of the fellows of one of the Yale colleges. Having demonstrated their devotion to nonconformity and appeased the more vocal undergraduates by electing Norman Mailer to their scholarly fellowship (a particularly splendid gesture, in view of the facts that one of their principal social activities is drinking and that Mailer is notoriously ugly in his cups), they refused even to vote on William Buckley because he was too controversial.

Jessica Mitford and the
End of the Spock-Coffin
Affair

TRANS-ACTION, 1970

I DON'T KNOW if there is such a thing as a chromosome which transmits the tendency to develop heavy crushes on charismatic leaders. If there is, it runs strong in the Mitford family, like the Hapsburg lower lip. Sister Diana was not merely dazzled by Adolf Hitler and his circle; she actually married Sir Oswald Mosley, the Führer of the British Union of Fascists. Sister Unity Valkyrie fell for *schöne Adolf* with a crash whose reverberations reached even the transatlantic backwater in which I was living at the time. Fascism, *eo nomine*,[1] has been distinctly non-U since 1943 or thereabouts, and in any case Sister Jessica's weakness has always been for the Messiahs of the Left, beginning with the late J. V. Stalin.[2]

1. There are, of course, plenty of governments—notably in the Arab countries—which today describe themselves as "socialist," but which thirty years ago would have proudly proclaimed that they were "fascist" —meaning pretty much the same thing in each case.
2. See generally *Hons and Rebels* (1960), Miss Mitford's autobiography. It was published in the United States as *Daughters and Rebels*, probably because naïve Americans would have been likely to suppose that "Hons" meant "Honeys," which was not the case.

161

In *The Trial of Dr. Spock, the Reverend William Sloane Coffin, Jr., Michael Ferber, Mitchell Goodman, and Marcus Raskin* the objects of her incandescent affection are Dr. Benjamin Spock ("the great eagle") and the Reverend Mr. Coffin ("the noble lion").

Miss Mitford is a remarkable example of the peculiarly British ability to combine ultra-Left political views with traditional snobbery, and Spock and Coffin get extra marks. Spock has "patrician New England forebears." Coffin is credited with having been educated at Exeter [3] and Yale; his nephews are "handsome prep-school boys in Brooks Brothers jackets" and his nieces "elegant debs in Italian knits"; ultimate accolade, his house is like "an English rectory." The other three defendants are undoubtedly good-thinkful, and Miss Mitford duly gives them their meed of praise, but it is plain that her real adulation is reserved for the genteel Spock and Coffin. Conversely, Judge Ford, who is characterized in terms distantly reminiscent of Macaulay's description of Judge Jeffreys (I intend no other comparison between Miss Mitford and Macaulay), is "an Irish Roman Catholic" (as distinct, I suppose, from all those Greek Catholic Irishmen); everyone knows that the only patrician Irish Catholics are the Kennedys.

Having introduced her cast of heroes and villains, Miss Mitford describes the trial at some length. The defendants (whom Miss Mitford naturally dubs "the Boston Five" [4])

3. Actually, it was Andover. Accuracy is not among Miss Mitford's passions; the book is full of similar instances of slipshod reporting. At one point, in what seems to be an effort to elevate Professor Abraham Goldstein to the patriciate, she reports that Coffin "phoned the Goldstein house and left a message with the maid." Few members of the Yale faculty have a maid, and I am reliably informed that the Goldsteins are no exception to the general rule.

4. An interesting subject for speculation is the ideological basis, if any, of the left-wing polemicists' habit of identifying defendants whom they regard as martyrs by place and number—Scottsboro Seven, Chi-

were, as most people remember, indicted for conspiring to "counsel, aid and abet" draft-eligible young men to violate the Selective Service Act. One was acquitted; Spock, Coffin, and two of the less prominent defendants were convicted. While their appeal was pending Miss Mitford, who seems to have taken for granted affirmance and ultimate review by the Supreme Court, sent her book to press. To her unconcealed dismay, the United States Court of Appeals for the First Circuit ruthlessly reversed all four convictions.[5] It directed the acquittal of Spock and Ferber because the Government's evidence in support of the offense charged was insufficient to warrant submission to a jury. The convictions of Coffin and Goodman were reversed because the trial judge, by submitting to the jury specific questions to be answered "Yes" or "No," instead of asking merely for a general verdict, Guilty or Not Guilty, might have put pressure on the jurors to find them guilty, in effect depriving them of their Sixth Amendment right to trial by jury.[6] The Government has not sought review by the Supreme Court. It is still free to retry Coffin and Goodman, but it has so far shown no sign of doing anything so foolish. The upshot is that two of the martyrs cannot be thrown to the lions, and the other two probably will not be. Miss Mitford's tract has been deprived of most of its point. It is all *most* unfortunate and vexatious.

She does what she can to retrieve the fiasco by devoting

cago Eight, etc., etc. It seems to go back only to the 1930's—Sacco and Vanzetti were not, so far as I know, referred to as the Boston Two. Right-wing defendants are never so described; the *Daily Worker* did not call the Nazi saboteurs who were sentenced to death in 1942 the Washington Nine.

5. 416 F.2d 165 (1st Cir., 1969).

6. The dissenting judge, who would have dismissed the complaint as to all four defendants, thought that, on the evidence actually presented, the defendants could not constitutionally have been convicted of conspiracy.

the back of the dust jacket to a denunciation of the First Circuit for "a judicial cop-out" and by predicting bravely, but probably wrongly, that "There will be further appeals and the fate of the defendants will eventually be decided by the U. S. Supreme Court."

This indignation stems from what an American or English lawyer—anyhow, *this* American lawyer—would regard as her peculiar misconception of the purpose of the trial. I believe that the purpose of a criminal trial is to determine whether the defendant is guilty, beyond a reasonable doubt, of having violated a constitutional law. She believes—and, by the standards of her ideal polity, rightly—that its purpose is to allow the government, if it is the right kind of government, or the defendant, if he is the right kind of defendant, to make a political point. From her point of view (which, *mutatis mutandis*, is essentially that of Josef Goebbels and Andrei Vishinsky), the main purpose of the trial was not to determine the guilt or innocence of Spock, Coffin, and the rest, but to give them a forum in which to propagate the thesis that the United States' participation in the war in Vietnam was in violation of the Constitution and international law and generally immoral. The tragic, outrageous consequence of the defendants' subjection to the bourgeois-democratic system of justice was that, as she phrases it, "the exigencies of a conventional defense against the conspiracy charge often seemed on a direct collision course with the needs of the antiwar movement."

Much of her petulant disappointment is vented on the defendants' lawyers, most of whom seemed hopelessly committed to the old-fashioned notion that their prime duty was to get their clients off. Sadly, some of the defendants, especially the Reverend Mr. Coffin, seemed to share this unenlightened view. Although the John Chrysostom of Battell Chapel is not generally thought of by the adult members of

164

the Yale community as a profound thinker, he is not (nor should he be) without a sense of his own self-interest. The painful truth—at least it pains Miss Mitford—is that the noble lion roared somewhat pianissimo.

The jury (whom she dismisses as "twelve tractable men") likewise let her down by failing to perceive its proper political role, which was to acquit without regard to either the law or the evidence. She espouses the theory that "a jury has the right, and in some cases the duty, to ignore the judge's charge, to find according to its conscience, and by its verdict to nullify unjust laws, to repudiate unjust governmental policy." So stated, the idea has its attractions and has, indeed, seduced better intellects than Miss Mitford's. But, as she seems not to notice, it precisely describes the state of mind of a Mississippi jury when it acquits a Ku Kluxer charged with murdering a civil-rights worker.

To some extent Miss Mitford's views on the purpose of a criminal trial may rest on ignorance as well as ideology. She seems to have made little serious effort to listen to and understand the lawyers, some of them very good lawyers, with whom she came in contact.[7] She appears to have relied heavily on her husband, to whom she kittenishly refers as the Old Trial Hand. I have no knowledge of the Old Trial Hand's reputation as a lawyer, but the general opinion in the profession is that even the greatest advocates are not necessarily, or even usually, great lawyers.

All told, a bad and boring book. This is not entirely Miss Mitford's fault. The trial simply did not have, and could not be made to seem to have, the absorbing interest of the trials of Alfred Dreyfus or Alger Hiss. Nobody was sent to Devil's Island or even to the Federal Reformatory in Danbury, Connecticut. Nobody was branded as a criminal or

7. Exception: She has written a good short history and criticism of the amorphous crime of conspiracy.

triumphantly vindicated. The prosecution was a mistake in the first place (as we may hope the Government now recognizes); if it served any useful purpose at all, it was only to show that in this country it is still very difficult to send men to jail for political activities which do not please the Government. Rebecca West herself could not have made of the proceedings the superb story which she made, for example, of the trial of William Joyce. But even had Miss Mitford had better material to work with, I do not think her book would have been much better. Adulatory gush is boring, and so are Hymns of Hate.

The first reaction of a reviewer (or at least of one who is a lawyer and a believer in the Bill of Rights for good-thinkers and oldthinkers alike) is to describe *The Trial of Dr. Spock* as flatulent propaganda and its author as a sob sister of the Old and New Lefts. As to the book, my second thoughts are much the same as my first. As to its author, my second thoughts are kinder and perhaps fairer. She is a warm-hearted woman, easily roused by injustice to people with whose personalities and ideas she sympathizes. In her own vein, she is an entertaining writer, of more than average competence. But this book is not in her vein. It deals with subjects which are both more serious and more complex than the eccentricities of the Mitford family or the chicaneries of undertakers. The moral, I suppose, is that Miss Mitford is not Rebecca West, and that it is regrettable that she did not know it.

A month or so after this appeared, the Department of Justice announced that Coffin and Goodman would not be tried again. Attorney General Ramsey Clark's mysterious decision to prosecute the five thus produced nothing except lawyers' bills, large enough to make even Dr. Spock wince, and a quantity of journalism, none of it appreciably better than Miss Mitford's.

To some extent, she may have been a victim of her publisher's urgent need to get the book on the counters before the public lost interest in the affair. Her plight can be analogized to that of another sort of author, the lawyers and accountants who prepare the prospectuses for corporate securities being offered to the public. When an issue is "hot" —i.e., when it is tailored to high but fleeting investment fashion, such as public demand for stock in uranium mines, computers, or bowling alleys—the pressure to get the stuff on the market before the vogue changes often leads to brochures containing more of richly colored fancy than of the dry and detailed fact which the Securities and Exchange Commission insists upon. The result is litigation and liability, if not bad reviews, for the authors. Miss Mitford was not subject to suit, except possibly a class action by the people who paid $5.95 for the book, but her literary reputation was not improved. No doubt she would have written a more useful history of the trial if she could have awaited the outcome of the appeal. But if she had done that, she would probably never have written the book at all, for what she yearned for was martyrs.

The Right of Privacy

YALE LAW JOURNAL, 1964

———

VANCE PACKARD's calling is that of a Viewer with Alarm. He stands at the head of his profession. He has Viewed with Alarm, and soaring sales, such unpleasant and possibly malignant social ulcers as high-pressure advertising, planned obsolescence and social climbing. This time he has set out after bigger and uglier game—the increasing ability and proclivity of government (state and federal, executive and legislative), employers, the press and the schools, not to mention a horde of private Nosey Parkers, to snoop into what is none of their business.

The Naked Society, the latest volume in Mr. Packard's series, is vulnerable to criticism in a good many places, and I intend to have some whacks at its more inviting protuberances. But I must say at the outset that, all things considered, I wish it success as solid as its predecessors'; for its author's topic is of vast importance and his heart generally in the right place.

Whatever success *The Naked Society* may have will not be due to the beauties of its literary style, for it has none. Each chapter consists of a string of facts, near-facts and sometimes, I regret to say, non-facts, more or less related to the thesis of that chapter, inadequately connected by paragraphs of platitudinous moralizing. I am left with the impression that Mr. Packard has seized on a suggestion once thrown off by Edgar Allan Poe [1]—*i.e.*, he has composed his opus by hiring a clipping service, covering a large sheet of paper with mucilage, and blowing the clippings in the direction of the page. Moreover, he writes with a total lack of humor and more than his share of naïveté. He solemnly reports, for example, that the lack of privacy in modern families and houses has driven young people into using parked cars for their sexual experiments.[2] I yield to no man in resistance to the repulsive modern phenomenon known as "Togetherness," but I doubt that it is a substantial factor in the causation of such harm as there may be in vehicular venery.[3] I can bear witness that it was popular thirty years ago and more, in an era blessedly innocent of Togetherness, and no doubt it flourished in other forms in antediluvian times. Mr. Packard is guilty, in short, of a certain lack of selectivity and proportion in the things he Views with Alarm. This leads to chronic overstatement and consequent weakening of a case which is intrinsically extremely strong.

Mr. Packard seems to assume that respect for the individual's privacy is innate and natural, and interference with that privacy degenerate. Primitive societies, he supposes, are marked by respect for privacy.[4] But the truth is that in most

1. See *The Literary Life of Thingum Bob, Esq.*, in THE COMPLETE TALES AND POEMS OF EDGAR ALLAN POE 322 (Modern Library ed. 1938).

2. Pp. 149–50.

3. Mr. Packard seems somewhat opposed to sex, apparently on the ground that it involves a crossing of "the last frontier of privacy" of the participants. *Ibid.* The point is incontestable; worse, there seems to be no avoiding the danger, except possibly in the cases of earthworms and oysters.

4. P. 15. Justice Brandeis knew better when he said that the right most valued by *civilized* men is the right to be let alone. Olmstead v. United States, 277 U. S. 438, 478 (1928) (dissenting opinion).

such societies the individual's every action is regulated by tribal mores, and policed by the rest of the tribe, with a thoroughness which would seem oppressive to a denizen of Communist China. The Inquisitive Society is the aboriginal model. It may be that *homo sapiens* is beginning to develop an instinct for privacy. But the instinct to snoop is of his very essence, for he belongs to the ancient and noble order of primates. The cause of that order's pre-eminence is to be found above all in its insatiable, monkeylike curiosity about everything and everybody, including itself.[5] Among other animals, even other mammals, the faculty of inquisitiveness is comparatively feeble or nonexistent. Take cats: A deplorable zoological ignorance is implicit in the proverb about curiosity and the cat. Man's excessive curiosity about the insides of the atom, if it does not lift him to the stars, may at least blow him to hellandgone; but no such instinct ever troubled the *felidae*. A race of civilized cats would no doubt make respect for privacy the first article in its Decalogue. But there will never be a race of civilized cats, for they lack the first prerequisite, which is a consuming urge to stick their noses into what does not concern them.

Given this ineradicable and on the whole desirable simian instinct, it should be clear to any reader of *The Scarlet Letter* or *Main Street* that the itch to learn our neighbor's secrets, to explore the recesses of his personality and police his private morals, is hardly a modern phenomenon. What is modern, of course, is the enormous progress in techniques for the gratification of the itch. The explosive proliferation of relatively simple and efficient devices for eavesdropping, spying, and probing personality has made the preservation

---

5. The gorilla, it must be admitted, seems deficient in the urge to snoop; stately and aristocratic beast that he is, he shrinks equally from exposing himself to publicity and from intruding upon the privacy of others. And where is he? Marching, not without quiet dignity, toward extinction.

of privacy exceedingly difficult. Mr. Packard describes these devices at some length,[6] including a piece of fiendish Russian ingenuity—originally reported by *Time*—a martini whose olive was a tiny transmitter, the toothpick serving as antenna.[7] Mr. Packard favors more and tougher laws to regulate and restrict the use of such devices,[8] but I suspect that in the long run the answer will prove to lie in improved methods of defense. At present, Mr. Packard notes, defensive techniques are too expensive for anyone short of the United States Government or the holder of a Texas oildom,[9] but the demand is great, and it is very likely that comparatively cheap methods of detecting and neutralizing wiretaps and all the other contraptions for electronic eavesdropping will be developed. After which, of course, as with battleship shells and armor,[10] super-bugs will be developed, then new counter-techniques, and so on.

But as of now there is surely a problem, for nobody can doubt that the snoopers are abusing their advantage. Mr. Packard is right to ring the tocsin long and loud. His trouble, as I have suggested, is indiscriminate condemnation. Some invasions of privacy are desirable, or at least necessary. Thus, despite Mr. Packard's indignant objections,[11] an employer

6. Pp. 29–43.

7. But *Time* subsequently sneered at gulls foolish enough to believe such a story; anyone, it said, should know that the liquid would deflect sound waves and that Moscow bars are lavishly equipped with conventional bugs. *Time*, March 6, 1964, p. 55. The article failed to mention the source of the original report of bugged martinis.

8. Pp. 319–22, 326–27.

9. P. 337. But elsewhere he says that one company sells for $300 a kit containing "a host of tools for detecting bugging devices." P. 35.

10. There was a fascinating formula: One inch of armor would turn a one-inch shell at one thousand feet; two inches would turn a two-inch shell at two thousand feet; and so on up to sixteen- or eighteen-inch shells and armor. It seems a pity that battleships faded away before we had a chance to learn the upper limits, if any, of their development. The same thing happened with the armed and armored dinosaurs.

11. See Chapter 3, whose general tenor is sufficiently indicated by its title, "How to Strip a Job-Seeker Naked."

II: MORALITY AND POLITICS, OLD AND NEW

has a perfectly legitimate reason for finding out facts relevant to a job-seeker's probable performance. God Himself did it, in the well-known case of Gideon's Army,[12] by observation of the candidates' reactions to a contrived situation, or, as some psychologists would label it, a controlled two-variable experiment on naïve subjects.[13] Bank officers who treated as a cashier's private affair his dedication of his spare time to the theory and practice of the three-horse parlay would certainly be subject to criticism and possibly to liability.[14] The valid point is not that employers have no right to pry into employees' affairs, but simply that they ought to confine their prying to those matters which are actually relevant to the performance of the job, as they ought to limit themselves to methods which are actually likely to produce relevant information. It probably doesn't matter if a prospective shoe salesman is a homosexual, unless he is the blatant sort of fairy who might irritate heterosexual customers, in which case it doesn't take an FBI investigation to ascertain the fact. The lie detector (a cause of particular offense to Mr. Packard) is objectionable not because it is wrong to interfere with the right to lie, but because polygraphs, and still more their operators, are not really very good at telling liars from the merely nervous.

Similarly, I decline to register either surprise or shock when I am told that banks install hidden cameras to shatter the privacy of the bashful bank robber [15] or that other enterprises, instead of relying on the honor system to hold down shoplifting and employee pilferage, resort to closed-circuit television and plainclothes detectives.[16] I can think offhand

12. Judges 7:4-7.
13. For this gorgeous specimen of jargon, I am indebted to my colleague, Leon S. Lipson.
14. E.g., Bates v. Dresser, 251 U. S. 412 (1920); Gamble v. Brown, 29 F.2d 366 (4th Cir.), cert. denied, 279 U. S. 839 (1928).
15. Pp. 89-90.
16. See generally Chapter 4, "The Hidden Eyes of Business."

of only one sizable business, Exchange Buffet Corporation, which relied entirely on its customers' honesty; it recently went into bankruptcy. Such industrial spying and the need for it again go back to Old Testament times: it is written that a technique of clandestine surveillance devised by the prophet Daniel broke up a ring of threescore and ten priests of Bel who were stealing the King of Babylon blind.[17]

Likewise, Mr. Packard's lengthy report on the investigative activities of credit bureaus [18] arouses my indignation not at all: If you want to keep your finances private, you can always pay cash. Nor do I beat my breast and rend my garments in mourning for the Bill of Rights when Mr. Packard hands me the stunning information that the Bureau of the Census every ten years requires every fourth householder to spend thirty minutes filling out a questionnaire.[19] I feel no urge to rush to the barricades even when I am told that a securities salesman, resident in Briarcliff Manor, was fined $100 for refusing to comply; and I most certainly do not believe that "his offense, apparently, was that he wrote a sizzling article saying why he balked." [20] I note with some amusement that the said sizzling article appeared on the asbestos pages of William Buckley's *National Review*, whose editors and contributors were never known to share Mr. Packard's indignation at the really objectionable inquisitions of the House Committee on Un-American Activities, the late Senator Joseph R. McCarthy, or any of the other road-company Torquemadas, professional and amateur, who have infested the republic for the past thirty years.[21] But for some reason they regard the Census Bureau's relatively innocuous

17. This instructive tale is contained in the first twenty-two verses of the Apocryphal History of the Destruction of Bel and the Dragon. The King, an old-fashioned employer, slew the offenders on the spot.
18. Chapter 10, "The Unlisted Price of Financial Protection."
19. Pp. 268–72.
20. P. 269.
21. See Chapter 13, "The Right to Have Unfashionable Opinions."

questions about the number of your TV sets, radios, air conditioners, and children as intolerable "bureaucratic harassment." I am less amused by the fact that Mr. Packard seems to have bought another favorite grievance of the Birchers, Minute Men and similar Saviors of the Republic, for he denounces compulsory medication in the form of fluoridation of water.[22] How he manages to condone chlorine while condemning fluorine I can't tell you, but it is a fact that he does.

Mr. Packard sheds tears (and so drags in a little marketable dirt) for Elizabeth Taylor, Richard Burton, and other poor hams whose privacy has been invaded by the press.[23] Any reporter could have told him that they and their congeners have no more use for privacy than a fish has for fresh air. Whenever the interest of the press in their private lives shows the slightest sign of flagging, they commonly resort to frantic mugging and capering, and if the inattention continues they perish. I do not go so far as a theatrical lawyer of my acquaintance, whose considered opinion is that his clients ought to be compelled to seat from the rear in buses and otherwise be classified as subhuman; but I am not profoundly concerned about their struggles with the naughty news media.

In short, Mr. Packard's recognitions that there may be two sides to the privacy question are few and somewhat grudging. The law is not so certain of the merits. Although the Warren-and-Brandeis article on "The Right to Privacy" [24] has been called "probably the most influential law-review article ever written," [25] today, three quarters of a century later, not many jurisdictions go much beyond protecting an individual's right not to have his name or picture

22. P. 294.
23. Pp. 218–19.
24. 4 HARV. L. REV. 193 (1890).
25. GREGORY & KALVEN, TORTS 883 (1959).

exploited commercially,[26] and perhaps imposing liability for
the more outrageous and gratuitous exposures of the secrets
of people who have neither a craving for publicity nor legitimate news value.[27] Obviously, the right to privacy has in
such cases to be reconciled with the invader's no less important right to freedom of speech, and, equally obviously, the
line is very hard to draw, as the decisions demonstrate.[28]
Cases in which damages have been awarded for pure invasion of privacy, such as electronic eavesdropping or other
trespassory prying, not accompanied by publication, are still
distinct rarities.[29] Here, of course, there is no collision with
the First Amendment, and the fact that the judges are so
far behind the professors in protecting privacy in such cases
is probably attributable to reluctance to sanction damages
for purely emotional injury.

The problem is, of course, much more serious and much
more difficult in the criminal context. Mr. Packard is not
quite one of those who believe that it is unconstitutional to
introduce evidence against a person accused of crime. But he
does appear to believe that the prosecution of murderers,
extortionists, narcotics magnates, Mafiosi, and similar human sharks is a sport, rather like dry-fly trout fishing, whose
object is to exact the greatest possible skill from the hunters

26. E.g., Pavesich v. New England Life Ins. Co., 122 Ga. 190, 50
S.E. 68 (1904); see Prosser, Torts 635–44 (2d ed. 1955).
27. E.g., Melvin v. Reid, 112 Cal. App. 285, 297 Pac. 91 (1931);
Restatement, Torts § 867 (1939); *but cf.* Sidis v. F-R Publishing
Corp., 113 F.2d 806 (2d Cir. 1940).
28. There is a good collection in Gregory & Kalven, Torts 888–
95 (1959). As might be expected, there is no very coherent pattern.
29. E.g., Byfield v. Candler, 33 Ga. App. 275, 125 S.E. 905 (1924)
(intrusion in woman's steamer stateroom); McDaniel v. Atlanta Coca-
Cola Bottling Co., 60 Ga. App. 92, 2 S.E.2d 810 (1939) (microphone
in tort plaintiff's hospital room); Roach v. Harper, 143 W.Va. 869,
105 S.E.2d 564 (1958) (landlord's bugging of apartment). *But cf.*
Chaplin v. National Broadcasting Co., 15 F.R.D. 134 (S.D.N.Y.
1953); Schmukkler v. Ohio Bell Telephone Co., 116 N.E.2d 819
(Ohio C.P. 1953).

and to give the hunted the maximum chance of escape, by labeling as unfair and illegal such efficacious, if unsporting, equipment as worms and wiretaps. "Wiretapping," he says, "is a form of unreasonable search that should put it under the prohibitions of the Fourth Amendment," [30] and he criticizes the Supreme Court severely for failing so to hold. It is true that the present state of the law on electronic eavesdropping, which is based on the pharisaical reasoning that there is no search or seizure unless there is some sort of physical trespass,[31] and a somewhat strained and artificial construction of Section 605 of the Communications Act of 1934,[32] produces distinctions so fine-spun as to be preposterous.[33] The fact is, of course, that wiretapping, like other varieties of electronic eavesdropping and like other techniques of clandestine surveillance (such as mail covers and stakeouts with binoculars), is essentially a form of search and seizure. So far Mr. Packard [34] is right. But, though such eavesdropping may be peculiarly susceptible to abuse, it is not *ipso facto* unreasonable, and there is no reason to suppose that it is beyond legislative ingenuity to devise controls under which its use would be reasonable within the meaning of the Fourth Amendment. Even Mr. Packard concedes that Congress could constitutionally authorize wiretapping

30. P. 309.
31. Olmstead v. United States, 277 U. S. 438 (1928); Goldman v. United States, 316 U. S. 129 (1942); On Lee v. United States, 343 U. S. 747 (1952); Silverman v. United States, 365 U. S. 505 (1961). Mr. Packard ascribes Chief Justice Taft's decision in the *Olmstead* case, which involved bootleggers, to Taft's fanatic devotion to the cause of prohibition. P. 310. It would be painful to believe that a man of Taft's beatific appearance was a common wowser.
32. Nardone v. United States, 302 U. S. 379 (1937), 308 U. S. 338 (1939); Goldstein v. United States, 316 U. S. 114 (1942).
33. Compare, *e.g.*, United States v. Tane, 329 F.2d 848 (2d Cir. 1964); Cullins v. Wainwright, 328 F.2d 481 (5th Cir. 1964); United States v. Pasha, 332 F.2d 193 (7th Cir. 1964).
34. Or, more probably, the lawyers who educated him in this area. They included such able defenders of civil liberties as Morris Ernst, Frank Newman, Joseph Rauh and Harriet Pilpel.

and microphoning, pursuant to court order, in "cases involving espionage, sabotage, or treason." [35] He is probably right, but it seems to me that these three do not by any means exhaust the catalogue of crimes against which we need all the protection we can get.

On this question of the constitutional limits on wiretaps and the like, Mr. Packard has talked to well-informed people, and his treatment of the problem, however tendentious, is reasonably thorough and informative. This is not true in other areas. He has a habit of dragging in problems which are only remotely related to his major thesis. Even "the right to have unfashionable opinions" [36] is not so much a question of the right prudently to keep such opinions to oneself as of the right to express them freely without being penalized. This and some of the other problems over which Mr. Packard flies at a considerable height and with great rapidity, such as sterilization of the unfit [37] and the right to travel freely *in partibus infidelium*, [38] are great and complex issues. Others, such as the diagnostic methods employed by the more Freudulent psychologists, [39] and the increase in the amount of hide which motion-picture actresses are expected to expose, [40] have more entertainment value than real importance. But all alike are treated in a manner which may charitably be described as sciolistic. [41]

All the same, I am glad that Mr. Packard picked these

35. P. 322.
36. Chapter 13.
37. P. 276.
38. Pp. 225–28.
39. See, *e.g.*, pp. 141–42, for a description of tests solemnly instituted to detect among school children Oral Eroticism, Anal Sadism, Oedipal Intensity, Penis Envy and other fearfully and wonderfully named specimens from the neo-Freudian bestiary.
40. Pp. 220–21.
41. One of Mr. Packard's bits of doubtfully relevant information is, however, worth the price of the book. Any transistor radio within a "few feet" can be put out of action by dialing your own set (silently) to a point 460 kilocycles below the wave length of the station broadcasting the offensive noises. P. 339.

topics, and particularly the Bill of Rights, for the latest in his string of best-sellers. If the gap between *The Naked Society* and the polemics of James Madison is as the Grand Canyon, be it remembered that Mr. Packard's useful and unpretentious volume is aimed at a mass audience which, if it lacks the wit and education to read and understand the prose of the founding fathers, is nonetheless allowed to vote, and on whose understanding depends the survival of our ancient liberties. The defense of the first ten amendments has been too often left to eggheads, while such masters of the popular style as the late Joe McCarthy systematically downgraded them to a point where millions of honest, if not overly bright, citizens regard as subversive contemporary advocacy of the ideas contained in the First, Fourth, Fifth and Sixth amendments. If Mr. Packard can help to reverse that trend, he deserves well of the Republic.

―――――――――

The Supreme Court finally held, a couple of years after the appearance of this review, that electronic eavesdropping is a form of search and seizure and therefore covered by the Fourth Amendment's requirement of reasonableness. As chronicled in my article on "Electronic Eavesdropping and the Public Interest," which follows immediately, the Congress thereupon passed a statute subjecting to regulation the use of wire-taps and similar listening devices by federal agents. A number of states have passed or are debating similar statutes. Whether the eavesdropping thus allowed is "reasonable" has yet to be decided by the courts. Other varieties of clandestine surveillance by law-enforcers—hidden cameras, planted informers and the like—remain unregulated.

178

The individual's right to recover damages for invasions of his privacy is still in a state of flux. The Supreme Court has held in New York Times v. Sullivan and other cases that the right to publish even false information about politicians and other newsworthy people, so long as the publication is not motivated by "malice" (or an indifference to truth so reckless as to be tantamount to "malice"), is protected by the First Amendment.

General Motors' recent settlement with Ralph Nader, to the tune of $425,000, may reflect a growing opinion in the legal profession that unwarranted intrusions on privacy, not complicated by the constitutional issue of freedom to publish, may be highly actionable. But Nader also charged that GM's agents, in their clumsy efforts to get some dirt on him, had attempted an actual frameup, and GM's decision to pay rather than litigate may have been based less on its counsel's belief that the law protected Nader (a very public figure) from private investigation than on the company's intense reluctance to expose itself to further terrible publicity. Senator Dodd's right of privacy did not preclude the publication of documents stolen from his files, as he found out when he sued Drew Pearson.

Electronic
Eavesdropping and
the Public Interest

THE NEW YORK TIMES MAGAZINE, June 8, 1969

_____

*This piece, another effort to lay out a complicated constitu-
tional problem for the benefit of a large non-lawyer reader-
ship, probably drew more hate mail than anything else I ever
wrote, except my insufficiently laudatory remarks about the
beatified Bill Coffin. The more excitable civil libertarians
accused me of advocating a police state, along the lines of
1984. (Many of these same people, incidentally, regard
George Orwell as a reactionary, if not downright fascist,
writer.) But other readers—some of them politicians and
lawyers who had actually had to struggle with the problem
of balancing the citizen's interest in privacy against his interest in being protected from crime—thought it was objective and fair. I still think so myself.*

_____

"THE RIGHT TO BE LET ALONE," said Mr. Justice Brandeis
(dissenting, in 1928), is "the right most valued by civilized

men." The ultimate horrors of 1984 are the Thought Police and their ubiquitous instrument of surveillance, the tele-screen: "You had to live—did live, from habit that became instinct—in the assumption that every sound you made was overheard and, except in darkness, every movement scruti-nized." That is one horn of the dilemma.

On the other hand, Mafiosi, kidnapers, blackmailers, and terrorists are not civilized men, and their right to be let alone is clearly subordinate to the right of honest men to be let alone by them. The New Left to the contrary, the United States in 1969 is not the same as Oceania in 1984, and there are wickeder men outside the Government than in it. "Crimes, unspeakably horrid crimes, are with us in this country," said Mr. Justice Black (dissenting, in 1967), "and we cannot afford to dispense with any known method of detecting and correcting them, unless it is forbidden by the Constitution or deemed inadvisable by legislative policy—neither of which I believe to be true about eavesdropping."

Justice Black probably expressed a more ancient and deeply rooted opinion than did Justice Brandeis. Men have always wanted government and law to protect them from the depredations of other men; they have been willing to put up with some extremely nasty governments to get such protection. It is quite possible that Big Brother could win an honest election. The idea of a right of privacy, on the other hand, is a great deal newer and less widespread; it is probably still largely limited to the upper intellectual layer of the community. As Justice Brandeis noted, the right is prized by *civilized* men.

Given these strong and conflicting drives, it is easy to see why wiretapping has been as fruitful a source of con-stitutional litigation as the tenets of Jehovah's Witnesses or the malapportionment of state legislatures. Muhammad Ali, *geboren* Cassius Clay, has won a rehearing of his conviction for draft violation because the Government had tapped the phones of some people whom he had called. And it is likely that eavesdropping cases will continue to crowd the dockets, for what is at issue is the basic problem of privacy vs. protection. Which are we to weigh more heavily in the scales?

Respect for privacy is certainly not innate among the primates. Indeed, that order's pre-eminence seems to rest largely on the insatiable simian curiosity of most of its members. Physics, astrology, theology, mathematics, and psychoanalysis—all the sciences and quackeries which make man the Lord of Creation, and also its prize laughingstock—rest upon the monkey's consuming urge to stick his nose into things which are none of his business. Among primates, only the gorilla and the orangutan seem deficient in the urge to snoop; these dignified and noble beasts shrink equally from exposing themselves to publicity and from intruding upon the privacy of others. Both are near extinction.

As anyone may learn by observing a cageful of rhesus monkeys, the manners, morals and personal hygiene of other members of the community are prime objects of pithecoid inquisitiveness. Primitive human societies are not much different. There have been (and are) many societies, not primitive nor even barbarous, which placed privacy very low on their scale of values. The Spartans, whom the other Hellenes regarded as models of antique virtue, treated privacy as a positive evil. Spartans lived and messed in barracks; men visited their wives rarely and by stealth, and had small part in the raising of their children. The Romans in their great days were no better. As Plutarch tells us in his life of the elder Marcus Cato, the Censor, "the Romans thought that no marriage, or rearing of children, nay, no feast or drinking bout, ought to be permitted according to everyone's appetite or fancy, without being examined and inquired into." Cato, elected on a platform of "great and thorough purgation," expelled one Senator for having kissed his wife in daylight and in the presence of his daughter. I suspect that he would not have concurred in the recent decision of the Supreme Court of the United States that a citizen has a constitutional right to keep dirty movies in his own house and for his own edification.

Cato, like every other inquisitor before the end of the nineteenth century, had to rely on rumors, spies, informers and almost unlimited powers of search and seizure. What makes the assaults on privacy so formidable in our own time and country is not an increase in the itch to snoop and pry, but the explosive proliferation of efficient and relatively simple means of gratifying that itch.

Justice Brandeis suggested (in 1928!) that "ways may someday be developed by which the Government, without removing papers from secret drawers, can reproduce them in court, and by which it will be enabled to expose to a jury the most intimate occurrences of the home." The prophecy has very nearly come true. Infrared-light techniques permit a room to be watched and photographed from an adjoining room through apparently opaque walls. Closed-circuit TV and other cameras have been so miniaturized that they are easy to conceal in a room. If windows are open, or the subject seeks privacy in his garden, cameras with telescopic lenses can take useful pictures of him or his face-up documents from half a mile away. (The cameras in spy satellites are said to be able to identify objects on the ground which are not much larger than a telephone book.) Orwell was, in fact, uncharacteristically sanguine: You *can* be observed and photographed in darkness if a source of infrared light has been placed in the room.

Wall microphones, of course, can hear and record anything said in an adjoining room. Concealed microphones ("bugs"), broadcasting to a nearby (or even distant) listener or tape recorder, are as small as matchheads and as easy to conceal. Parabolic microphones ("big ears") can monitor conversations in the open air, or in rooms with open windows, from hundreds of yards away. A new building (such as a foreign embassy) can be thoroughly wired for sound when it is built.

The art of shadowing has been greatly improved by ingenious devices which turn the suspect into a walking broadcasting station. If the spy has access to the subject's clothing, a mike can be disguised in a button. If there is access to his lunch or his medicine cabinet, he can be fed a "radio pill," which will broadcast for six hours or so.

This alarming catalogue could be greatly expanded, and has been in a number of books (the best of which is Alan F. Westin's *Privacy and Freedom*). In short, modern optics and electronics have done for man's eyes and ears what the ICBM has done for his throwing arm. There are, of course, countermeasures—rooms within a room, scramblers, jamming devices, bug detectors. Although reasonably effective, they are likely to be expensive and cumbersome. Their worst drawback is that they interfere seriously with the normal conduct of business and pleasure. It is hard to whisper soft nothings in your mistress's ear if you have reason to believe that they are being picked up, amplified and recorded by people who do not wish you well.

Along with the increase in the efficiency of the techniques of spying has come a corresponding increase in the number of people eager to employ them. The Crime Control Act of 1968 having legalized electronic eavesdropping by law enforcers, the Attorney General tells us that he will take full advantage of the new statute. State law enforcers are not likely to show more restraint. Moreover, electronic eavesdropping by private persons, while generally illegal, is still very popular. Aside from all the industrious blackmailers, and the perverted practical jokers who bug bedrooms, there are strong commercial motives for industrial and labor espionage. Some members of the working press seem to feel that the public's right to be informed rises above any interest in privacy; a federal grand jury recently indicted one of NBC's news directors for bugging Chicago hotel rooms in which the Democratic Platform Committee was meeting.

Mention should be made also of a class of private policers of morality, lay and clerical, who prefer the ancient and time-tested techniques, such as breaking and entering. Their activities, which are usually carried out as publicly as possible, for some reason appear to draw less condemnation from professional civil libertarians than the arcane and covert techniques of the minions of the law. There seems, however, to be a certain degree of intrusion on privacy when a gang of dervishes, acting in the holy name of morality and in the great tradition of the Rev. Elmer Gantry, kick in the door of a person whose ideas and activities they judge to be immoral, rifle his files, destroy some of his papers and publish others. But these zealots, though public nuisances, are no more than a sideshow; they account for a very small part of the total assault on privacy.

We are faced with the painfully familiar problem of a technology which has outstripped our knowledge of how to use and control it; once more the scientists have beaten the lawyers. The public is of several minds about the proper use of electronic spying in law enforcement. At one end of the spectrum is what may be termed the Dick Tracy view: Only criminals talk about their constitutional rights, from which it follows that it ought to be a crime to invoke the protection of the Constitution. At the other end is the school of opinion (ably represented by a large faction within the American Civil Liberties Union) which, if it does not quite believe that it is unconstitutional to introduce evidence against people accused of crime, is at least willing to allow human tigers a sporting chance by forbidding the use of high-powered rifles and telescopic sights. I once heard an eminent American professor of criminal law tell an audience of European lawyers that the only sure way to eliminate the Mafia would be to suspend the Constitution for twenty-four hours. He did not, however, favor such a remedy—which, after all, is rather like Mark Twain's suggestion that all the ills of humanity could be cured by withdrawing the oxygen from the air for a period of five minutes.

In between the two extremes stand the Congress (and probably most of the state legislatures), the Department of Justice and other law-enforcement agencies, most of the courts and most of the citizens. The legislative psychology is complicated; the usual Congressional enthusiasm for law and order is tempered by the conviction of many Congressmen that they are themselves prime targets of electronic eavesdropping.

The framers of the Constitution were naturally familiar with the networks of police agents, spies and informers with which the European monarchs of the seventeenth and eighteenth centuries kept tabs on their foreign and domestic enemies. Some of them were very efficient: John Thurloe, for example, seems to have supplied Oliver Cromwell with more reliable intelligence than most subsequent British (or American) Governments have had at their disposal, and Joseph Fouché did so thorough a job of scotching conspiracies against the Consulate and the First Empire that Napoleon made him not merely Minister of Police but also Duke of Otranto.

The activities of Thurloe, Fouché and the rest of their ilk may have been necessary to the security of the state, but they were at best annoying and at worst oppressive, especially when they took the form of searching the house and rifling the papers of a suspect. The Fourth Amendment to the Constitution of the United States attempted to balance the interests of the Government against those of the citizen by providing that "the right of the people to be secure in their persons, houses, papers and effects, against unreasonable searches and seizures, shall not be violated, and no warrants shall issue, but upon probable cause, supported by oath or affirmation, and particularly describing the place to be searched, and the persons or things to be seized."

This provision, plus a series of acts of Congress forbidding both private persons and agents of the Government to open other people's letters, took care of the problem for more than a century. But the first telephones had hardly been installed before the police, the Pinkertons [1] and purely private snoops began to tap them. The concealed microphone is almost as old. Many of the states passed statutes outlawing wire-tapping. Congress did nothing, and federal agents continued merrily to tap the wires of suspected violators of federal law—on an increasing scale after Prohibition had doubled or tripled the number of practicing federal criminals. They were deterred not at all by the fact that their own activities were frequently violations of state law. All things considered, it is surprising that the question did not reach the Supreme Court until 1928, in a case called *Olmstead v. United States*.

Olmstead led the Supreme Court (and the inferior federal courts, which had to tag along) into a morass rivaled only by the Great Dismal Swamp of obscenity. They were to flounder in it for forty years. The decision affirmed the conviction of a titan of the bootlegging industry, on evidence obtained by tapping the telephone wires leading to his prem-

1. This statement drew an indignant letter from a vice-president of the Pinkerton organization, asserting that no Pinkerton operative had ever tapped a wire. I had used "Pinkerton" loosely as a synonym for private detective and so couldn't contradict his statement, which I received with equal parts of gratification and skepticism.

ises—without, however, any physical entry on those premises. Chief Justice Taft and four of his brethren found no violation of Olmstead's constitutional rights. They read the Fourth Amendment literally—a house could not be "searched" without being entered and there could be no "seizure" of incorporeal things like words.

Brandeis dissented because he thought the Fourth Amendment applied to "any intrusion by the Government upon the privacy of the individual," Holmes because he thought that illegal wiretapping by law enforcers (*not* wiretapping per se) was a "dirty business." Taft's opinion has been ascribed to zeal in the cause of Prohibition. Although it is difficult to believe that one who had been a professor of law at Yale shared the morality of the Anti-Saloon League and the Methodist Board of Temperance and Morals (and equally difficult to believe that he achieved his girth and complexion without the help of malt or vinous liquors), the tone of the opinion does suggest that he disliked bootleggers. He referred, for example, to a lady who opened the door of a liquor seller's house as "a woman who claimed to be his wife," although there was in fact nothing to suggest that the couple were not lawfully wedded.

Whatever its motivation, Taft's opinion was a disaster. The Court had, to be sure, conceded that Congress could restrict wiretapping. But when Congress, six years later, made it illegal to "intercept and divulge" communications without the sender's consent, the principal result was to compound the confusion, for the statute was full of holes and ambiguities. The courts shortly became entangled in distinctions of preposterous, almost theological, subtlety—the kind of distinctions which allow an orthodox Jew to shave with an electric razor but not a blade. A wiretap was an "interception," but a concealed microphone was not. A microphone attached to the wall of adjoining premises did not trespass and, therefore, was not a "search"; a spike mike trespassed, but only if the spike penetrated through more than half the thickness of the common wall. The courts split on the portentous problem of jurisprudence raised by dangling a microphone down a ventilating shaft in an apartment house. A mike concealed on the person of an informer was perfectly constitutional, because the informer (although not his bug) had been invited onto the suspect's premises and, therefore, committed no trespass.

And so on and so forth. Only the most astute judges could thread their way through the maze; cops, criminals and lawyers were thoroughly bewildered. People went to jail or went free unpredictably, without rhyme or reason.

By 1967 even the Supreme Court had had enough. In *Katz v. United States,* the Court finally held—as Justice Brandeis would have had it hold in 1928—that electronic eavesdropping amounts to search and seizure, which the Fourth Amendment permits only under a warrant issued by a judge. But about the same time the Justices also held, in *Berger v. New York,* that a New York statute which provided for just such warrants was unconstitutional because it gave the state courts too much discretion. The opinions in these cases did, however, suggest—although not with great precision—warrant procedures which would satisfy the Bill of Rights and (more to the point) the Supreme Court itself.

The invitation was quickly accepted by the Department of Justice and Congress. Title III of a statute with the mouth-filling name of the Omnibus Crime Control and Safe Streets Act, passed in June, 1968, set up a procedure (in the case of state law enforcers, a minimum procedure) whereby the police may use bugs and taps—constitutionally, one hopes—pursuant to judicial warrants. It may be assumed that both federal and state police will take the fullest possible advantage of the new authority—Attorney General

Mitchell has said as much—and that, in so doing, they will produce plenty of grist for the Supreme Court's mill.

With *Katz* and *Berger*, the Court swept away the debris of the *Olmstead* doctrine. In *Katz*, the FBI had planted a mike on the roof of a public telephone booth which bookie Katz used to phone his bets from Los Angeles to Miami and Boston. Mr. Hoover's men had not set foot in the telephone booth or any other premises used by Katz; under the *Olmstead* rule the Fourth Amendment had no application, and they were under no obligation to obtain a warrant or otherwise make sure that their intrusion on Katz's privacy was legal or reasonable. The Supreme Court, at long last, overruled *Olmstead*: "The Fourth Amendment," it declared, "protects people, not places." Katz went free.

(It may be noted in passing that only Katz himself benefited from the holding in his case, for the Court held three months later that the new construction of the Constitution should be prospective only; all the other people who, prior to its decision, had been convicted on evidence supplied by nontrespassing taps and bugs stayed convicted.)

Only Justice Black dissented from the majority's proposition about people and places. The older he gets (and he is now eighty-four), the more set he becomes in his conviction that the Constitution means precisely what its authors said —no more and no less. If the Constitution says that freedom of speech cannot be abridged, then every man has a constitutional right to slander any other man. It is entirely possible that he would argue that, since the Constitution empowers Congress to provide only for an Army and Navy, there is no warrant for an Air Force—unless the planes and pilots are sneaked in as parts of the Army or Navy.

In this particular case, however, the Justice did not have to rest on the argument that the framers of the Bill of Rights knew nothing of electronics and so could not have intended to limit the use of that science. He argued, more plausibly, that they *did* know about eavesdropping with the naked ear, but said nothing about it; they decided to protect the citizens against having their doors kicked down without a warrant, but not against less oppressive forms of prying. If the Constitution furnished no protection against the kind of listening with which its draughtsmen were familiar, how can it be held to cover other varieties they never heard of? (Perhaps the pragmatic answer is that if Jefferson, Franklin and the rest could have foreseen modern improvements in the art of listening and peeping through keyholes they might well have equated them to search and seizure.)

But whatever the merits of Justice Black's reasoning, it did not prevail. It is now clear (unless the Supreme Court changes its mind again) that the citizen is constitutionally secure from eavesdropping, if done without a warrant which meets the Fourth Amendment's tests.

As the Court took pains to explain, the fact that wiretaps, concealed microphones and all the other varieties of electronic prying became "searches and seizures" as of December 18, 1967, when Katz's case was decided, did not make them *ipso facto* illegal, nor did it mean that the use of evidence so obtained necessarily violates the accused's right to due process. The Supreme Court, indeed, pointed out in that case that the FBI could have obtained a warrant to listen in on Katz's phone calls (without notifying Katz) and that, if it had done so, the search and seizure would not have been the "unreasonable" kind which is condemned by the Fourth Amendment. The *sine qua non* of reasonableness, said the Court (which has great faith in judges), is the interposition of an impartial *judge* between the citizen and the police, instead of leaving to the cops themselves, or even to the District Attorney, the decision to bug or not to bug.

But, the Court went on, not even a judge can be given

carte blanche to grant the law enforcers' request that they be allowed to listen in. He must be satisfied that there is "probable cause" to believe that the subject is up to something criminal, and his warrant must "particularly describe the place to be searched, and the persons or things to be seized." In effect, that means that he must set some bounds on the premises and people to be monitored, and also on the duration of the surveillance. The D.A. cannot simply be given a license to go fishing. New York, like many states, had a statute which allowed its police to use taps and bugs pursuant to court order; the Court in *Berger* held it unconstitutional simply because it allowed the magistrate to give the police authority to bug Berger's offices for a period of sixty days.

Thus, the Court blocked out for Congress and the states the broad outlines of a regulation of electronic search and seizure which would satisfy the Constitution. Unfortunately, the Justices at the same time placed a limit on the Fourth Amendment's protection (and, therefore, on the need for legislative restriction of eavesdropping) which may contain the seed of a bramble bush as tangled as that which grew out of Olmstead's case. The Government made much of the fact that Katz was telephoning from a sort of goldfish bowl —a glass telephone booth—and so could hardly have expected much privacy. The Court's answer was that "what he sought to exclude when he entered the booth was not the intruding eye—it was the uninvited ear." Presumably, if the FBI had posted at a nearby window a lip-reader with a pair of binoculars, Katz would have had no complaint.

The Court thus seemed to concede that the Fourth Amendment protects only that privacy which a person reasonably expects. A man and his wife have a constitutional right to quarrel or make love in their bedroom without unwarranted observation, but no such right surrounds their activities on the front lawn. As every small-towner knows, people with party lines can expect the substance of their conversations to be all over town within the hour. The dilemma is simply that, as the science of surveillance develops, the difference between the bedroom and the front lawn becomes less and less obvious: The more sophisticated the techniques of spying, the less reasonable is a man's belief that he is unobserved.

Could Katz, a professional gambler, really have been startled when he learned that his phone calls were overheard? Can the staff of a foreign embassy *ever* reasonably suppose that their telephone conversations are not monitored? But, as I have previously suggested, the United States in 1969 is not Oceania in 1984, nor even the People's Republic of China in 1969, and there are still many situations in which its people expect privacy and in which that expectation is justified. A jail, for example, differs in some respects from a home; it may even be thought of as open to the public; but the courts have held that a prisoner can fairly expect that his talks with his lawyer will not be overheard.

Title III of the Crime Control Act of 1968 represents Congress's effort to take advantage of the helpful hints on constitutionality which the Court supplied in *Berger* and *Katz*. Its object, in simplest terms, is to permit federal and state law enforcers to use taps and bugs subject to regulations which it is hoped will satisfy the Fourth Amendment and the Supreme Court. (Electronic eavesdropping by private persons is practically outlawed—a part of the act which may be easier to pass than to enforce.) No warrant is required if one of the parties to a conversation consents to its being overheard—for instance, when the police listen in on threatening or obscene phone calls at the victim's request. Otherwise, federal or state agents may use hidden listening devices to obtain evidence of serious crimes (particularly those, like kidnaping, bribery, and extortion, in which electronic evidence has been most often used), but only under a warrant issued by a judge. Whether the limits which the act places on that judge's discretion are strict enough to satisfy the Supreme Court remains to be seen.

The act, like the Court, treats electronic eavesdropping as a variety of search and seizure, which it is. The subject does not know that his conversations are being searched and seized, to be sure, but he may not know that his house has been searched and his papers copied. In neither case is he given advance warning. A hidden listening device may uncover evidence of crimes other than the one the tapper is investigating (in which case the warrant can be amended to cover the new crime), but so may any search. The judges may be less impartial than they ought to be (although the bias of judges does not invariably run in favor of the police), but they are certainly more so than the cops or the D.A. At any rate, they are the best we have. All in all, the act, putting limits on the freedom of the police to listen to anyone, any time, any place (and on their freedom to use evidence so obtained), seems to me a long step in the right direction.

It leaves a lot of questions unanswered. It protects only "oral communications." But the telescopic lens, the see-through wall panel and the other devices for optical spying seem to me (although so far not to the Supreme Court) as much within the spirit of the Fourth Amendment as are the hidden listeners. Following the Court's construction of the Fourth Amendment, the act protects only those words which are "uttered by a person exhibiting an expectation that such communication is not subject to interception, under circumstances justifying such expectation"—and that, as I have suggested, may pose some pretty questions of fact.

It exempts altogether the acts of the President in national-security cases: So far as Congress is concerned, the Justice Department and military intelligence can eavesdrop on suspected spies and subversives, or foreign embassies, without first telling a judge. What the Supreme Court thinks about national security is not so clear. Justice White has said that in such cases it is reasonable to search without a warrant, and Justices Douglas and Brennan that "spies and saboteurs are as entitled to the protection of the Fourth Amendment as suspected gamblers"; the rest of the Court has said nothing. It is safe to guess that the surveillance of the Soviet Embassy's telephones continues. (It must be dreadfully dull work for the listeners.)

One other serious problem both Court and Congress have left untouched: the use of the planted informer, whom the British call a "copper's nark." (The flower children are, incidentally, quite wrong in supposing that the word "nark" is a contraction of "narcotics agent." It is far older than heroin, pot or the Narcotics Bureau; it probably comes from the Romany word "nak," meaning "nose.")

The informer is still the most effective weapon of the police detective. In 1984 it was not the telescreen which trapped Winston and Julia, but Mr. Charrington, the informer and *agent provocateur*. Logically, the planted informer seems to me to differ from the disguised microphone principally in that he is less accurate and truthful; he is likely, moreover, to try actively to elicit damning evidence. But in 1966 the Supreme Court held, affirming Jimmy Hoffa's conviction for jury tampering, that the Fourth Amendment did not protect Hoffa against a planted informer. Hoffa, said the Court, had not relied upon the security of his hotel room, but on his misplaced confidence in the spy. We shall learn in due time whether the foundation of that opinion was eroded by the Court's subsequent decision that it is people, not places, that are protected.

The contending forces which are shaping our policy on electronic eavesdropping are, of course, on the one hand, the desire to catch criminals, or at least some kinds of criminals, with any weapons available; on the other, a developing belief that privacy is a very important right. A few years ago, when the Supreme Court struck down a Connecticut statute prohibiting the dissemination of birth-control information, some of the Justices talked grandly and vaguely of a *constitutional* right of privacy. But there is, of course, no mention of any such thing in the Bill of Rights, and the Court's most recent pronouncement, in *Katz*, said clearly that it does not exist. Except for the Fourth Amendment, the Constitution leaves the protection of privacy largely to Congress and the law of the states—as it leaves the protection of property and life itself.

Despite the fervent protests of those who think that even legal wiretapping is a dirty business, I think Congress has struck a reasonable balance between the people's interest in being let alone by government and their interest in being let alone by criminals. There *is* something distasteful about wiretaps and hidden microphones, but, on reflection, I find something even more distasteful about kidnaping and heroin peddling.

196

III

The Law and Language
of War

The Legal Status of
Berlin

THE NEW REPUBLIC, October 2, 1961

———

This is an updating, revision, and documentation of an article which I wrote for The New Republic at the height of the Berlin crisis of 1961. There have been no significant changes in the legal situation since then, so it can be re-used if the Russians should decide to re-ignite the fuse on that particular powder keg. Although they and Mr. Ulbricht have continued to harass the lines of communication between Berlin and the West at irregular intervals, the latest discussions between the Western powers and the Soviet Union on the status of Berlin (initiated in conjunction with the negotiation of the 1970 treaty between the Federal Republic and the Soviet Union) seem to have had as legalistic a flavor as the former ones. Novoye Vremya, the Soviet journal of international affairs, now suggests that West Berlin might be allowed to exist as an autonomous city-state, something like the Vatican. This po-sition, although it is described by Klaus Schütz, Willy Brandt's successor as Mayor of West Berlin, as unrealistic, and although it is still accompanied by Russian assertions that the Western powers are entitled to no say in the matter, does seem at least to represent a modification of the hard Russian position of the early Sixties.

———

A NECESSARY PRELIMINARY to a discussion of the legal status of Berlin is a consideration of the question whether these points of law really matter and, if they do, why. The Soviet government did not attempt to strangle the city in 1948 because a study of treatises on international law had convinced it that the Western allies had no legal right to remain in the city, and it did not give up that attempt because the cogent arguments of Western lawyers had persuaded it otherwise. The Russians turned off the blockade because it was not working and because the Allied counterblockade was putting a severe strain on the feeble economy of East Germany. (Of course, it may well be argued that the abandonment of the blockade itself proved something about the rights of the parties in the city, just as the event at Appomattox elucidated once and for all some basic questions of Constitutional law which had theretofore been regarded as at least doubtful.) At no time since 1958, when the U.S.S.R., announcing that it could no longer tolerate the Western occupation of Berlin, inaugurated the flexible campaign of pressure, threats, sweet reasonableness, and blackmail which has continued intermittently to the present day, did Mr. Khrushchev or his successors evince any disposition to take the case to the International Court of Justice. For that matter, neither did Mr. Kennedy, or even Mr. Macmillan, and certainly not General de Gaulle or Dr. Adenauer or *their* successors. And yet all of the governments concerned clogged the air waves and stuffed diplomatic pouches with thousands of words intended to demonstrate that international law solidly supports, on the one hand, the exclusion of the Western forces from Berlin and, on the other, their continued presence there. My own file, which is very far from complete, contains several hundred pages of the tedious, repetitious, and somewhat flatulent notes, aide-memoires, memoranda, etc., etc.—all of them heavily larded with legal argumentation—in which the disputants have put their cases to each other and the rest of the world. I may note in passing that they make very hard and indigestible reading indeed. I am not privy to the contents of the apparently interminable talks among the four governments which started in 1961 and which were most recently resumed in March, 1970, but I think it safe to guess that much of what has been said has had a strong legal flavor.

Thus, I am brought up short at the outset of this examination of the law of the case by the question of *why* parties who will not go to court have put so many lawyers to work. The question, of course, is one which bedevils any consideration of international law in the context of an actual and important dispute between nations, and of course I can give no pat answer. The best I can do is to suggest that the motives of Messrs. Kennedy, Khrushchev, *et al.* were not essentially different from those which led the saintly statesmen of the Papacy, in the darkest of the Dark Ages, to forge the Donation of Constantine as a legal basis for their claims to temporal sovereignty. (I do not suggest, of course, that any of the disputants have actually resorted to such doctoring of the record.) Men who are even moderately civilized prefer, by long habit and training, to have the law on their side, even if there are no policemen to enforce that law. Moreover, neither the NATO powers nor the Communists have any desire to seem lawless in the eyes of the neutral nations or their own people. Indeed, I think there is more to it than a mere desire to keep up appearances. One of the many qualities which made Adolf Hitler unique among modern rulers was his quite genuine and open contempt for law, domestic or international. He really seems never to have bothered to convince himself that what he wanted to do had any legal justification. But the heads of state chiefly concerned in the Berlin dispute were and are essentially sane and normal men, and I suspect that each of them, including the Soviet leaders, preferred to believe, and probably did believe, that his political goals and his methods of achieving them were legal and even equitable. In general, the Communists are probably a good deal less devoted to the concept of the rule of law than are democratic statesmen, but in a batch, selected more or less at random, of four speeches made by Mr. Khrushchev at the height of the Berlin crisis of the summer of 1961, I find no less than fourteen appeals to international law, which in each case turned out to support the Soviet position. It goes without saying that these contentions have not passed unchallenged by the West. Indeed, about the only propositions on which the two sides concur is that West Berlin is now under military occupation by the armed forces of France, the United Kingdom, and the United States and that its situation is peculiar.

Let us try then, as dispassionately and objectively as possible, to assess the legal situation. That, of course, requires a statement of the facts. Those facts are pretty well known and, generally speaking, are not in dispute. For present purposes they can be summarized with comparative brevity. The same thing is true of the contents of the various documents which are relevant to the question of the right of the Western powers to be in Berlin; [1] there has been no opportunity,

---

1. The relevant documents up to 1959, which include practically all of those germane to the problem, are reprinted in UNITED STATES DEPARTMENT OF STATE AND STAFF OF SENATE COMMITTEE ON FOREIGN RELATIONS, 86TH CONG., 1ST SESS., DOCUMENTS ON GERMANY, 1944–1959 (Comm. Print 1959). See also A *Decade of American For-*

and perhaps no occasion, for fakery.

By late fall of 1943 the defeat of Germany seemed sufficiently certain to call for advance planning of the occupation. The United States, the United Kingdom, and the Soviet Union at the Moscow Foreign Ministers Conference, held in October of that year, set up the European Advisory Commission (composed of representatives of the three prospective victors), whose job was to recommend terms of surrender and methods of enforcing Allied policy in Germany. Its terms of reference optimistically assumed a joint, tripartite occupation and a joint, tripartite policy. By the fall of 1944 it was apparent to almost everyone except Adolf Hitler and the more bemused of his disciples that the disintegration of the thousand-year Reich was imminent. On September 12, 1944, the three powers signed a protocol, prepared by the European Advisory Commission, providing for the division of Germany into three zones of occupation, one per ally, "and a special Berlin area, which will be under joint occupation by the three powers." In November of the same year this was supplemented by an agreement among the three powers on control machinery for Germany, also prepared by the Advisory Commission. That agreement created the Allied Control Council, composed of the military governors of the three zones of occupation, and an "Inter-Allied Governing Authority"—the so-called Komendatura [2]—con-

---

eign Policy: Basic Documents, 1941–1949, S. Doc. No. 123, 81st Cong., 1st Sess. (1950). An extraordinarily comprehensive collection of documents bearing on Berlin, including statements of the position of the Federal Republic of Germany, and including also some papers of relatively subordinate importance that are not readily available elsewhere, is DOCUMENTS ON THE STATUS OF BERLIN 1944–1959, prepared and edited by the Forschungsinstitut der Deutschen Gesellschaft für Auswärtige Politik under the direction of O. M. von der Gablentz, and published in Munich in 1959. All of the documents therein reprinted are in English.

2. Among the subjects of disagreement in Berlin is the spelling of this Russian term. The original documents spell it "Komendatura";

sisting of the military commandants in each sector of the city, to rule Berlin, subject to the general direction of the Control Council. Each Berlin commandant governed his nation's sector, subject, of course, to the direction of his nation's commander-in-chief in Germany; "questions of principle and problems common to all zones" (*i.e.*, sectors of the city) were to be decided by the Komendatura. As might have been expected, both the Control Council and the Komendatura, like the Security Council of the United Nations, could act only by unanimous vote. It is somewhat remarkable that the application of the veto principle to the workings of the Komendatura was not made explicit until July 7, 1945, although it was no doubt implicit in the subjection of that body to the direction of the Control Council. In July, 1945, these agreements were amended to include France as a fourth occupant of both Berlin and Germany. Its zone and sector were carved out of those allotted to the other two Western powers, and the addition of French members to the Control Council and the Komendatura did not, of course, affect the fundamental balance of power between the Western allies and the Soviet Union—or at least has not so far done so.

When the Nazi government finally evaporated and the four powers, on June 5, 1945, assumed "supreme authority with respect to Germany," the Red Army was in exclusive possession of Berlin. Why that was so has been the subject of a good deal of non-legal discussion, most of it partisan and polemical. General Eisenhower, who ought to know, says that he had decided, for military reasons, that the city "was not the logical or the most desirable objective for the forces of the Western Allies." [3] On the other hand, United States

---

later ones, such as the Resolution of Representatives of the Allied Commands on the quadripartite allied administration of Berlin of July 7, 1945, spell it "Kommandatura."

3. EISENHOWER, CRUSADE IN EUROPE 396 (1948).

forces occupied most of Saxony and Thuringia to the Elbe River, some two hundred miles inside the Russian zone. On June 14 President Truman offered Stalin a trade whereby the American forces would be pulled back to their own zone "in accordance with arrangements between the respective commanders, including in these arrangements simultaneous movement of the national garrisons into Greater Berlin and provision of free access for United States forces by air, road and rail to Berlin from Frankfurt and Bremen." Stalin accepted, agreeing to take "all necessary measures" in accordance with the plan. Similar agreements were concluded between Stalin and Churchill—against the better judgment of the latter prescient statesman, for he had viewed the location of the United States forces as conferring a heaven-sent opportunity for "the settlement of many great things which would be the true foundation of world peace"—*i.e.*, an opportunity to bargain, realistically and from a position of strength, with the Russians on some of the questions of the future of Germany which the various protocols and declarations had passed over in silence or wrapped in woolly ambiguities.[4] In the succeeding weeks the four zone commandants filled in the details of these basic agreements by arranging for the use by Western forces of the Helmstedt-Berlin railroad and autobahn, these being the most direct routes across the Soviet zone to Berlin. Access was to be subject only to "normal traffic regulations," which, as General Clay recalled Marshal Zhukov's oral gloss, would include such matters as road signs and document checking, "but no inspection of cargo—the U.S.S.R. is not interested in what is being hauled, how much or how many trucks are moving."[5]

4. See 6 CHURCHILL, THE SECOND WORLD WAR: TRIUMPH AND TRAGEDY 443–52, 522–88 (1954); 1 TRUMAN, MEMOIRS: YEAR OF DECISIONS 60–61, 210–19, 297–304 (1955).

5. See the statement by Ambassador Philip C. Jessup to the UN Security Council, October 6, 1948, 19 DEP'T STATE BULL. 485 (1948); CLAY, DECISION ON GERMANY 25–26 (1950).

By November, 1945, quadripartite agreements had created three air corridors across the Russian zone to Berlin with unrestricted flight, subject only to agreed safety regulations. There were in addition less important agreements dealing with canal traffic, mail, telephone and telegraph, and so forth.

These fundamental agreements obviously left open many topics for future discussion and agreement. Nevertheless, particularly with respect to Western access to Berlin, they were reasonably explicit and unambiguous. They were at least adequate to the situation with which they were intended to deal and for the assumptions upon which they were predicated. Those assumptions appear clearly in other contemporary agreements. The United States, at least, and probably the British, supposed that the situation was essentially what it had been after World War I and after most previous wars: a military occupation of comparatively short duration—perhaps five years—followed by the establishment of a new central German government with its capital in Berlin and the termination of the occupation by a peace treaty with that new German government. Thus, the agreement of November 14, 1944, which created the Control Council and the Komendatura, specified that they were to "operate during the initial period of the occupation of Germany immediately following surrender," and "the question of the Allied organs required for carrying out the functions of control and administration in Germany at a later period" was left to subsequent agreement. The closest thing to such a subsequent agreement is the Potsdam Protocol of August 2, 1945, which has not proved to be very close. Although the heads of state grandly announced in that protocol agreement "on the political and economic principles of a coordinated Allied policy toward defeated Germany during the period of Allied control," they did nothing further to define how that control was to work. They dealt with the problem of the creation of a new German government by postponing it: "For the time being no central German government shall be established"— although they agreed to set up "essential central German administrative departments" to handle economic matters (finance, transport, trade, etc.) under the direction of the Control Council, which, it will be recalled, could only act unanimously. The problems of ending the occupation and signing a peace treaty were postponed even further; the newly created Council of Foreign Ministers (which replaced the European Advisory Commission) was instructed to prepare "a peace settlement for Germany to be accepted by the government of Germany when a government adequate for the purpose is established." In short, the parties set up temporary arrangements for the occupation of the defeated enemy and agreed to agree later on the long-range solution.

I think it not beyond the bounds of possibility that the Russians themselves shared the optimistic illusion that some such solution might actually be reached. As is well known, one who properly applies the science of Marxism-Leninism cannot err in political diagnosis; but as is also well known (since 1953), the late J. V. Stalin occasionally displayed a defective understanding of Marxism-Leninism. Communists, like other men, often come to believe their own slogans, and it may be that the Russians really did suppose that the German Communist Party could clamber into control of the central government with no more than an initial leg-up from the Red Army. If that had happened—and it is very easy to forget how likely it seemed, before the Marshall Plan, that the Communists really might win elections all over Western Europe—it might have been very difficult for the United States and Great Britain to refuse to sign a peace treaty with the new and honestly elected German government.

The point is that the present legal situation of Berlin was

not planned by lawyers; it was not planned by Americans, Englishmen, or Frenchmen; and it was probably not planned by Russians. It just happened—as is the case with many other tangled legal problems. Moreover, it is unprecedented. The original interest and policy of the United States, to which it still clings in all its formal pronouncements, was to arrange for the occupation and reconstruction of Germany, pending the creation of a new central government and a peace treaty. Two-thirds of Germany has now been reconstructed to our satisfaction, and the other third to Soviet satisfaction. The problems implicit in mixing this oil and water to produce an homogenous, reunified whole need not be stated here. The United States' real policy now, as far as it has one, is to keep the people of West Berlin out of the clutches of the German Democratic Republic.

The original assumptions of quadripartite control of Germany and the creation of a central German government broke down early, because of the total inability of the four victorious powers to agree on anything at all. That history is well known and need not be recapitulated here. Developments in the Berlin microcosm naturally paralleled those in Germany as a whole—and, incidentally, furnish some support to the hypothesis that the Soviet Union, like the West, entered into the arrangements of 1944 and 1945 on the basis of a major political miscalculation. The Russians had utilized their brief period of exclusive occupation to install in Berlin a German administration dominated by the Socialist Unity (Communist) Party. In October, 1946, the Russians made the never-to-be-repeated mistake of permitting honest elections in Greater Berlin; the Socialist Unity Party took a fearful drubbing, and the German administration of the city became anti-Communist. The Soviet authorities were reduced to the chronic use of the veto in the Komendatura, which (like the Allied Control Council) practically ceased to

208

function. The Soviet delegation formally walked out of the Komendatura on July 1, 1948, the immediate cause being the introduction into West Berlin of the currency reform already effected in the Western zones. These developments were accompanied by the blockade (and counterblockade) of 1948 and the Berlin airlift. In November of the same year the Russians set up a Magistrat (city government) in their sector, purportedly the lawful government of the whole city. The original Magistrat moved to West Berlin, where it has functioned ever since. Thus, there were and are two separate and hostile city governments, each claiming to be the lawful government of Greater Berlin and each, of course, exercising actual authority only in its own bailiwick.

The Western Allies, of course, promptly and repeatedly denounced the blockade as a violation of their rights stemming from the defeat and surrender of Germany—rights of access to Berlin which, they argued, were not only implicit in their status as military occupants of the city but confirmed both by the agreements already described and by usage. The Russians did not—and apparently do not to this day—deny the existence of these agreements nor even seriously contest the construction given them by the West. *Their* legal answer was that the four-power agreements on Berlin were no more than an "inseparable component part" of the broader agreements on Germany as a whole and that the frustration of these agreements by the Western powers—particularly their transformation of their zones into a separate economic and political unit and their failure to carry out the disarmament of Germany—destroyed the whole system of four-power agreements on Germany and "thereby undermined as well the legal basis which assured their right to participation in the administration of Berlin."

This dispute, it goes without saying, was not resolved by the two quadripartite agreements—the last agreements which seem relevant—made in connection with the ending of the blockade. That of May 4, 1949, simply provided for the simultaneous removal of "all the restrictions imposed since March 1, 1948, by the Government of the Union of Soviet Socialist Republics on communications, transportation, and trade between Berlin and the Western zones of Germany and between the Eastern zone and the Western zones" and the corresponding restrictions placed by the West on such traffic. On June 20, 1949, the four powers agreed that the May agreement should be "maintained." They announced their intention "to continue their efforts to achieve the restoration of the economic and political unity of Germany" and to that end to consult together "to mitigate the effects of the present administrative division of Germany and Berlin," particularly by (a) "Expansion of trade and development of the financial and economic relations between the Western zones and Berlin and between Berlin and the zones"; (b) "Facilitation of the movement of persons and goods and the exchange of information between the Western zones and the Eastern zone and between Berlin and the zones"; and (c) "Consideration of questions of common interest relating to the administration of the four sectors with a view to normalizing as far as possible the life of the city." They agreed further that, in order to promote these laudable purposes "and in order to improve and supplement this and other arrangements and agreements as regard the movement of persons and goods and communications between the Eastern zone and the Western zones and between the zones and Berlin and also in regard to transit, the occupation authorities, each in his own zone, will have an obligation to take the measures necessary to insure the normal functioning and utilization of rail, water and road transport" for the movement of persons and goods between East and West zones and between the zones and Berlin. Nothing was said about air traffic (presumably because it had not been affected by the blockade), and no time limit was set on the "maintenance" of the agreement to lift the blockade.

Despite these virtuous intentions, or at any rate virtuous protestations, the polarization of Germany proceeded apace. In September, 1949, the Federal Republic of Germany was established in the Western zones and accorded a high degree of autonomy, though the occupation was not ended.[6] A week or so later the German Democratic Republic appeared in the East zone and got about the same degree of autonomy as other Communist states in Eastern Europe.[7] But both sides were chary of drastic tampering with the status of Berlin; the relationship of these German governments, particularly the Federal Republic, to the city was and is complicated and somewhat obscure. The *Grundgesetz* (Basic Law) of the Federal Republic (not called a constitution because that august title is to await the reunification of Germany) listed greater Berlin as one of the twelve *Laender* (states) to which it applied. But the Western military governors, when they approved this basic law, made reservations on Berlin: It was neither to be given voting representation in the federal parliament (though it may and does send non-voting representatives) nor to be governed by the Federal Republic. Likewise, West Berlin's own constitution now describes it as a *Land* of the Federal Republic governed by the latter's *Grundgesetz* and other laws, but the Western Komendatura limited their approval by stipulating that Berlin should have none of the attributes of a *Land* and that the Federal Republic's laws should not apply of their own force to Berlin.

6. I have described the creation of the Federal Republic and its relations with the Western Allies in my article on *The "Contractual Agreements" with the Federal Republic of Germany*, 49 AM. J. INT. LAW 125 (1955).
7. See Simpson, *Berlin: Allied Rights and Responsibilities in the Divided City*, 6 INT'L & COMP. L. Q. 83, 98–99 (1957).

These laws have to be enacted by Berlin's own city government—which, however, can be simply and expeditiously accomplished by a *Mantelgesetz* (cover law) incorporating by reference a law of the Federal Republic or a group of such laws. Under this system Berlin has, in fact, pretty well homologized itself to the Federal Republic in financial and judicial matters: In taxation and public expenditure it is practically a twelfth *Land* of the federation, and it has the same currency. The decisions of its courts are subject to the appellate jurisdiction of those of the Federal Republic. But the *Bundesverfassungsgericht*, the Federation's supreme constitutional court, held in 1957 that so long as the Allied reservations remained in force Berlin was not one of the *Laender* and constitutional questions arising in that city were not within its jurisdiction. The Western Allies were sedulous not to disturb this delicate balance by their 1954 Contractual Agreements (so-called to make sure that nobody confused them with a Peace Treaty) with the Federal Republic. These agreements, though they terminated the occupation in West Germany, changed the mission of Allied forces from occupation to "the defense of the free world, of which Berlin and the Federal Republic form part," and gave the Federal Republic "the full authority of a sovereign state over its internal and external affairs," reserved to the Western powers their rights as military occupants "insofar as they are required for the exercise of the rights" relating to Berlin, Germany as a whole, reunification, and a peace treaty. Passing rapidly over the concept, intelligible only to the *hochgelehrte* among international jurisconsults and not to all of them, that West Germany ceased to be occupied territory but the three Allies continued to be occupants for certain purposes, the intent is tolerably plain—to change radically the relationship between the Western Allies and the West Germans without affecting their status vis-à-vis the Soviet Un-

212

ion. Although Berlin, not being part of the Federal Republic, was not within the scope of these agreements, the Three Powers took the occasion further to increase the control of the city government over its own affairs. But the Allied authorities retained power, *inter alia*, in matters affecting the security of their own forces, the relations of Berlin with authorities abroad, and authority over the Berlin police to the extent necessary to assure the city's security. Moreover, they kept the right to take "such measures as may be required to fulfill their international obligations, to insure public order and to maintain the status and security of Berlin and its economy, trade and communications." As to Berlin, the Western ambassadors continued to be High Commissioners —*i.e.*, military governors—and Berlin continued to be under military occupation. It may well be the only belligerent occupation ever heard of whose continuance is acceptable to the inhabitants of the occupied territory, with the exception of a small group of radicals centered in the university, who would like to incorporate West Berlin (and probably West Germany as well) into the GDR.

Parallel subtleties occurred in the East zone. In 1949 a constitution was promulgated for the German Democratic Republic, declaring Berlin to be its capital, although the allocation of powers and duties between the Soviet occupants and the GDR was left undefined, at least by any published document. The Soviet government seems to have followed the Western example in allowing the laws of the GDR to become effective in East Berlin only when adopted by the municipal authorities. In September, 1955, the Soviet signed a treaty with the GDR, allegedly granting it "unrestricted sovereignty." Accompanying letter agreements stipulated that the GDR would exercise "watch and control" over its borders, "the demarcation line between the German Democratic Republic and the German Federal Republic, the outer boundary of Greater Berlin, in Berlin," and the communication lines between the Federal Republic and West Berlin. The tortuous quoted language appears to be intended to emphasize that, while there may be *de facto* boundaries between the GDR, the Federal Republic, and West Berlin, these lines do not exist *de jure*: They are not international borders. But control of the transport of personnel and material of the West Berlin garrisons was "temporarily" reserved to the Soviet High Command "until a corresponding agreement has been reached"—with whom was not stated.

These are the principal facts pertinent to the question of Berlin's status under the law of nations. The main legal questions, as I see them, are these:

What is the source of the rights of the Western Allies? The Soviet Union argues that since the Red Army actually conquered Berlin and is, therefore, its original and sole lawful occupant, Western rights to be there stem from Russian consent and thus depend upon the continued validity of the four-power agreements. The West replies that its rights, though reinforced and confirmed by these agreements, "derive from the total defeat of the Third Reich and the subsequent assumption of supreme authority in Germany"; the right of free access to Berlin, implied as an essential corollary to the right to occupy it, rests on the same basis. Russia, it concludes, cannot retract rights which were not hers to grant or deny in the first place. If the Soviet view were good law, added the United States (presumably with tongue in cheek), it could adduce Russian violations of the four-power agreements as a ground for their nullification and insist that Saxony and Thuringia, which were conquered by the United States forces, be returned to Western control. The fact seems to be that the Western armies played as important a role in the capture of Berlin as the Red Army did in the conquest of Saxony and Thuringia. Militarily, it is unrealistic to say that any part of Germany was conquered by the particular regiment or division or army or nation which happened first to overrun it.

What is the present status of the agreements providing for Western access to Berlin? The Russian notes of November 27, 1958, denounced the 1944 and 1945 agreements, described above, as "null and void." Are they? These agreements were no doubt intended to be temporary and provisional, from which the Soviet argues that they have expired by their own terms. But this is exceedingly doubtful. The control machinery agreement of November 14, 1944, was to last, if not forever, at least until a central German government had been established and had signed a peace treaty, an event which has certainly not come to pass. Moreover, the protocol of September 14, 1944, the basic agreement on the joint occupation of Berlin, contains no time limitation at all. The Russians argue further that these agreements are merely component parts of the whole structure of four-power agreements for the unification, demilitarization, and general reconstruction of Germany, constituting in effect one big treaty, and that the foundation of this structure has been destroyed by the Western powers' repeated and gross violations of these agreements. International law, like orthodox domestic contract law, does indeed support the proposition that a material breach of a treaty by one of the contracting states, though it does not automatically and instantly terminate that treaty, gives the other party a right to do so—if it acts within a reasonable time and if the first party's failure to perform was not attributable to the complaining party's own wrongful prevention of that performance.[8] If the Soviets' factual premises were correct, the argument that it is entitled to annul the Berlin agreements would have considerable

8. 1 OPPENHEIM-LAUTERPACHT, INTERNATIONAL LAW § 547 (7th ed. 1948).

strength, although it would still not meet the fundamental Western argument that the American, British, and French forces occupy Berlin by right of conquest and not by grace of these or any other agreements with the Soviet Union. The difficulty is, of course, that the factual question of which side bears the responsibility for the collapse of quadripartite control and the failure to reach agreement on a permanent settlement is not so easily determined. Both the Western powers and the Soviet Union have done a good many things since 1948 which are hard to square with the language of the original scheme as spelled out in the political and economic principles of the Potsdam Protocol of August 2, 1945, even allowing for the ambiguities of that language. Among the major principles therein agreed upon were, *inter alia*, "the complete disarmament and demilitarization of Germany and the elimination or control of all German industry that could be used for military production"; the "decentralization of the political structure"; and the allowance and encouragement throughout Germany of "democratic political parties with rights of assembly and of public discussion." Each side has turned its zone into a separate economic and political entity, and each has permitted and encouraged its German government to rearm. The Federal Republic clearly corresponds more closely than does the German Democratic Republic to the original conception of the reconstructed Germany. Its political structure, in which the *Laender* have in fact considerable autonomy, is certainly more decentralized than that of the GDR, which is a typical totalitarian state of the Stalinist variety. The GDR can be said to allow and encourage "all democratic political parties with rights of assembly and of public discussion" only if these words are construed in a highly Pickwickian, or Marxist-Leninist-Stalinist, sense—*i.e.*, by definition a party is not "democratic" if it is not Communist. The Federal Republic ac-

216

quired armed forces, *eo nomine*, a trifle sooner than the
GDR, but the latter's so-called *Volkspolizei* were training
with tanks at a time when the Federal Republic had no
paramilitary forces more formidable than *Grenzpolizei*
armed with rifles and pistols—although, of course, it may be
argued that tanks are to be regarded as normal police equipment in most of the Communist states. In short, the foundation of the four-power arrangement for the occupation, control, and reconstruction of Germany was an agreement to
agree, and it is notoriously difficult to assess the blame for
the failure of such an agreement or even to determine when
there has been a failure to bargain in good faith. If, as the
West insists (and not without plausibility), it was the Russians whose intransigence first frustrated the consummation
of the four-power agreements, the Russians are in no position to cancel any part of that complex of agreements.

The Russians have subsidiary arguments. There is an ancient, rather disreputable, principle of international law, dat-
ing at least from Roman imperial times, which is summed
up in the phrase *"conventio omnis intelligitur rebus sic
stantibus,"* the English of which, in very free translation, is
that a substantial and material change of circumstances may
justify the demand of a party to a treaty to be released from
its obligations.[9] It corresponds, of course, to a familiar principle of domestic contract law. If, for example, Germany had
agreed as a disarmament measure not to build aircraft fac-
tories, and if aircraft lost their military significance, a German government might invoke the doctrine; if such a change
in circumstances really had occurred, the other parties to the
treaty could not well object. But no such obvious change in
circumstances has here taken place; it is hard to see why the
presence of the Western forces in Berlin is more onerous for
the Russians, or less important to the West, in 1970 than it

9. See *Id.* § 539.

was in 1945. It is impossible to take seriously the argument that the small Western garrisons constitute a military threat to the Red Army. In any case, even if it is assumed that the principle is tacitly incorporated in every treaty, it seems clear that a party to a treaty cannot normally constitute itself the sole judge of when circumstances have so changed as to bring the clause into play; if it could, there would be an end to a far more important bit of Latinity, *pacta sunt servanda.* Certainly the mere fact that compliance with a treaty has become inconsistent with the expansionist goals of one of the parties has never been considered the kind of change in circumstances which justifies breach of the treaty.

Does the West's right of access include German civilian traffic? The Western Allies say that their rights exist by right of conquest, are those of military occupants, and endure as long as may be necessary for the fulfillment of their responsibilities as occupants. Under Article 43 of the Hague Regulations a military occupant has the duty to "ensure public order and safety," a phrase which includes at least the physical well-being of West Berlin's population and the maintenance of its economy. It probably includes a good deal more, for "public order" is not a very happy translation of the phrase in the French text (which is the controlling text), *"la vie publique."* A better translation might be "normal public life." The Russians do not appear to have contested this interpretation; indeed, the Soviet authorities, simultaneously with the entry of Western forces into Berlin, requested that the latter assume responsibility for the physical care of civilians in the Western sectors. The Russians do object violently to the introduction into the city of "spies, revanchists, and provocateurs," and others bearing choice names from the Marxist *schimpflexikon.* These terms, in this context, seem to refer to the West German politicians who make frequent symbolic visits to West Berlin, which the

Federal Republic regards as its real capital.[10] If *vie publique* means normal public life, such political visits seem a reasonable and permissible implementation of the occupant's duty. On the other hand, in the absence of any precedent which is even remotely analogous, it is not crystal-clear that the public order and safety, or even *la vie publique*, of West Berlin require the importation of politicians from the Federal Republic, for this commodity is locally in long supply. At any rate, the view that the Western occupants' responsibilities do entail a right to maintain whatever communications are necessary to the normal life of the population is confirmed by the 1949 agreements ending the blockade. They provided for the removal of all restrictions on communications, transport, and trade between Berlin and the rest of Germany and for the maintenance of that free traffic; they were certainly not limited to the supply of the Western garrisons.

What would be the effect on the West's rights of a peace treaty between the Soviet Union and the GDR? Mr. Khrushchev, stating his legal premise that "it has always been the case that after the signing of a peace treaty the conditions of capitulation lose force in the entire territory which the treaty covers, and throughout this territory the occupation terms are lifted," bounded nimbly to the conclusion that "the occupation rights, of course, would discontinue with the conclusion of a German peace treaty, no matter whether it is signed with both German states or only with the German Democratic Republic, inside whose territory West Berlin lies." This seems to slur over the very substantial distinction between *a* peace treaty and *the* peace treaty. It is certainly true that peace treaties have been an accepted and traditional means of ending belligerent occupations, although

10. See, for example, an exchange of notes between the United States and the Soviet Union in 45 DEP'T STATE BULL. 397, 431, 433, 511, 513 (1961).

there is nothing to prevent such a treaty from providing for a continuance of the occupation. As phrased by Colonel Winthrop, whom the Supreme Court sometimes describes as the Blackstone of military law, "The status of military government (i.e., occupation) continues from the inception of the actual occupation until the invader is expelled by force of arms, or himself abandons his conquest, or till, under a treaty of peace, the country is restored to its original allegiance or becomes incorporated with the domain of the prevailing belligerent." [11] Passing over the question whether either the Soviet or the Western Allies can unilaterally sign a peace treaty with either part of Germany, there is no precedent for the idea that a treaty between one belligerent and the *de facto* government of that part of the conquered territory which it occupies can end the occupation by that belligerent's allies of another part of the conquered territory, particularly when those allies do not recognize the local signatory government. In the past the peace treaty which terminated an occupation has invariably been one between the occupier of a particular territory and a government which the occupier recognized as the lawful sovereign of such territory. The case of the United States on this point, however solidly founded on law, is not much helped by the fact that it signed a separate peace treaty with Japan, as the Russians have not failed to point out on every possible occasion. In fact, however, the Declaration of the United Nations of January 1, 1942, did *not* obligate the United States not to sign a peace with Japan separately from the Soviet Union: It affected only those enemies with which the signatories were then at war, and to Japan Russia was then—and until 1945 —a neutral. Moreover, the Russians, though they were uninfluential members of the Allied Control Council in Japan,

11. WINTHROP, MILITARY LAW AND PRECEDENTS 801 (2d. ed. 1920); see Madsen v. Kinsella, 343 U. S. 341 (1952).

were not in actual occupation of any part of that country; there was only one Japanese government; and the treaty certainly did not purport to bind the Soviet Union or abrogate such rights as it had.

What is the effect of the "sovereignty" of the German Democratic Republic? The Russians say that after the signing of a peace treaty the GDR will be even more sovereign than it is now. Therefore, since control over air, land, and water communications across its territory is "an inalienable right of any sovereign state," access to West Berlin must, under "generally accepted international norms," depend upon the GDR's consent. I accept as good international law the premise that a sovereign state normally has a right to control its territory. But, even assuming that the GDR is a *de facto* "sovereign state" (only the Communist states and a few of their friends recognize it as such *de jure*), the rights of such a state are by no means "inalienable." The territory of a sovereign may be, and often is, subjected to a "state servitude," defined by the late Sir Lawrence Oppenheim as "an exceptional restriction made by treaty on the territorial supremacy of a State by which a part or the whole of its territory is in a limited way made perpetually to serve a certain purpose or interest of another state." [12] The commonest example is a right of transit, and to just such a servitude did the victors in World War II, including the Soviet victor, subject the territory of Germany in the exercise of the supreme authority which they had assumed. Moreover, since state servitudes are "rights *in rem*, they remain valid and may be exercised however the ownership of the territory to which they apply may change." [13] There is, in short, no precedent for the idea that State A, by recognizing a new "sovereign"

12. See generally 1 OPPENHEIM-LAUTERPACHT, *op. cit. supra* note 8, §§ 203–208.
13. *Id.* § 207.

over territory, can cut off the rights of states B, C, and D to
that territory. If, under customary international law or the
existing four-power agreements, the territory in question is
subjected to such servitude, it is not lifted by the transfer of
sovereignty to the GDR any more than A's common law
easement to use B's driveway to get to his own house is
abolished when B deeds his land to C. It may be a trifle
cavalier of A to use the driveway of one whom he is unwill-
ing to meet socially, but it is not illegal. Finally, it should be
noted that the blockade-lifting agreements of 1949 speak
only of the restrictions imposed by the U.S.S.R., and so
might arguably not be directly applicable to a new and different sovereign. But, even if the Soviet Union were willing to
rely on so hair-splitting a textual argument, it could not be
applied to the original access agreements or to such rights as
are inherent in the Western powers' status as occupants.

*How about communications between East and West Ber-
lin?* Here the U.S.S.R. and the GDR seem to be on firmer
ground, at least in so far as the letter of the law is concerned.
I find nothing in the four-power agreements that explicitly
and unambiguously obligates the Soviet authorities to permit
free circulation *within* the city: The agreements refer in
terms only to communication between zones and between
the zones and Berlin. I note that, although Secretary Rusk's
statement of August 13, 1961, described the sealing-off of
East from West Berlin by the Berlin Wall as "a violation of
the four-power status of Berlin and a flagrant violation of the
right of free circulation throughout the city," he did not cite
chapter and verse for these rights, whereas he termed the restrictions on travel between East Germany—itself a "zone"
—and Berlin a "direct contravention of the four-power agreement reached at Paris on June 20, 1949." [14]

14. *New York Times,* August 14, 1961, p. 7.

History never repeats itself precisely, and the legal problems arising out of the four-power condominium—if that is the right word—over Berlin have no exact precedents. Nevertheless, accepted international law seems on the whole to justify the conclusions that the Western powers have now, as military occupants, valid rights of access to West Berlin (including access for the purpose of maintaining the normal life of the city) which are reinforced by, but do not depend upon, the four-power agreements; that these agreements cannot be unilaterally abrogated by the Soviet Union; and that these rights cannot be annulled by a treaty to which the Western powers are not parties. This does not mean that no different or better solution can be devised. I hope and believe that in the long run—perhaps I should say the very long run—it will be, although not in all probability along the lines which the parties envisaged, or said they envisaged, in 1944 and 1945. It does mean that such a solution must, as a matter of law, be based on agreement among the states now having rights in Berlin. And perhaps I ought to add that one of those states is the Soviet Union.

Governing the
Vanquished

YALE LAW JOURNAL, 1957

—————

"Silent enim leges inter arma," wrote Cicero.[1] He could have added—doubtless in more Ciceronian Latin—*sed non iurisconsulti.* Long before the end of World War II, scholars of all belligerent and many neutral nations had begun to pour forth a mighty torrent of words on the laws of war, a gloss bearing about the same quantitative relationship to the rather skimpy texts of the Hague and Geneva Conventions that the literature of Christian apologetics, exegesis, and hermeneutics bears to the New Testament. In *The Occupation of Enemy Territory*, Professor Gerhard von Glahn has set himself the task of seining in this turbid flood, apparently with the praiseworthy intent of reducing to manageable size the consensus of more or less civilized nations on what the law of belligerent occupation is or ought to be.

The role of the writer on international law, and particularly on the law of war, is, at least in common-law countries, unique. The law of war has essentially two sources: treaties and custom. The treaties are of unquestioned authority but

1. M. Tullius Cicero, Pro Milone § IV, ¶ II.

full of deliberate ambiguities [2] which can only be elucidated —given solid content and accepted meaning—by the decisions of courts, the practice of nations, and the opinions of savants. The first are scanty, and the second is often deplorable, if not actually in violation of those treaty provisions which are explicit. Hence, a gratifying and unusual weight is accorded to the views of scholarly writers—mostly, to be sure, by other scholarly writers, but sometimes by the authorities who shape the policies of belligerents and the statesmen who draft new treaties. If the hardships of war and occupation have been appreciably lessened over the last few centuries, much of the credit must go to the writers.

The experience of the last few decades might well conduce to the dismal conclusion that no such lessening is noticeable and that the labors of Professor von Glahn and his fellows have been so much intellectual *brutum fulmen*. One has to go far back indeed to find anything comparable to the occupation regimes of the Nazis and Japanese. But the saving point is that the mass killings, deportations and systematic looting practiced by those governments in occupied territory represented a sharp deviation from what had by their day become the practice of civilized nations—a deviation which was denounced not only by their victims but by most of the rest of the world, and which was punished after the war with remarkably little dissent, and even with the acquiescence of a substantial number of Germans and Japanese. Such enlightened views are not innate in mankind. The Old Testament, of course, is full of appalling massacres, some of them

2. See, *e.g.*, articles 43, 52 of the Hague Regulations of 1907, the former obligating an occupant to respect "unless absolutely prevented, the laws in force in the [occupied] country" and the latter providing that "a receipt shall be given [for requisitions in kind], and the payment of the amount due shall be made as soon as possible"—by whom is not stated. See Scott, The Hague Conventions and Declarations of 1899 and 1907 123, 125 (1915).

not only tolerated but prescribed by the mores of the time.[3] Nor would it have occurred to a statesman of classic antiquity to question the legality of such conduct. In the course of the Peloponnesian War, for example, the Athenians determined, not by the act of any dictator but by the direct vote of the enlightened democracy, to discipline Mitylene, an ally which had defected, by putting to death the entire adult male population—including those who had remained loyal to Athens—and enslaving the women and children. They reversed the decision the next day by a very close vote, largely on grounds of expediency, and contented themselves with the execution of about a thousand Mitylenians who had in fact been active in the rebellion.[4] The Spartans were no better.[5] So far as history records, neither of these glories of Hellas was subjected to reproach from any quarter for their treatment of the conquered. The repressive measures taken against partisans and guerrillas by Nazi occupants were undoubtedly harsh, but Himmler himself would probably have hesitated at the steps taken by Marcus Licinius Crassus to suppress the servile revolt led by Spartacus.[6] Crassus was not regarded as a monster of cruelty; he was, in fact, awarded

3. See, e.g., I Samuel, 15:3, 8–11, 32–34.

4. THUCYDIDES, PELOPONNESIAN WAR 193–205 (Crawley transl. 1874). The Athenians, having changed their minds, dispatched a second galley to overtake the one which had sailed the day before to carry the original order to the Athenian commander on Lesbos. Stimulated by the promise of a substantial cash bonus (and possibly by considerations of humanity) the rowers of the second galley bent to their oars with such effect that they arrived just in time to stop the massacre.

5. On the urging of their Theban allies, the Lacedaemonians actually meted out such treatment to the little city of Plataea, which had so distinguished itself in the Persian wars. *Id.* at 216–18. It is interesting to note that Thucydides condemns as cruel the first Athenian vote on Mitylene but chronicles without comment the fate of Plataea—which suggests that, in his view, the vice of the Athenian policy lay only in the fact that it contemplated the massacre of friends as well as enemies.

6. He crucified 6,000 captured slaves along the road from Capua to Rome. See 3 MOMMSEN, RÖMISCHE GESCHICHTE bk. 5, c. II (1885).

a triumph. Many similar examples could be cited, down to comparatively modern times. The distinction between those ages and this lies in the creation of a climate of world opinion in which the commission of an atrocity is at least embarrassing, and possibly dangerous, to the committer. The conduct of the Soviet government in Hungary, for example, though bad enough, might well have been very much worse if its desired action had not been so obviously inconsistent with the appearance it wished to present to the world. And the existence of international standards, to which that government was reluctant to do more extreme violence than required by its estimate of the political situation, is in some measure due to the accumulated weight of works like Professor von Glahn's.

That weight is considerable. Professor von Glahn has performed the remarkable feat of producing a ponderous tome in a mere 350 pages weighing no more than two pounds. He has done this partly by weighting down his text with 896 footnotes and a bibliography containing some 700 items, and partly by the employment of a singularly heavy-footed style; [7] but it must be conceded that in large part the feat is attributable to sheer slogging scholarship and the compression of voluminous materials into a comparatively small space. If *The Occupation of Enemy Territory* does not contain a great deal of original thought, it is at least a desk-size encyclopedia of learning on its topic. Here and there one finds a dogmatic statement of a debatable proposition—for example the flat assertion that "indigenous courts have no right whatsoever (during belligerent occupation) to try enemy

7. See, *e.g.*, p. 23: "[N]o advocate of revision of the laws of war in favor of collective security forces can deny that armed action against an aggressor, whether it is labeled a war or a police action, is not an armed conflict in the meaning of those 1949 instruments." The meaning of this cumbrous sentence is the exact opposite of what the author probably intended.

persons (that is, individuals of the occupant's nationality or that of any of his allies in the war) for any and all acts committed by them in the course of hostilities in the broadest sense of the term, even if such acts are in the nature of war crimes." [8] It is doubtful whether that immunity extends beyond members of the occupant's armed forces,[9] regardless of their nationality; and it is probable that the occupant can subject members of his forces, and a fortiori persons of his nationality, to the jurisdiction of the local courts.[10] Equally dubious is the unqualified statement that "decisions handed down by the military tribunals of the occupant lose their validity at the end of the occupation unless otherwise provided for in a treaty of peace." [11] It would seem more reasonable to hold that a decision of a military government court, made in a case within the jurisdiction lawfully conferred on it by the occupant, should be accorded the same treatment as any other decision of a competent court in the occupied territory.[12]

8. P. 112.
9. See Coleman v. Tennessee, 97 U. S. 509 (1878); cf. In re Lo Dolce, 106 F. Supp. 455 (W.D.N.Y. 1952).
10. Cf. Madsen v. Kinsella, 343 U. S. 341 (1952); Neely v. Henkel, 180 U. S. 109 (1901). In both cases, American citizens were held triable by courts of the American military government of occupied foreign territory; and in the Madsen case, the petitioner was deemed to be a member of the occupying forces. Both courts applied the indigenous law of the occupied territory. In neither is there any suggestion that the result would have been different if the military government had provided for trial by the indigenous courts. The Court regarded both situations (Germany after World War II and Cuba after the Spanish-American War) as cases of belligerent occupation of enemy territory, although in both hostilities had ended.
11. P. 258.
12. Cf. Mechanics' and Traders' Bank v. Union Bank, 89 U. S. (22 Wall.) 276 (1874). A caveat must be entered with respect to criminal sentences imposed by an occupation tribunal for an offense against the occupant's security regulations, however lawful those regulations might be, especially if the act were not otherwise criminal. It would be too much to expect a returning sovereign to leave in jail one who is, from its standpoint, a patriot. Yet this caveat has an unfortunate corollary:

228

These are comparatively minor matters. More fundamental is the author's espousal of the doctrine that neither the Hague Regulations nor the customary law of belligerent occupation apply after the end of military operations against an enemy still in the field.[13] Specifically, as applied to Germany, he believes that "only limitations resting on grounds of humanity could be said to have been binding on the victorious Allies during the post-surrender period." [14] He arrives at this conclusion by a somewhat curious route. He appears to believe that most of the American denazification program in Germany—including the eradication of Nazi influence on education, the repeal of characteristic Nazi laws, such as the Nürnberg racial laws, and even the abolition of the totalitarian form of government—would have violated the Hague Regulations and the customary law of belligerent occupation, had those laws been applicable.[15] But he balks, very rightly, at saying that international law forbade the Allies to achieve the very purposes for which they fought the war unless they took the extreme step of an outright annexation of Germany.

an occupant may be expected to resort freely to the death penalty for offenses against its security, on the ground that nothing else can be expected to stick. Article 68 of the 1949 Geneva Convention Relative to the Protection of Civilian Persons in Time of War attempts to counteract this practical consideration by prohibiting the infliction of the death penalty under the ordinances of the occupant except where the accused is guilty of espionage, "serious acts of sabotage against the military installations" of the occupant or "intentional offences which have caused the death of one or more persons, provided that such offences were punishable by death under the law of the occupied territory in force before the occupation began." Aside from the fact that some signatories, including the United States, made reservations to this article, the phrase "serious acts of sabotage against . . . military installations" leaves a good deal of leeway for construction. See U. S. DEP'T OF STATE PUB. No. 3938, GENERAL FOREIGN POLICY SERIES 34, 185 (1950).
  13. See, e.g., pp. 27–28, 117, 281.
  14. P. 283.
  15. See, e.g., pp. 57–67. Rather inconsistently, he makes an exception of the suspension of the Volksgerichtshöfe and other peculiarly Nazi courts. Pp. 106–07.

He resolves the dilemma by concluding that the law of belligerent occupation ceases to be effective the moment that one party surrenders. This is dangerous doctrine. Precisely at that time, the conquered and occupied territory stands in most need of whatever protection is afforded by international law.[16] It would be safer to go a little more slowly and to assume as a first proposition that international law draws no sharp line between occupation *durante bello* and occupation after the end of hostilities but prior to definite settlement of the status of the occupied territory.[17] It can be further argued that nothing in the corpus of the law of belligerent occupation was inconsistent with the Allies' abolition, for example, of the Nürnberg racial laws; in light of their war aims and the very broad construction traditionally given the phrase, they can fairly be said to have been "absolutely prevented" from respecting such a law.[18] The reform of the German educational system and the abolition of totalitarian forms of government can be similarly justified.[19] The laws of war are likely to do more real good if they set themselves the modest goal of protecting the persons and property of noncombatants, and do that at all times, than if they purport to circum-

16. The 1949 Geneva Convention Relative to the Protection of Civilian Persons in Time of War specifically provides (art. 6) that it shall apply for a year after "the general close of military operations"—whatever that means—and that certain of its more fundamental provisions shall apply for the duration of the occupation. But that convention falls far short of protecting all the rights covered by the pre-existing law of belligerent occupation. See U. S. DEP'T OF STATE PUB. No. 3938, GENERAL FOREIGN POLICY SERIES 34, 166 (1950).
17. Madsen v. Kinsella, 343 U. S. 341, 360 (1952); Burke v. Miltenberger, 86 U. S. (19 Wall.) 519, 524 (1873). See Cobb v. United States, 191 F.2d 604, 610 (6th Cir. 1951).
18. See note 2 *supra.*
19. It must be admitted that the decartelization laws of the Western Allies present a tougher exercise in casuistry—although, insofar as they contributed to the economic resurgence of West Germany, they might be brought within the occupant's duty to restore and ensure public order and safety.

scribe a belligerent's achievement of his political aims until actual hostilities have ended and then vanish altogether. For similar reasons, Professor von Glahn's thesis that the law of war ought to distinguish between aggressor nations and their victims—as, for instance, by giving lawful combatant status to guerrillas fighting for the latter and leaving the former's partisans in their present unprotected status [20]—seems of dubious practicality. The trouble is that in the last century, at least, there has been hardly any belligerent which did not claim to be a victim of aggression. It is hard enough to enforce the laws of war without having to determine, as a preliminary, who started the particular war.

Professor von Glahn devotes a chapter to an admittedly summary examination of the subject of punishment of violations of the laws of war. This topic has not escaped the attention of other writers, and his chapter is mainly useful for purposes of reference. But he has largely ignored the potentialities of judicial enforcement of those laws through civil courts which are independent of the occupant, either because they are sitting in another country, or because their proceedings take place after the end of the occupation or because they are the occupant's own domestic courts, exercising under the occupant's own polity some power of control over the actions of its military and political authorities. There is, for example, a small but growing body of case law in the United States which suggests that its courts will apply the law of war to the acts of an occupant very much as they would apply the Constitution to an act of Congress or the President: that is to say, an ordinance or other act of military government will be treated as valid, and binding on parties affected, if it does not exceed the powers allowed by treaties and customary law, and will be treated as void if it

20. See, *e.g.*, pp. 53, 171.

contravenes international law.[21] No American court has yet
struck down an act of American military government on
such grounds,[22] but, if such an act could be brought within
the jurisdiction of an American court,[23] there is no compel-
ling reason why it should have greater immunity from review
than one of a foreign occupation authority. Professor von
Glahn has also ignored—reasonably enough, since he had
ample ground to cover without getting into the maze of
American constitutional law—the related question of the ap-
plicability of the Constitution of the United States, and particularly the Bill of Rights, to the actions of American military government in occupied foreign territory. The orthodox
view would certainly deny any application;[24] but there have
been indications that the classic rule might be subjected to

21. See, e.g., State of the Netherlands v. Federal Reserve Bank, 201
F.2d 455 (2d Cir. 1953); Aboitiz & Co. v. Price, 99 F. Supp. 602
(D. Utah 1951).
22. See, however, Ochoa v. Hernandez, 230 U. S. 139 (1913). The
Court held an ordinance of American military government invalid because inconsistent with the President's orders to the Military Governor;
but the Court laid some stress on the fact that the President's order
was an expression of accepted principles of international law. The
point at issue would have been raised if the President had authorized
or tolerated military government ordinances in violation of international
law. To the same effect, see also MacLeod v. United States, 229 U. S.
416 (1913).
23. In Johnson v. Eisentrager, 339 U. S. 763 (1950), the Court
held, through Justice Jackson, that the writ of habeas corpus was not
available to a nonresident enemy alien and said, in a dictum which was
probably not very carefully considered, that rights of alien prisoners
of war under the Geneva Convention of 1929 could be "vindicated . . .
only through protests and intervention of protecting powers." Id. at
789 n.14. There was a vigorous and cogent dissent. I find it hard to
believe that if a prisoner of war were, let us say, sentenced to death
for attempting to escape, in violation of the explicit provisions of the
Convention, the present Court would thus wash its hands of the
matter.
24. See, e.g., Neely v. Henkel, 180 U. S. 109 (1901); Mechanics'
and Traders' Bank v. Union Bank, 89 U. S. (22 Wall.) 276 (1874).
See also Fairman, Some New Problems of the Constitution Following
the Flag, 1 STAN. L. REV. 587, 623–26 (1949).

some alteration if a proper case were presented.[25] The development in civilized nations of a concept that the occupant's domestic courts have a duty and power to check violations of the law of war is greatly to be desired. Otherwise, enforcement of the law of belligerent occupation, so carefully collated in Professor von Glahn's pandect, must continue to rely on the self-restraint of occupants, which is risky, and postwar prosecution of the losers, which is effective but one-sided. Of course, it will be long before any such judicial independence can be expected to develop in some countries, but that is no reason why the seed should not be sown in soil where it has a chance to grow.

Professor von Glahn has produced a well-digested and well-organized compendium of the substantive law of belligerent occupation. Its virtues considerably outweigh its defects. To all those who have the responsibility of applying or enforcing that part of the law of war, *The Occupation of Enemy Territory* will be a convenience.

———

In the light of the events of the past thirteen years, my mild optimism about the beneficial effects of the laws of war may seem excessive. Those laws have been broken by all parties to the Vietnam conflict, although in the Middle East Israel, Egypt, and Jordan do not seem to be guilty of really flagrant

25. See Black, J., dissenting in Johnson v. Eisentrager, 339 U. S. 763, 791 (1950); *cf.* Best v. United States, 184 F.2d 131 (1st Cir. 1950), *cert. denied,* 340 U. S. 939 (1951). As Justice Black made clear, not every part of the Bill of Rights would be held applicable in occupied territory. For one thing, it seems probable that the introduction of some of the refinements of the Bill of Rights in favor of criminal defendants might, in countries where criminals have traditionally been given shorter shrift, collide with the occupant's duty to restore and ensure public order and safety.

violations. The Palestinian guerrillas, like guerrillas every-
where, necessarily violate the law of war, because their tac-
tical doctrine (the only one which offers them any chance of
success) rests on repudiation of the basic principle of the
conventional law of war that combatants are to wear uniforms, carry arms openly, and generally be easily distinguish-
able from noncombatants. Likewise, guerrillas rely heavily on
assassination, the seizure of hostages, and the use of neutral
territory as a sanctuary—all practices expressly forbidden by
the Hague and Geneva Conventions.

The fact is, of course, that the law of war as it now exists is
designed for the sort of grand-scale warfare between sovereign states, carried on by large, well-organized, and well-
disciplined armies, which was standard in Europe from the
time of Louis XIV to World War II. Soldiers, statesmen,
and lawyers have scarcely begun to consider what sort of rules
might be devised to mitigate the brutality of what Chairman
Mao calls "wars of national liberation," which are a mixture
of domestic insurrection and more or less covert belligerency
by a neighbor sovereign friendly to the rebels. Similarly, in
an age when armies are supplied with a variety of lethal
chemical and bacteriological agents, intercontinental missiles,
and hydrogen bombs, it hardly seems worthwhile to prohibit
dum-dum bullets and lances with barbed heads.

Although the Vietnam fighting is today regarded as unusually dirty, its worst atrocities would not have stirred much
outcry a couple of centuries, or even a quarter century, ago.
The massacres at Songmy, or even Hue, would have been
only an ordinary day's work at Auschwitz. More important,
there is some evidence that the United States, at least, may
actually intend to do something to deter the commission of
war crimes by its own forces—a novel and hopeful development.

The Quality of Military
Justice

THE NEW YORK TIMES MAGAZINE,
February 22, 1970

———————————

*This is another of my efforts to describe a controversial area
of the law in such a way as to give an educated layman a
basis for intelligent discussion. Naturally, it produced squeals
of indignation from the sort of libertarian bigot who feels
there is something disreputable in actually studying any subject having to do with the military and who disposes of the
problem by quoting Clemenceau's remark that military justice is to justice what military music is to music. (In the first
place, the Tiger of France was talking about the nineteenth-
century French variety of military justice, as applied to Captain Alfred Dreyfus, which has about the same relation to
modern American military law that a French elevator of the
period has to the ones in Rockefeller Center. In the second
place, what's so bad about John Philip Sousa, or "Taps"?)*
    Nevertheless military justice is different from the civilian
variety. Since its prime purpose is to preserve discipline and
efficiency among several million vigorous young males who
have ready access to deadly weapons, it ought to be swift and

sure; it is less able to afford the luxury of acquittal of the guilty. This does not mean that it need be so structured as to produce conviction of the innocent. It does mean that it should be limited to cases having a clear connection with the maintenance of military discipline. The Supreme Court's decision in the O'Callahan case, no matter how sleazy its reasoning and rhetoric, was thus in the best interest of both the law and the armed services.

The time-honored practice of entrusting the assessment of guilt and punishment to a panel appointed by the officer who is responsible for the discipline of the command, whose members are themselves generally part of that command and concerned with its efficiency, inevitably raises suspicions that a court-martial is even less likely than a jury to take seriously the presumption of innocence. Giving the accused in non-capital cases the right to demand trial by a military judge, altogether independent of the chain of command, was a long step in the right direction. I see no reason why it should not be extended to capital cases. The new French Code of Military Justice provides for the trial of all military offenses by permanent tribunals composed of military and civilian judges, responsible only to the Minister of Defense, with a right of appeal to the civilian Cour de Cassation.

THE NORMAL ATTITUDE of the American public toward military justice is compounded of equal parts of indifference and ignorance. In what used to be normal times, this was natural enough. Before World War II, the peacetime military establishment was small and composed entirely of regulars—a caste that tended to be distinct from the rest of the population. Its officers came from West Point or Annapolis, married the daughters of other regulars and sent their sons to West Point or Annapolis. Enlisted men got drunk on payday and drunker at the expiration of every hitch, after which they staggered back to the post and reenlisted. When they landed in the brig or guardhouse, which was frequently, the civilian public cared about the fairness of the proceedings no more than it cared about the system of criminal justice applicable to other foreigners, such as Chinese coolies. Neither the Supreme Court nor anyone else ever supposed that the Bill of Rights applied to soldiers. Chief Justice Salmon P. Chase said in 1867 that "the power of Congress in the government of the land and naval forces . . . is not at all affected by the Fifth or any other amendment," and the proposition was scarcely challenged until after World War II.

The indifference is rapidly dissipated, of course, when millions of career civilians find themselves suddenly subjected to the Articles of War, as they did in the Civil War and the two world wars and as they do now. The ignorance is more stubborn than the indifference; even today, when the Songmy (or Mylai, or Pinkville) incident produces millions of words on the chances of prosecuting the alleged culprits, ignorance seems as widespread and opaque as ever. Examples abound. The usually careful and accurate *Wall Street Journal* leads off a feature story on military justice with the statement that Congress enacted the Uniform Code in 1950 "to introduce due process into a system that hadn't been altered since the Revolutionary War." As a matter of fact, there were major revisions of the Articles of War, which steadily increased the rights of soldier defendants, in 1806, 1874, 1916, and 1920. The *Journal* went on to quote Charles Morgan of the American Civil Liberties Union as having made the somewhat sweeping statement that "it's impossible to have true justice in the military, because courts-martial are almost totally dedicated to the preservation of discipline at the expense of justice."

Mr. Morgan is primarily a zealous partisan, who (to do him justice) has never made any pretense of objectivity, who has recently defended the accused in widely publicized courts-martial, and who heartily agrees with the West Point doctrine that the best defense is a blitz attack. Nevertheless, he probably expresses the orthodox opinion of pious liberals. Professor Alan Dershowitz of Harvard, who is certainly more scholarly than Mr. Morgan and at times a temperate and balanced commentator, is quoted by *Time* magazine as saying, "I don't think any court-martial can be fair with the kind of control the military has over its men."

Aside from the fact that such a judgment ignores the existence of the Court of Military Appeals, whose civilian members are subject to no sort of military control, it rests on the unarticulated premise that the ordinary member of a court-martial is either a sadistic martinet or a servile lackey, or both, quite ready to violate his oath and such shreds of conscience as his military service has left him, in order to gratify his prejudices and further his career. I could tell Professor Dershowitz that I have seen some courts-martial and have read the records of many more, and that my experience leads me to the conclusion that most are as fair as most civilian criminal trials (for what that is worth) and their members as fair as civilian jurors (for what *that* is worth). But I do not think I would affect his opinion, for his statement is, I suspect, simply a profession of belief in the Devil, a fundamentalist left-liberal's version of *"Credo quia absurdum est."*

The orthodox view has deep historical roots. Although the idea of a separate and draconian system of justice for the military is almost as old as war and armies, which is to say almost as old as human society, it was never a part of the common law of England. From medieval (and probably

Saxon) times the King could deal rough military justice to his soldiers in time of war or when they were serving outside England. Richard Coeur de Lion's Ordinance of 1190, intended to discourage brawling among his Crusaders, is a representative specimen of medieval military justice: "Whoever shall slay a man on shipboard, he shall be bound to the dead man and thrown into the sea. If he shall slay him on land, he shall be bound to the dead man and buried in the earth."

By the seventeenth century there were considerably more sophisticated military codes, but not of English origin. Macaulay sums it up: "The common law of England knew nothing of courts-martial and made no distinction, in time of peace, between a soldier and any other subject. . . . A soldier, therefore, by knocking down his colonel, incurred only the ordinary penalties of assault and battery, and by refusing to obey orders, by sleeping on guard or by deserting his colours, incurred no legal penalty at all."

Given the necessity of a standing army—a necessity that faced the British from the time of William of Orange and which, I fear, will be with us for a good many years to come —such a situation was intolerable. In 1689, Parliament passed the original Mutiny Act, which empowered courts-martial to punish mutiny, sedition and desertion. (Although it accorded the accused fewer rights than he would have had in a civilian court, it provided one protection not found in modern criminal codes, military or civilian: "Noe Proceedings, Tryall or Sentence of Death shall be had or given against any Offender, but between the hours of eight in the morning and one in the afternoone." The holders of the King's commission included plenty of eight-bottle, ten-bottle and even twelve-bottle men, and a court that met after dinner would have been likely to lack the judicial temperament.)

239

In 1775 the Continental Congress enacted Articles of War, largely borrowed from the British. Later, the framers of the Constitution gave Congress power "to make Rules for the Government and Regulation of the land and naval Forces." From 1789 to 1950, Congress steadily expanded the jurisdiction of courts-martial over both persons and offenses. The Uniform Code of 1950 covered not only the traditional military offenses—such as absence without leave, desertion, insubordination, cowardice and mutiny—but also all the ordinary civilian crimes, from writing rubber checks to murder, whether committed in peace or war, inside or outside the United States. Moreover, it applied to sundry categories of civilians and quasi civilians, as well as to soldiers.

At this point the Supreme Court called a halt, beginning in 1955 with *Toth v. Quarles*. Congress, when it passed the Uniform Code, had been much disturbed by the possibility that a serviceman might commit a serious crime in a foreign country, conceal it until he was discharged, and thereafter thumb his nose at the law: American civilian courts cannot normally try offenses committed outside their territorial jurisdiction, and extradition would rarely be feasible.

The possibility was real enough. Captain Kathleen Nash Durant, who stole the crown jewels of Hesse, was brought to justice only because the Army's criminal investigators managed to get the goods on her a couple of days before she would have become a civilian. A few American servicemen literally got away with murder.

Congress might have given the Federal District Courts jurisdiction to try such cases; it chose instead to make them triable by court-martial. But when a court-martial convicted former Airman Robert W. Toth of murder committed in Korea before his honorable discharge, the Supreme Court held flatly that the power to make rules for the government and regulation of the land and naval forces could not be stretched to authorize the military trial of a civilian who was no longer a member of those forces.

Two years later, the Court struck down the ancient jurisdiction of military courts over camp followers when it held unconstitutional the convictions of a couple of ladies who had murdered their soldier-husbands while "accompanying the armed forces outside the United States." (I hasten to add, however, that the decisions did not confer on soldiers' wives a license to terminate distasteful marriages in the quickest and cheapest way, for the self-made widows can still be tried in the courts of the country in which the domestic disagreement took place.) It is now clear that a court-martial cannot try a civilian in peacetime, and at least doubtful that it can do so in time of war.

Having thus limited the military's jurisdiction over persons, the Supreme Court in 1969 pruned back the list of offenses for which it could try soldiers. Historically, courts-martial could try soldiers only for offenses having a demonstrable impact on military discipline. When Sergeant Mason, assigned to guard Charles J. Guiteau, the assassin of President Garfield, anticipated Jack Ruby by "willfully and maliciously discharging his musket, loaded with ball cartridge, at said Guiteau," he was not court-martialed for attempted murder (unlike Ruby, he missed), but for what the Supreme Court called "an atrocious breach of military discipline."

Inability to punish soldiers for common crimes committed when the Army was engaged in hostilities outside the United States posed serious problems, as General Winfield Scott found out in the Mexican-American War. Scott (who must have had a resourceful Judge Advocate) solved them by creating military commissions to try such offenses, apparently as an exercise of his authority as military governor of occupied foreign territory. (The crimes punishable included not only "assassination, murder, poisoning, rape" and the like, but also "wanton desecration of churches" and "interruption of religious services," which suggests that the Protestant zeal of some of his troops was making trouble for General Scott.)

When the problem recurred in the Civil War, Congress amended the Articles of War to allow courts-martial to try soldiers for ordinary crimes committed in time of war. In 1916, the Army persuaded Congress to grant such jurisdiction in time of peace, except for the capital offenses of murder and rape. Even these were covered by the Uniform Code; by 1950 a court-martial could try any soldier and many civilians for almost any transgression, including, at least in theory, a violation of the antitrust laws or the Internal Revenue Code.

Thus, when Sergeant O'Callahan, off-post, on leave and clad in civilian clothes, broke into a hotel room in Honolulu and attempted to rape the occupant, he was duly convicted and awarded ten years' confinement at hard labor by a court-martial. (He could, of course, have been tried in a Hawaiian court, but the Honolulu cops elected to turn him over to the Army.) But when his case reached the Supreme Court in 1969, a majority of the Justices held that a court-martial could not constitutionally try a soldier for a peacetime offense which was not "service-connected."

Both the reasoning and the scope of Justice Douglas's opinion were uncommonly obscure; in the last few months, the Court of Military Appeals seems to have spent most of its time attempting to figure out its meaning. As the situation stands now, the military can still try a soldier for a non-military offense which is committed, for instance, on the post, or against another serviceman or Government property, or whose commission is aided by his military status. If Sergeant O'Callahan had raped a WAC or a visitor to Fort

Shafter, or had used his rank and uniform to obtain admission to his victim's room, his conviction might have been sustained.

Moreover, since Justice Douglas's conclusion seemed to be based largely on the consideration that O'Callahan had been deprived of his right to a jury and other attributes of American due process, a soldier can still be court-martialed for any offense committed outside the jurisdiction of American courts.

The disposition of today's Supreme Court to limit military jurisdiction to the smallest compass needed to preserve discipline is based on its belief that, in Justice Black's words, "Traditionally, military justice has been a rough form of justice, emphasizing summary procedures, speedy convictions and stern penalties," so that "military tribunals have not been and probably never can be constituted in such way that they can have the same kind of qualifications that the Constitution has deemed essential to fair trials of civilians in Federal Courts."

Macaulay put it still more forcefully: "The machinery by which courts of law ascertain the guilt or innocence of an accused citizen is too slow and intricate to be applied to an accused soldier. For, of all the maladies incident to the body politic, military insubordination is that which requires the most prompt and drastic remedies. . . . For the general safety, therefore, a summary jurisdiction of terrible extent must, in camps, be entrusted to rude tribunals composed of men of the sword."

Writing when he did, in the middle of the last century, Macaulay's rhetoric was not much exaggerated. Consider, for example, the case of Lieutenant Keyes of the 5th United States Cavalry, decided in 1883. The colonel commanding the regiment had preferred the charges, had appeared as a prosecution witness, and as a member of the court-martial had voted to convict and cashier Keyes. But when Keyes challenged the proceedings by a suit for back pay in the Court of Claims, the Supreme Court gave him short shrift: "Whatever irregularities or errors are alleged to have occurred in the proceedings, the sentence of dismissal must be held valid when it is questioned in this collateral way."

There are later cases nearly as hard. Not until after World War II did the Federal Courts begin to suggest that at least the more basic parts of the Bill of Rights might apply to courts-martial. The Supreme Court has not to this day freed a military convict because of unfairness in his trial.

Nevertheless, Justice Black's strictures seem somewhat excessive, in the light of the "military due process" which Congress, if not the Constitution, now accords to accused soldiers. Most of the basic protections of the Bill of Rights are present in the Uniform Code. The code prohibits compulsory self-incrimination, double jeopardy, and cruel or unusual punishments. The accused must be apprised of the charges against him. He is entitled to compulsory process to obtain witnesses and to counsel of his choice or, if he has no money, to assigned counsel—a right which indigent defendants in state felony trials did not get until 1963, when the Supreme Court decided *Gideon v. Wainwright.*

The principal exceptions are the Fifth Amendment's requirement of grand-jury indictment in a "capital, or otherwise infamous, crime," the Sixth Amendment right to trial by "an impartial jury of the State and district wherein the crime shall have been committed" and the Eighth Amendment's prohibition of "excessive bail." The Fifth Amendment expressly excludes cases arising in the land or naval forces. In lieu of bail, the code provides that confinement of an accused pending trial and appeal shall be no stricter than is necessary to ensure his presence—which seems to me a considerably fairer and more rational test of a defendant's right to freedom than his ability to raise high bail.

The language of the Sixth Amendment would be impossible to apply to soldiers stationed overseas and difficult in other cases; even Justices Black and Douglas have conceded that soldiers have no right to jury trial for military offenses.

The value of rights to due process, in military as in civilian jurisprudence, depends on the vigilance with which trials are policed. In the inferior military courts, as in the inferior state criminal courts, that vigilance is frequently nothing to boast about. But a general court-martial—the only one that can impose more than six months' confinement—must be presided over by a military judge, responsible not to the commander who convened the court and preferred the charges, but only to the Judge Advocate General of the service concerned.

Taking one day with another, military judges are likely to be at least as honest and competent as the judges of state criminal courts. Moreover, the code provides that a serious sentence—one that includes a dishonorable discharge (or the hardly less punitive bad-conduct discharge), or confinement for a year—must be reviewed by a Court of Military Review, whose members are likewise beholden to no military authority except the Judge Advocate General. From its decision, appeal lies to the Court of Military Appeals, the major innovation of the Uniform Code, whose members are civilians appointed by the President with the advice and consent of the Senate.

COMA (a somewhat unfortunate abbreviation) is no rubber stamp: it busts about half the convictions it decides to review—although, like the Supreme Court itself, it normally takes only those cases in which the judges think there is a substantial question as to the rightness of the verdict. At both stages of military review the accused is entitled to free appellate counsel, in most cases eager young beavers—which is more than a moneyless civilian appellant can be sure of.

In theory, the Court of Military Appeals is the "Supreme Court of Military Justice"; alone among the courts of the United States, its decisions cannot be appealed to the Supreme Court. But in practice, and despite Congress's explicit provision that court-martial sentences affirmed by the military reviewing authorities are "final and conclusive" and "binding upon all courts of the United States," military justice is no longer a law unto itself.

The Supreme Court refused to construe the code as denying to people convicted by court-martial the right to challenge the validity of their convictions by seeking writs of habeas corpus in the Federal Courts; if Congress had intended to abolish the great writ in such cases, it would have exceeded its constitutional powers. The Supreme Court itself has gone no farther than that.

Habeas corpus is, however, of no use to a military convict who is not deprived of his liberty, but who wants a dishonorable discharge nullified. A dishonorable discharge, though no longer accompanied by drums, button snipping, sword-breaking, and the rest, is still highly punitive. Not only does it deprive the recipient of the pension or other benefits that he would get with an honorable discharge, but it is also a brand that makes it hard for him to find a job.

The inferior Federal Courts have developed a variety of techniques for policing military justice (as they police the criminal justice of the states) in order to make sure not only that the court-martial had jurisdiction over the accused and the offense, but also that no serious violence was done to the defendant's constitutional rights.

He can, for example, attack the validity of his discharge by bringing suit for his pay in the Court of Claims, or by asking a Federal District Court for a writ of mandamus ordering the Secretary of the Army, Navy or Air Force to issue him an honorable discharge, complete with spread eagle and Old English type. A number of such suits have succeeded when the civilian court was persuaded that the military trial's unfairness was of "constitutional magnitude."

How big is "constitutional"? A museum specimen of unfairness of constitutional dimensions is the case of Lieutenant Shapiro—which, it should be emphasized, took place in 1943, before the Uniform Code and the Court of Military Appeals. Shapiro, a zealous defense counsel for a soldier accused of rape, made a farce of the court-martial by bringing before the court (without informing its members of the deception), instead of the real defendant, another soldier with an ironclad alibi—whom the prosecuting witness identified as her attacker.

At 12:40 P.M. a couple of days later, Shapiro was charged with the horrendous military offense of making his superior officers look foolish, given until 2 P.M. to find a lawyer (which he was unable to do) and prepare his defense, and by 5:30 on the same day was convicted and sentenced to be dismissed from the service, which is the officer's version of a dishonorable discharge.

President Roosevelt, on the recommendation of the Secretary of War, gave him a full and unconditional pardon—but that did not quite nullify the sentence. Shapiro sued in the Court of Claims for his pay from the date of his dismissal. That court, outraged by a "flagrant case of military despotism" and "an almost complete denial of constitutional rights," held the sentence void and the dismissal illegal.

Unfairness need not be quite so gross as this to reach "constitutional" size, but it must be more than common, garden-variety error, such as the admission of incompetent evidence. As noted above, the Supreme Court has yet to find a fatal denial of constitutional rights in a court-martial—in large part, no doubt, because such unfairness would be unlikely to get past the Court of Military Appeals.

Thus, an examination of military criminal procedure as it exists in 1970, produces a picture rather different from the peace marcher's cherished tintype of drumhead courts-martial inflicting savage punishment on poor privates whose only offense is an attempt to claim their rights as men and citizens. If most military defendants, like most civilian defendants, plead or are found guilty, the principal reason is the simple one that military prosecutors, like civilian prosecutors, rarely bring charges unless they think they have the evidence to convict.

It has been suggested that the "atmosphere" of a court-martial differs from that of a civilian criminal court. It does, but I am not sure how that difference affects the grade of justice dispensed. The military court is neater, more formal, more inclined to go by the book, perhaps (except in the case of a semipermanent court-martial sitting in a place like World War II London or Saigon) more amateurish.

By the same token, it may be less likely than a big-city criminal court with an endless docket to grind out verdicts and sentences without much attention to differences among the pieces of raw material fed into the machine.

Nonetheless, a hard basis of reason underlies the Supreme Court's policy of confining courts-martial as closely as possible to the disciplining of soldiers for military offenses. For one thing, there is nothing to keep Congress from curtailing the protections provided by the code. For another, though the members of a court-martial (as distinct from the military judge) perform the functions of a jury (and, in addition, decide the punishment, if the accused is found guilty), they differ radically from a civilian jury. They are appointed by the military commander, and they are not the peers of the accused. (The code entitles an enlisted man to demand that

248

enlisted men be among the members of the court-martial that tries him, but he knows that what he will probably get are first and master sergeants, who are likely to be rougher than commissioned officers.) The members may be, and I believe usually are, honorable men, unlikely to perpetrate deliberate injustice merely to curry favor with the commanding officer. Moreover, Congress has done about as much as Congress can to eliminate his influence, by making the exertion of such pressure itself a violation of the code and by providing in the 1968 amendments that the accused in a noncapital case may elect to be tried by a military judge, whose efficiency reports are not written by the commander who convened the court.

The Court of Military Appeals has consistently reversed convictions when it scented a whiff of the outlawed command influence. Some of these cases reveal crude attempts by the commander to pressure the members of the court; others seem to manifest a commendable hypercaution on the part of the judges, such as their reversal of a conviction on rubber-check charges because the commanding general, concerned about the relations of his command with the civilian community, had issued a bull on "dishonored checks," exhorting his men to recompute their bank balances after every check. But illegal command influence is often intangible and hard to find in the record.

Even when the members of the court are not subjected, or do not yield, to command pressure—which I think is the usual situation—they cannot forget that the prime purpose of military justice must be deterrence, which means the swift and certain suppression of misconduct. The principle that it is better that ninety-nine guilty men go free than that one innocent man be convicted is hard to square with Army discipline. If a soldier who runs away is shot, in Voltaire's expressive phrase, *"pour encourager les autres,"* the heartening effect is much diminished if 99 percent of the deserters go unpunished. (The severity of military justice should not, however, be exaggerated: Exactly one American soldier was executed for a military offense in World War II, and none since.) I doubt that a court-martial is much, if any, more likely than a civilian jury to convict an innocent man, but it is less inclined to deal mercifully with a guilty one.

Whatever trials come out of the Songmy episode will pose appalling problems. War crimes, of course, are nothing new. I think it safe to say that in *every* war the forces of *all* the belligerents commit violations of the laws of war, usually by mistreating prisoners of war or civilians. The difference—and it is an exceedingly important difference—is one of degree and government policy.

In World War II, Germany and Japan (and Russia, when the Red Army got out of its own territory) simply threw away the rule book and committed atrocities on a scale unheard of since the time of Genghis Khan. The British and Americans, though far from spotless, behaved very much better. Indeed, the Songmy charges are the most serious to be leveled against American troops since the Fort Pillow massacre of 1864.

There is an abundance of credible evidence that the Vietcong and the North Vietnamese have systematically butchered civilians more brutally and on a much larger scale than anything plausibly charged against the Americans or even the South Vietnamese—without shocking David Dellinger, Jean-Paul Sartre or anyone else, except possibly the victims. Indeed, the theory of what Chairman Mao calls "wars of national liberation" rests on repudiation of the fundamental principle of the conventional law of war that combatants are to be distinguished from civilians.

It is significant that North Vietnam and its friends did not seem to focus their propaganda on Songmy (although the

North Vietnamese would almost certainly have had knowledge of such an occurrence) until it became an enormous issue in the American press. The really extraordinary (and, in fact, unprecedented) feature of the incident is the spectacle of a great power, in the midst of hostilities, investigating and proposing to try war crimes alleged to have been committed by its own forces.

The development is all to the good. I earnestly hope that the investigation will be pushed hard and charges preferred against anyone, at any level, who may be responsible. But there are formidable obstacles. Courts-martial have jurisdiction to try any participants in the massacre who are still in service. The deliberate killing of noncombatants by soldiers is certainly murder, whether or not pursuant to orders. (The Uniform Code enjoins obedience only to *lawful* orders, and the Court of Military Appeals has several times held, in relatively unpublicized cases, that a soldier charged with such a crime cannot plead as a defense an order that an ordinary man should have known was illegal.)

The Supreme Court's decision in the *O'Callahan* case probably does not apply to crimes committed outside the United States, and in any case the offenses charged at Songmy were pretty clearly "service-connected." But Lieutenant William L. Calley, Jr., and any other soldiers who may be charged before they are separated from the Army, ought to have as much constitutional right as Dr. Sam Sheppard not to be tried and convicted by newspapers and television.

The problem, of course, is the head-on collision between the defendant's right to a fair trial and First Amendment freedom of the press. There is no easy solution. On the whole, I do not share the view of the American Civil Liberties Union that a fair trial is now impossible and that only the Army itself (always a favorite whipping boy of the Union's professional staff, whose constitutional dislike of uniforms is by no means limited to the police) should be given a fair trial and sentenced to the pillory. I would *also* favor investigation by a commission of disinterested civilians (preferably with some tincture of military experience), not of the guilt of individuals, but of the Army's handling of the matter at brigade and higher levels. By "disinterested" I do not mean either the Army secretariat or Dr. Benjamin Spock.

As the Supreme Court suggested in Dr. Sheppard's case, there are ways of mitigating the effect of publicity without resorting to censorship. The judge can place limits on the presence and activities of newsmen in the courtroom. He can insulate the witnesses from enterprising reporters. He can at least try to control leaks of prejudicial information by witnesses and counsel and to minimize the jurors' exposure to the news media. Perhaps a military judge can use these tools more effectively than a civilian judge can; in this context, the Army's control over some of the participants in the trials may conduce to more fairness, not less. At any rate, the effort should be made.

Even tougher legal knots must be untied before there can be trials of those who were discharged from the Army before the story broke. Unless the Supreme Court overrules its holding in the *Toth* case, which is neither likely nor desirable, they cannot be court-martialed.

Nevertheless, the reliance on *Toth* may be misplaced. A court-martial is not the only kind of military tribunal. The Constitution gives Congress power "to define and punish . . . offenses against the Law of Nations," and the code expressly saves the concurrent jurisdiction of military commissions over "offenders or offenses that . . . by the law of war may be tried by military commissions." The wanton killing of a noncombatant by a soldier is not only murder under the Uniform Code, but also a violation of the international law of war.

In 1942, President Roosevelt created a military commission to try nine Nazi saboteurs who had been landed by submarine on the beaches of Long Island and Florida, with the mission of blowing up American munitions plants. They wore civilian clothes, which made their passage through the military and naval lines of the United States a violation of the law of war. The military commission convicted all nine and sentenced them to death; in *Ex parte Quirin*, the Supreme Court unanimously upheld its jurisdiction.

None of the nine were members of the American armed forces, but one was assumed to be a citizen of the United States. The fact that the violation was committed on American soil does not distinguish the precedent, for the jurisdiction of a military commission to try war crimes has no territorial limitation. If *Quirin* is still good law, there is no apparent reason why a military commission could not try an American civilian for a war crime committed in Vietnam.

If *Quirin* seems vulnerable in the light of the Court's more recent reluctance to permit the trial of civilians by military courts, the Government may consider asking Congress for a statute giving Federal Courts jurisdiction over war crimes committed by Americans outside the United States—although there may be doubt as to the constitutionality of such a retroactive grant of jurisdiction.

Despite all these difficulties, it seems to me of paramount importance that the United States apply to its own forces the standards that it applied to the Germans and Japanese after World War II; the possibility of bringing offenders to justice should be thoroughly tried out in the courts. The Department of Justice is rumored to be much more reluctant than the Army to embark upon this sea of legal troubles. If so, the Attorney General should be reminded that, assuming the murder of noncombatants in Vietnam to be a violation of the 1949 Geneva Convention on Protecting Civilian Persons, as I think it is, the United States is under a treaty obligation to bring alleged violators "regardless of their nationality, before its own courts." The crimes alleged to have been committed at Songmy are, I think, the kind that are peculiarly fit for trial by a military court, as are other military offenses.

In the light of the Supreme Court's restriction of courts-martial to their proper business, of Congress's provision of a reasonable facsimile of constitutional due process for soldiers and of the disposition of the Federal Courts (including, in all probability, the Supreme Court itself) to police the fairness of military trials, I would not favor radical changes in the system of military justice. In the cold light of military reality, it seems doubtful that the discipline and efficiency of an armed force would be promoted by requiring that a private who slugs the first sergeant be convicted by the unanimous vote of twelve other privates.

This is not, of course, to say that the system is incapable of improvement. It still suffers not only from the infirmities and injustices that plague civilian criminal justice, but also from a few of its own. For example, the stiffness of a sentence is likely to depend on the idiosyncrasies of the particular human beings who assess it: One court may hand out ten years where another would think three was plenty.

The military's elaborate system of review probably militates in favor of equalization of punishment, but this advantage, if it exists, is counteracted by the improper but common tendency of courts-martial to impose sentences that leave plenty of room for clemency by the reviewing authorities. (General courts-martial in World War II regularly sentenced deserters to death, relying on higher authority to see to it that no one was actually shot—a confidence that in the case of Private Eddie Slovik proved misplaced. The fifteen-year sentences recently imposed on some of the Presidio mutiny defendants reflected this custom, as well as the military's inveterate prejudice against mutiny. They were greatly reduced on review, although the reductions naturally received far less publicity than the original sentences.)

To cite another example, the jurisdiction of courts-martial over people who are essentially civilians, but who have some military status, seems to me rather broader than necessary. I can see no good reason for court-martialing retired regulars —a jurisdiction that the Navy (although not the two other services) has used on several occasions, apparently for no better purpose than to deprive the man of the pension earned by his years of honorable service.

The most serious complaint against the services' treatment of soldiers who get in trouble has nothing to do with courts-martial or the Uniform Code. The "undesirable" discharge, which for all practical purposes is as heavy an albatross around the recipient's neck as is the dishonorable or bad-conduct discharge, can be given administratively, without any of the process due the accused in a court-martial.

This may not be unfair when the ground is conviction by a civilian court. But the services have regularly resorted to the device in cases—many of them involving draftees and other young and inexperienced recruits—when the evidence of misconduct was not judged solid enough to go to a court-martial. Senator Sam Ervin, who, although not generally regarded as a flaming radical, has a healthy respect for the Bill of Rights, has for years sponsored legislation that would in substance forbid the military to hand out a discharge less than honorable except after proceedings in which the soldier is given such basic rights as a free lawyer. The proposal deserves more serious Congressional consideration than it has so far received; indeed, it should be made law.

I have serious doubt about the constitutionality of the ancient article that forbids commissioned officers to use "contemptuous words" against the President, the Vice President, Congress and a long list of other civilian officials. The only person to be convicted under it in recent times was Lieutenant Henry Howe, who accused President Johnson of "facist agression." (He should have been charged with spelling unbecoming an officer and a gentleman.) The very infrequency of its use suggests that it serves no disciplinary purpose sufficient to justify its possible inconsistency with the First Amendment.

Likewise, the general article, which denounces "all disorders and neglects to the prejudice of good order and discipline in the armed forces, all conduct of a nature to bring discredit upon the armed forces, and crimes and offenses not capital," is on its face so general that it would be unconstitutionally vague if it were part of a civilian penal code. (In practice, however, its coverage is pretty well understood: a Navy airman named Sadinsky, for instance, was probably well aware that he was doing something illegal when he won a bet by executing a back flip off the flight deck of the U.S.S. *Intrepid*, then under way in a rough sea, and put the Navy to the inconvenience and expense of dispatching a destroyer to fish him out.)

An enumeration of all the defects that Congress could and should do something about would require a good many pages, some of them full of indigestible technicalities.

Steering, as is my wont, a course somewhere between the A.C.L.U.'s Mr. Morgan and Senator Eastland, I conclude that modern military justice is, despite its blemishes, about as fair as the brand of criminal justice dispensed in most of the states, and that there is solid constitutional and political justification for its application to military personnel who commit military offenses.

Footnote to the History
of World War II

This one was written neither for money nor out of the usual lust to see my stuff in print, but simply because it asked to be written—to be precise, because some law students to whom I told it thought it ought to be committed to writing before it perished from the memory of man. Neither they nor I had any idea what to do with it after that; I simply shoved it in a file marked "Military Law—Miscellaneous" in the vague hope that it might some day come in handy. It was written more than twenty years after the fact, and my memory may have embroidered on some of the details, but mainly it is true.

I SPENT most of World War II as a Judge Advocate, or Army lawyer, in what was then called the European Theater of Operations. I was supposed to be furnishing General Eisenhower (on whom I never laid eyes) with advice on international law, which (being fresh out of law school) I regarded as a very intellectual and high-toned field. But vulgar Army crime accounted for most of the business in the office, and pretty often the flood of criminality rose so high that all the lawyers in the Hotel Majestique, no matter how eggheaded, had to turn to and review court-martial records. Every death sentence, of which there were a great many, had to be confirmed or commuted by Eisenhower himself, which meant that some military lawyer had to review the record exhaustively. Generally speaking, the crimes were tedious and unimaginative murders, rapes, and desertions, and only the most ferocious of the murderers were actually executed, for the Army, despite the slamming around it took at the hands of platoons of angry young novelists, and despite the blood-curdling menaces which filled the Articles of War, was usually fairly humane in applying its criminal law.

Taking one day with another, it was monotonous work, and only occasionally was the reviewer's day brightened by some touch of macabre comedy, such as the truck driver who, having silenced the squawks of a rape victim by driving his truck over her a couple of times, attempted to account for the state of his wheels by pleading a severe nosebleed. There was, in fact, only one case which struck me then and strikes me now as worth remembering and recounting. The record, which was about eighteen inches thick, is probably moldering in a warehouse in the Middle West, but it was unusually full of fascinating details, and, at least as to its highlights, I have practically total recall.

The criminal, whom I'll call Smith, because I have forgotten his name, had never done anything interesting until the spring of 1944, though he had been in the Army for a couple of years before that. Having been expensively educated at several rather snobbish prep schools and colleges, from some of which he had been expelled, he was inappropriately sent to the Adjutant General's Officer Candidate School and commissioned. An officer of the Adjutant General's Corps is in effect a practicing expert on Army red tape, which is on the whole a little more tangled than the civilian kind. When this method of winning the war began to pall on Smith, which was almost immediately, he simply went AWOL. For this he was court-martialed and busted out of the service. Thereupon he either re-enlisted or was drafted and, having had his fill of *papierkrieg*, volunteered for the paratroops.

Since Smith was a man of first-rate intelligence, physique, and enterprise, it is just possible that, could he have been kept busy, he might have had a gallant military career and maybe accumulated four or five rows of polychromatic ribbons. But the ennui of the months in England before D-day gnawed at his vitals, and presently he planned and nearly, but not quite, brought off a daring coup, the theft of a whole case of Scotch from an Officers' Club. This was in time of war a grave military offense, more to the prejudice of good order and military discipline than dueling or the use of contemptuous words against the Vice President—almost, in fact, comparable to mutiny. Smith should have thought himself lucky to get off with six months in the stockade, which was a couple of acres of mud, sprinkled with tarpaper barracks and inadequately fenced with barbed wire—sufficiently dull, but by no means a Devil's Island. There were no floodlights, because of the blackout, and the guards were far from alert, because they figured, reasonably enough, that the prisoners had no place to go anyway. As a jail, the stockade bore about the same relation to Alcatraz that an Army mess hall bears to the Tour d'Argent.

This pathetic amateur Bridewell presented hardly any challenge to a man of Smith's parts, and he was under the fence and out of it within a night or so of his incarceration. More, he took with him three of the other inmates. His reasons for taking them are to this day somewhat of a mystery

to me, for all three were unmitigated slobs, criminally inclined, no doubt, but congenitally incapable of achieving
eminence in that or any other endeavor. One was big and
dumb, a former strongman in small gyp carnivals, doubling
as bouncer and complaint silencer when not lifting weights
or challenging the burlier apple-knockers to wrestling
matches. The second had had an undistinguished civilian
career as an auto thief; the only unusual episode in his military career was an ill-conceived effort to throw the MPs off
his trail by peroxiding his hair. This had left him with a
streaky brown and yellow thatch, like the tresses of the
more sluttish sort of Piccadilly Commando. The third was
undersized and generally ratlike; I can't remember his civilian calling—something on the order of a pool shark or numbers runner. Such talents as these three had, they had duti-
fully turned from civil to military crime, but none had
achieved greater dignity in the Army than out of it: Though
each had a longish record, none had been thought worthy
of anything higher than a special court-martial. As I said,
it is hard to see what Smith wanted of them. Perhaps he was
vain enough to relish the swift obedience and doglike admiration which these *untermenschen* seem always to have
given him; perhaps he had a streak of softheartedness; perhaps—which is the likeliest explanation—he had already
cast them as useful stage properties in the spectacular drama
of fraud which he projected.

At any rate, by 3:00 A.M. of a drizzling April night the four
of them were buried under a heap of blankets in the back
of a 4 x 4, 2½-ton truck, bound for London. So far, a sufficiently commonplace escape from confinement, of a kind
which took place by the thousand and nearly always ran a
course as predictable as measles—a few weeks or months of
furtive liberty in the half-world of the bomb-battered,
blacked-out city, living on the black market, shacked up per-

haps with a friendly streetwalker, maybe doing a little stealing, inevitably terminating in routine questioning by a London police constable or an MP patrol, unsatisfactory answers, swift return to military custody, and a new and longer court-martial sentence. But here began the truly brilliant part of Smith's career, the swift attainment of its full powers by a seminal mind, possibly the only seminal mind in the whole long history of the art or science of AWOL and desertion.

Arriving in London, Smith marched his men to the nearest Red Cross club. They shaved, they showered, they pressed their uniforms and they shined their shoes, for Smith well knew that in all places more than a mile from actual fighting a snappy appearance is the first of military virtues, instantly disarming suspicion and highly conducive to an attitude of sympathy and benevolence on the part of brass of high or low degree. He himself was from policy and predilection at all times and in any circumstances neater than a cat, or even than a Fifth Avenue floorwalker—as neat, say, as a junior partner in a Wall Street law firm, which I take to be the approximate pinnacle of neatness. Incredibly, he seems to have kept his slobs looking like a West Point color guard during all their adventures; more, his ascendancy over their dull minds and brutish natures was such that he actually kept them sober and out of trouble so long as they remained under his command—both feats far beyond the capacities of the duly constituted authorities.

Following the great military principle of conservation of effort, Smith used the shower for more than sanitation, picking up (in addition to some loose currency) four sets of dogtags, hung on nails by soldiers heedless of the Army's injunction that dogtags (like a Skull and Bones pin) should never be removed from the person. Having thus acquired for his Freikorps new names, new serial numbers and even new blood types and religious preferences, and having parked them in the coffee-and-doughnut bar, with strict instructions neither to stray nor open their mouths, he turned to the execution of his plan. That plan can fairly be described as Napoleonic—bold and simple in concept, thorough and precise in detail. He intended, in short, to go home, in style and at the expense of the Army. For that he needed orders, which were to the traveling soldier of World War II what his horse was to the Mongol warrior or his long rifle to Daniel Boone.

Mechanically speaking, these required only a typewriter, a stencil, a mimeograph machine, and a stack of paper. Where Smith got these I do not know, for he was close-mouthed on this point, but there were several possibilities. It would not have been hard for a man of Smith's address and plausibility simply to walk into one of the Army administrative offices, which proliferated in London in those days, and borrow the use of the necessary equipment; he might have had a friend in such an office (which would explain his taciturnity); conceivably, he obtained his equipment from civilian sources. Whatever his method, he managed to lay hands on the raw materials and had only to work them into suitable orders.

This was by far the most complex part of the maneuver, for orders had to be composed in the bizarre Newspeak which the Army mistook for efficient abbreviation, and arranged according to a rigid convention, all of which made their preparation a task comparable to the writing of a Japanese *tanka*. Moreover, they had to be peppered with such esoterica as appropriation symbols and tables of distribution, an operation as impossible to the layman as surgery on the optic nerve.

Smith had not wasted his opportunities at the Adjutant General's school; his knowledge of this appalling bureaucratic vernacular was encyclopedic, and he rattled off its formulae with ease and correctness. What is more, he did it in the authentic style—a style as indescribable and inimitable as that of Tacitus (though not otherwise similar) but recognizable by anyone who ever saw it. With superb inventiveness and consummate crust he ordered himself and his squad—under their new names—to the Military Intelligence School, Washington, D. C. (There was no such school, but it sounded reasonable. No one ever questioned it.) He authorized travel by air or water and the maximum per-diem allowance en route; and, while he was at it, he promoted himself to staff sergeant and the least dense of the slobs to corporal. His Extract Orders, copies of which were introduced in evidence and thoroughly flyspecked by me, were magnificent specimens of their genre; there was, indeed, nothing whatever about them to excite suspicion— with the possible exception of their total freedom from error; not many adjutants were such masters of their craft as Smith.

One detail remained: Soldiers returning to the Zone of the Interior had to carry their service records. Smith took four large brown manila envelopes, inserted in each a comic book (with which the Red Cross was well supplied), typed on each "Service Record and Allied Papers of ___," sealed them and, in a final burst of creativity, stamped them "CON- FIDENTIAL" in letters half an inch high and tyrian purple in color.

To soldiers armed with such credentials, the Army Finance and Transportation Officers were not obstacles, but simply a combination of bank and travel agency, olive-drab versions of the American Express Company. It would be tedious to chronicle the details of their trip home (in a comfortable cabin on a luxury liner turned troopship), for it seems to have been as enjoyable and tranquil as a cruise.

The only problem, indeed, was an eager and rather high-ranking representative of the OSS, who seems to have concluded that soldiers who said so little about themselves and where they were going (for the American soldier of World War II, despite the rash of posters depicting wooden crosses, sinking transports, and other alarming sequelae of loose talk, was normally extremely gabby) must be intelligence agents of a superlatively secret sort. Smith had a dreadful time convincing him that he was nothing more than an honest, dumb and slightly bewildered sergeant, traveling to the Zone of the Interior for a routine, low-level intelligence course.

Arrived in New York, they drew a substantial amount of partial pay and rested from their adventures in a comfortable, though not ostentatious, hotel suite. For reasons of morale, Smith at this point allowed his returned heroes a little relaxation; at least they ran up a $300 hotel bill in three days, which (at 1944 prices) suggests intensive relaxation. But three days was all he permitted them, for he believed in celerity of movement and was uncertain how long the partial-pay vouchers would take to bounce. Besides, he was tired of the Army. Pausing only to tap the complacent Finance Office for another partial pay, and the Transportation Office for railroad tickets, they proceeded to Washington. Smith parked his task force in Union Station, instructing them to keep their noses buried in comic books, and took a taxi to the War College, where he found an unoccupied typewriter and some blank requisition forms. From there, armed with his requisitions, he went to the Pentagon, where (for what seems to have been the first and only time in the whole hegira) he had a little trouble with a WAC receptionist. But he got past her, handed in his requisition, and presently emerged with four Honorable Discharges, needing only to be filled out and signed by an officer not below the rank of colonel. Smith had a fountain pen, and the Pentagon was full of typewriters. By 1700 hours each of the four was honorably discharged from the Army of the United States and had a handsome certificate to prove it, testifying to numerous battles, campaigns and skirmishes, and signed by a nonexistent colonel of Infantry.

At the same time Smith dismissed his irregulars; it must have been a strain to look after them, and it is improbable that he valued their company. He headed for New York alone, and they went their various ways. Left to their own moronic devices, they didn't last long. One stole a car and was picked up; one got drunk and was picked up; the third lost his nerve and turned himself in.

And even Smith made a mistake: He called his girl. She loved him still, but her mother did not. The old lady called the cops, who called the FBI, who called the Army. Smith rejoined the slobs for the trip back to Europe, to face a general court-martial. They could, of course, have been tried on forty or fifty charges apiece, some of them real rarities, but there would have been no sense in such a procedure. The desertion count, which could be proved with ease and dispatch, carried in time of war a maximum penalty of death and so was perfectly adequate. Within a couple of weeks, all of them had been tried, found guilty and sentenced to be shot to death with musketry.

This was a good deal less fearsome than it sounded, for Smith at least was well aware that the odds against his really being shot were astronomical. On the other hand, he was also aware that the sentence probably did mean something like a decade in the federal pen or a disciplinary barracks. This remarkable man was by no means at the end of his rope. The French prison where serious offenders were confined was a good deal more formidable than the English stockade, but Army routine was still Army routine. He took thought and went to see the chaplain, who possessed both a typewriter and a mimeograph. The chaplain was out. The next morning at 0800 hours the in-basket of the prison adjutant contained a General Court Martial Order, signed by Dwight D. Eisenhower, confirming the sentence in the case of Private John C. Smith but, because of special circumstances, commuting it to five years' confinement at hard labor, suspended. By 1300 hours Smith was out. So far as I know, he's still out. Should he see this, he may be interested to know that General Eisenhower actually did commute the sentence to dishonorable discharge, total forfeitures, and confinement at hard labor for the term of his natural life.

I find myself quite unable to draw an instructive moral from all this, other than the obvious one that an intelligent man with good nerve can always make a monkey of any bureaucracy, military or otherwise. At the time, I thought the moral was that the Army should have known how to make better use of Smith's undoubted talents. Twenty-odd years later, having practiced a lot of law and seen a lot of crooks, I suspect that he was probably what some of the baffled psychiatrists call a "constitutional psychopathic inferior," and others diagnose as "sociopathic personality disturbance, antisocial reaction," meaning in either case that the patient is a no-good bum. Desertion in time of war is not really a comic offense; in Smith's case, at least, it argues an egocentricity which I do not find sympathetic. But all I am sure of is that his offenses were picturesque and vastly amusing. For that I was and am grateful to him.

Remember the Repple
Depple: American Army
Speech in World War II

―――――――

This was the first piece I ever published (other than unsigned and unreadable student contributions to the Harvard Law Review) and about the only one having nothing to do with law or politics. Its genesis was a long letter to H. L. Mencken, pursuant to the general invitation to readers contained in his preface to The American Language. Mencken, a very kindly man in such relationships, sent me a friendly reply, which swelled my ego to insufferable proportions by suggesting that I turn the thing into an article for American Speech, which he described as "the only publication that ever pays any serious attention to the language spoken by 140 million Americans." Since this was roughly equivalent to the Pope's suggesting to a Jesuit (of the old-fashioned variety) that he pray for the papal intentions, the article was promptly submitted to that scholarly magazine, where it must have been read by several dozen people. I did not crave a larger audience. The paragraphs on "forbidden phrases," which today would attract no attention in the Ladies' Home Journal, seemed pretty risqué in 1946, and I would have been uncomfortable had I thought they were likely to be read by any of the senior partners in my law firm. As a matter of fact, I have never since used a Dirty Word in print: There has been no kick in it for years.

THE AUTHOR of this article concedes in advance his lack of scholarly qualifications. This is his first venture in philology, if you can call it that. But it seems desirable that someone, interested rather in what was actually said than in the publicization of his own pet witticisms, set down his impressions while they are still fresh in memory. They may at least be useful as checks on the findings of more learned writers, or as source material.

Most of the things which I have so far seen printed on the subject have been ephemeral collections of vaudevillesque patter, some of it fairly clever, but little of it bearing much relation to the ordinary language of the troops. My own observations are limited to what I have actually heard in fairly common use—i.e., in use not only by the gifted individuals who invent neologisms, but also by the rest of us who adopt them, if they are good enough.

Undoubtedly, many usages exist which are not familiar to me, and some of them may be widespread. Most of my service overseas (commencing in April, 1944, and continuing until the summer of 1946) was in rear echelons, and my occasional tours of duty in combat areas were not extended enough to permit me really to familiarize myself with the prevailing dialect up there. Similarly, my acquaintance with the Air Force and the Navy was limited. But so far as my observation goes, the speech of infantrymen, airmen, and sailors does not differ radically from the norm, except for the ordinary amount of professional jargon.

I have tried to eliminate all locutions which are not peculiar to, or a product of, the Army. In some cases, inevitably, I will have erred and included phrases which, while new to me, are old stuff. Most soldier talk is the same as civilian talk except, perhaps, that certain meritorious localisms have caught on with men from all parts of the country. In fact, my principal emotion when I had completed the search of my own memory, those of my friends, and such files as were available of *Yank* and *Stars and Stripes*, was surprise at the smallness of the number of new words and phrases (aside from the technical, never part of the vulgate and not likely long to survive the individual's return to civilian life) the war had introduced. Perhaps it is because very few aspects of this war were conducive to high spirits and excess energy of the sort which produces new language. It is significant that the cartoons of Bill Mauldin, among the most accurate impressions of the war, almost never introduce new words. Mauldin's characters are ungrammatical, and they employ slang of the sort which is part of the American language, but they rarely say anything which would not be perfectly intelligible to any normal American. Willie and Joe were usually much too tired to wisecrack. So far as my recollection serves, Mauldin introduced but one new word, *garritrooper* (a portmanteau from *garrison* and *paratrooper*), which he defined in substance as one too far forward to wear a necktie and too far back to be shot at; but this, while received with amusement, never passed into everyday speech. It cannot be too strongly emphasized, for the benefit of future playwrights and novelists, that real soldiers never sound anything like some of the current comic-strip and Hollywood syntheses. It may be that some immature individuals do talk in this extraordinary fashion—I have heard none, personally—but if they do, the odds are that they brought it into the Army with them, from the zoot-suit period of civilian life. (As a matter of fact, despite the lapse of time, the speech of Stephen Crane's soldiers is remarkably like that of modern ones.) In any case, I have tried to err on the side of inclusion, excluding words and phrases from the list which follows only if I myself had heard them in civilian speech, before the war.

I. CATCH PHRASES

Only six of these seem to me to be sufficiently long-lived and widespread to merit comment. These are:

1. *Oh my aching back* (often contracted to *Oh my back*, or simply *My back*). This is used in a variety of situations; *e.g.*, upon the receipt of bad news, especially if such news entails labor for the speaker; to express general discontent, tempered by resignation; to express sardonic amusement at a gaffe or piece of naïveté (presumably because the aching back—*i.e.*, war-weariness—prevents the hearty laughter which would otherwise be called for). It has become a counter phrase, but in the right circumstances it can be pungent. Its genesis, while obscure, is probably connected with the fact that an aching back, which cannot be expected to produce visible symptoms, is the common complaint of soldiers seeking light duty or no duty at all.

2. *Things are rough in the ETO.* This is obvious in origin and meaning, *rough* (or *rugged*) being the adjective of all work for anything dangerous, difficult, or unpleasant. It is standard comment in all adverse circumstances and has consequently been worked very hard. It will be noted that although, when actual shooting stopped, the designation of this area was reduced from "European Theater of Operations" to "European Theater," it continued to be the ETO to all soldiers.

3. *Whaddya want—an egg in your beer?* Properly, this is the retort courteous to a gripe, or bitch, which is not fully justified. By loose usage, it has become an answer to any and all complaints. I do not know its etymology, but my assumption has always been that it is based on the fact that fresh eggs and real beer were two of the scarcest desiderata in the ETO, the possession of either one of which ought to have sufficed any man. There is some evidence that it has been prevalent around Brooklyn for years, but, at any rate, it has certainly had wider currency in the Army than ever before and has been more apt.

4. *You've had it.* (Also, of course, *I've had it, he's had it,* etc.) This convenient phrase is an Anglicism. It is used in a great variety of situations, most of them unpleasant, as when one has been swindled or summarily treated; when an effort to obtain some desired thing has failed; when, in general, no hope of improvement exists; or when a leave (for example) which has been disappointing or brief has ended. It connotes finality. It is the standard retort when stocks of some desired article are exhausted. "Got any Scotch today?" Answer: "You've had it."

5. *Blow it out your ass.* This, used in lieu of "nuts," etc., or sometimes as an urgent invitation to shut up, is by no means limited to the ETO. It may be old, but the author has never heard it in civilian life, despite a good deal of experience as an ordinary seaman and in other walks of life where no inhibitions stood in the way of its free employment had it been known. In print it is softened to "Blow it out your footlocker" or "Blow it out your B-Bag." (The B-Bag was a denim barracks bag which, with the A-Bag, contained the government and personal property of the traveling soldier before the handier duffel bag was introduced.) In fact, *Stars and Stripes* for some time printed a column of letters from readers (mostly gripes, of course) known as "The B-Bag." It used to be subheaded "Blow It

Out Here," but this vanished from the masthead of the column some time after V-E Day—perhaps due to the post-hostilities influx of herds of female civilians.

6. *You never had it so good.* This is a sardonic response to complaints about the Army; it is probably supposed to represent the attitude of a peculiarly offensive type of officer. It was probably true of a substantial number of recruits in the early days of training, featured by good food and plenty of it, modern barracks, etc., but it became a bitter and popular jest in the foxhole and K-ration areas. In spirit it is closely allied to No. 3 above.

II. ARMS, EQUIPMENT, ETC.

The remarkable thing in this category is the paucity of terms of the soldier's own invention. In general, he is content to accept whatever nomenclature is in official use, although he usually selects the shortest form or himself shortens a longer form. Thus, his rifle is always referred to as an *M-1* or *carbine*, as the case may be, which is perfectly correct; a truck having six wheels, all powered, is a *6-by-6*, which is what Ordnance calls it; even the odious C and K rations are either given their full titles or referred to as *C's* and *K's*. I heard little approximating the *goldfish* and *monkeymeat* of the last war. An exception may be made as to the powdered synthetic lemon juice, alleged to contain vitamin C and very prevalent in K rations, which I have sometimes heard called "battery acid" and "bug juice." Of course, I have heard many derogatory epithets applied to standard items of Army chow (an old word, but current)—as, for instance, the usual designation of scrambled (powdered) eggs on toast—but all of these were familiar to me from my days on shipboard, in college commons, and even in secondary school. Perhaps another exception should be made in favor of *Spam,* as used; it was usually applied to any canned, processed meat, and was almost invariably used as a pejorative. The shoulder patch of the Army Service Forces was sometimes known as a *spam cluster.*

Among Army vehicles, only the jeep seems to have passed into the language. (Such terms as *Weasel, Duck, Buffalo,* etc., were official or semi-official designations and can hardly rank as part of the demotic speech. They refer to highly specialized types of vehicle, having no civilian equivalents, and are not likely to be heard after the war.) *Jeep,* which may come to be applied to any small, powerful vehicle, is, of course, the common name of the ¼-ton truck, 4-by-4. I am not sure of its derivation. I have heard that it is based on "G.P.," meaning general purpose, but I am doubtful of this, for several reasons. "G.P." is not a normal Army abbreviation, so far as I know, and the jeep is, in fact, not a general-purpose vehicle—at least, in theory. My own opinion is that it comes from a character in the comic strip "Popeye," Eugene the Jeep, a small, fantastic animal possessing practically magical powers. *Jeep* also became an adjective; thus, a small traveling camp show, the entire staff and paraphernalia of which could theoretically be loaded into a jeep, was a "jeep show," and this term was likely to be applied to any not very elaborate enterprise, even though it required a couple of 6-by-6's as transportation. It should be noted that in the Armored Force, for reasons unknown to me, the ¼-ton 4-by-4 is always a *peep,* the term *"jeep"* being applied to the command-and-reconnaissance car—the latter an awkward, high-silhouetted cross between a truck and an old-fashioned touring car. But this usage is peculiar to the tankers, clung to as a matter of esprit de corps, and is not likely to make progress or even to survive.

Although perhaps not strictly relevant, it is noteworthy that a riotous fancy was displayed in the individual christening of vehicles, guns, tanks, aircraft, and any other piece of equipment having some individuality. Especially was this true of jeeps. I saw, for example, such typical specimens as "Displaced Person," "Toujours l'Amour," "She's Old But She Can Still Get Hot," "Our Lady of Victory" (driven by a Catholic chaplain), "Gwendolyn Feinschreiber" (driven by an admirer either of Miss Feinschreiber or of the S. J. Perelman school of humor), and even the ineffable "Wacky Wabbit" (driven, inevitably, by a WAC). Jeeps, perhaps because of their prominence in the public and official eye, have rarely been given improper or risqué names, but aircraft often were. In particular, I remember noticing in a Munich illustrated paper published in October, 1943, a photograph (in violation of the rather explicit provision of the Geneva Convention) of a captured U. S. airman whose flight jacket bore the device of his aircraft—a nude holding a bomb, and the words "Piccadilly Commando." This combination of naked *mädel* and bomb was seized upon by the editorialist as an outstanding example of the New York and Hollywood Jewish (the German word was, I think, *verjudeten*) cynicism of these murderers of German children. Unfortunately, the propagandist apparently did not know that a "Piccadilly Commando" is a London prostitute and so missed an excellent opportunity for further homiletics in his peculiar vein.

Nor have new weapons produced as much new popular nomenclature as might have been expected. The *bazooka* (the correct name of which is "rocket-launcher") derives its name from its obvious resemblance to Bob Burns's musical instrument; but I am not sure that the War Department did not invent and popularize the term as a sort of code word, just as the British originally used *tank*, for the weapon was very secret in its early days. The Germans, with characteristic Nazi grandiosity, labeled a similar weapon *panzerfaust*, and this term was known to most G.I.'s. Aircraft were always known by their official names or, interchangeably, their official numbers—*e.g.*, B-17 or Flying Fortress, B-24 or Liberator, P-47 or Thunderbolt, etc. Often, of course, these were contracted to "Lib," "Fort," and so forth. Almost any type of portable automatic weapon, including the Thompson submachine gun, was likely to be called a *Tommy gun*, except the Browning Automatic Rifle, which was always a *BAR*. The standard hand grenade seems rarely to have been called a "pineapple," despite the Chicago use of that term. None of these words, of course, is novel.

Not much more inventiveness was displayed with respect to enemy weapons. The V-1 was in the U. S. and British official parlance a *flying bomb*, after an original sporadic use of "pilotless aircraft," and the former name remained in fairly common use. The troops, however, generally called it a *buzz bomb*, probably because it normally came in at rather low altitude, reminiscent of an airplane "buzzing" the ground. The name may, however, refer to the sound of the V-1's jet engine—a resonant buzzing, rising to a shattering roar. I have never heard a soldier call one a *robomb*; *robot* (pronounced "rowboat") and *robot bomb* I have heard but rarely. So far as I know, the V-2 was always referred to as a V-2; it was employed principally against civilians and did not become familiar to most troops. A type of multiple-rocket projector, called *nebelwerfer* by the Germans themselves, was sometimes called *screaming meemie* by American troops, from the noise it made—or rather, its projectiles were so called. Practically any type of German automatic or semi-automatic small arm was apt to be described as a *burp gun*, presumably from the resemblance of shots or short bursts of fire to hiccoughs; but I have been told by a combat infantryman that the name is properly applicable only to the Schmeisser machine pistol. (Similarly, any German pistol was

275

likely to be called either a *Luger* or a *P-38*, no matter what model it was or who had manufactured it.) German aircraft were generally so rare, at least in so far as the average U. S. soldier in France or Germany was concerned, that I don't believe any of them ever acquired nicknames, although the Germans seem to have had a number of slang terms for our aircraft. German soldiers themselves were, as in the last war, usually known as Jerries or Krauts; when in particular disfavor they might be referred to as Nazis or supermen. "Heinie," "Fritz," and "squarehead" were relatively rare and "Dutchman" almost unknown, perhaps because real Dutchmen were respected allies.

Ribbons representing decorations and campaign medals were sometimes called *fruit salad*, but I have never known them to be called *brag rags* except in the funny papers. The Good Conduct Medal, awarded to enlisted men for twelve months of exemplary behavior, was frequently called the *no-clap medal*, in allusion to a principal prerequisite to its award. The Bronze Star Medal, supposedly in recognition of heroic or meritorious achievement, which blossomed profusely on the chests of staff officers not having sufficient rank to receive the Legion of Merit, was often known as the *Officers' Good Conduct Medal*, sometimes, more bitterly, as the *Brown Nose Medal* or *Brown Star*. The Air Medal, the award of which to combat fliers was more or less routine, was often referred to (both by themselves and by ground troops) as the *Junior Birdman Badge*. Other decorations, more respected, had no derisive appellations that I know of. The gold bars, worn on the sleeve at the rate of one for each six months of service overseas, were frequently spoken of as *Hershey bars*, for obvious reasons.

The war of course introduced a great many new technical terms, in connection with radar, aviation, and the like. Most of these were current only with the very limited groups who engaged in these highly technical pursuits and cannot in any case be regarded as peculiar to the Army. Practically every specialized activity had its own jargon. The author, for example, spent the latter part of the war as a Judge Advocate. Terms peculiar to military justice include such specimens as *bust* (court-martial conviction disapproved by higher authority), *DD, TF, and CHL* ("dishonorable discharge, total forfeitures and confinement at hard labor") and the like.

III. G.I.

These letters were undoubtedly the major addition to the vulgate of the World War II Army. They represent, of course, an abbreviation of "Government Issue," but this may not be their only meaning, or even the original one. I have been told by a Regular Army sergeant of many years' service that many years before the war the large ash-, garbage-, etc., can used by the Army was known as a *G.I. can* (as it still is) not because it was Government Issue, but because it was galvanized iron. According to this source, a man who was G.I. was crude or uncouth, and the term was considered insulting.

At any rate, the adjective G.I. is now applied to all items of army equipment, generally to distinguish them from civilian analogues; *e.g., G.I. truck, G.I. shoes, G.I. soap, G.I. glasses, G.I. cognac* (purchased through official sources and hence probably potable), *G.I. insurance*—the list is very long. So pervasive an adjective was bound to become a substantive; thus, in the proper context, "my G.I.'s" may mean the wearer's shoes or woolen underwear. (*The G.I.'s* is—or are—diarrhea; the phrase is a contraction, probably, of "the G.I. trots." The malady is cured or aggravated by a *G.I. pill.*) It would have been tautologous to refer to a *G.I. soldier*, but he could be called simply a G.I., and the name, although originally more popular with civilians than soldiers, has stuck. There are a few others; infantrymen and, by extension, more or less all front-line soldiers are sometimes called *doughs* or *dogfaces*, although both of these are commoner in the newspapers than in the mouths of the troops themselves; Air Force flying personnel are sometimes labeled *birdmen* or *flyboys*; but by and large a U. S. soldier is a G.I. G.I. *Joe* is frowned upon (although a soldier unknown to the speaker may be, as in civilian life, referred to as "a Joe" or "some Joe") and is found only in advertising copy, the stories of the sloppier sort of correspondent, and the orations of Clare Boothe Luce. It should finally be noted that G.I. almost invariably denotes an enlisted man, as distinguished from an officer—the latter are usually *the brass* or, if of high rank (very senior, in official jargon), *the big brass*. This may be a contraction of *brass hat*, but I rather think it refers solely to the heavier load of insignia sported by officers.

As an adjective, G.I. also means strict, addicted to the enforcement of (or personal compliance with) regulations. Thus, the statement that an officer is G.I. means that he enforces regulations to the letter, insists upon a snappy appearance and observance of the canons of military courtesy, and generally tolerates no laxity. The adjective is used similarly in reference to an entire command; the Third Army, under General Patton, had the reputation of being extremely G.I. A less courteous word for this sort of thing is discussed below.

To my knowledge, G.I. has but one meaning as a verb— to clean, polish, scour with G.I. brush and G.I. soap. (A G.I. *party* is an organized attack upon dirt, usually staged on the Friday night before a Saturday-morning inspection.)

IV. FORBIDDEN PHRASES

While all the ordinary forbidden words are employed in the Army and, indeed, badly overworked, I can think offhand of only three which I believe to be peculiar to the Army. These are:

1. *Chickenshit.* This graphic description, used both as noun and as adjective, signifies what is mean, petty, and annoying, especially as applied to regulations. Thus, when an infantryman in a rest area finds himself restricted because his dogtags are not worn around his neck, or his shoes are unshined, or he has been detected in the act of robbing the village bank, he complains that there is too damned much chickenshit around. If he puts the gripe in a letter to "The B-Bag," or otherwise feels it advisable to watch his language, the word is contracted to *chicken.* As an adjective it sometimes connotes cowardice, perhaps by confusion with chicken-livered or chicken-hearted. I have recently seen a quotation from a soldier newspaper published in 1919 by the then Army of Occupation which employed the word in its modern sense, but this seems to have been exceptional.

2. *Pissed off* (or *P'd off*). This means, roughly, fed up, irritated, depressed. I have no idea of its history. The British say *browned off,* and it may be that the Americans who borrowed the phrase simply felt that "browned" was not strong enough. The superlative is, for some reason, *highly pissed off,* which may also be a Briticism.

3. *Tough shit.* Something which is unfortunate, but about which nothing can be done. The phrase has been dephlogisticated to *T.S.,* and in this form is extraordinarily widespread, having many variations. A *T.S. ticket* is an imaginary form entitling the bearer to sympathy and nothing else. "All I can do is punch ya T.S. ticket (or slip) for ya." Some humorists, including chaplains, went so far as to print and distribute T.S. tickets with appropriate blanks to be punched.

V. BORROWINGS

This Army has had uncommon opportunities to add foreign words and phrases to its vocabulary, but (perhaps as a part of the normal disinterest of the American soldier in anything in any way different from himself and his background) there have been remarkably few such accretions. Most of the traffic has been the other way, at least in the areas of which I have had experience—the United Kingdom, France, and Germany.

The presence of more than two million Americans in the U. K. undoubtedly hastened the Americanization of the British vulgate. Certainly any ordinary Englishman is now familiar with (although he probably does not use) *elevator,* *gas, gum* (chewing), and a variety of acthronyms for "Negro," to select a few random examples. Possibly owing to the educational efforts of both the U. S. Army and the British Government, cases in which serious misunderstandings of each other's languages arose were very rare. (SHAEF, an organization in which U. S. and British personnel were carefully commingled, used sometimes to print its directives in both British and American, where the difference between the two was great—thus, such forms as "stores/supplies" and "other ranks/enlisted men" were common.) The use of a few Briticisms became common among Americans, partially displacing, even in speech among themselves, American analogues. Thus, *pub* and *fish and chips* became standard, perhaps because there were no exact American equivalents, and *flat* and *lift*—which can be upheld as better words than *apartment* and *elevator*—came into fairly common use, as did *queue* for line, although most of the boys would probably have spelled it "cue" and did so spell it in the instances in which I ran across it while censoring mail. The entire subject is, of course, too vast and complex to be discussed in this brief article and will probably furnish occupation to numbers of trained philologists for years after the war. My own opinion is that the war did a good deal to check the drift-apart of the two languages.

As for the Continent, it is now safe to say that no Frenchman, Belgian, Dutchman, Luxemburger, Dane, Norwegian, or German, and hardly any Pole or Russian, is ignorant of *O.K.*, *G.I.*, and *jeep*. So far as I know, practically no French locutions passed into the language of the troops, other than such old familiars as *bowkoo*, *parleyvoo*, *vooleyvoo coushay*, and others which also served honorably in the last war. An exception might be made in favor of *zig-zig*, used either as noun or as verb, and implying sexual intercourse. (French friends, however, inform me that *zig-zig* was imported into France from North Africa, the source of a good deal of low French argot.) The following is taken verbatim from a record of trial by court-martial, which I myself have examined, in which the ability of the accused to speak French was relevant. A military policeman is on the stand.

Question: Did you actually hear the accused talking French to this girl?
Answer: Yes, sir.
Q: Well, what did he say, if you know?
A: He said, "No zig-zig ce soir, sweetheart."

German has contributed *kaputt*, meaning variously broken, dead, all up, etc.; *verboten*; and *schnaps*, meaning practically any type of strong liquor (including, for example, the liquid fuel used to propel V-2's) other than gin and whiskey. (Schnaps has a rival as a generic term in *calvados*; this beverage, of very high voltage, made a profound and possibly lasting impression on the troops in Normandy.)

Whether any Russian has seeped into the G.I. vocabulary is unknown to me; Berlin and Vienna are practically the only places where American and Russian troops in any numbers have been in prolonged contact, and I have been to neither.

VI. OFFICIAL JARGON

A number of words and phrases coined by or popular among administrative officers have been adopted by the troops, sometimes with substantial changes in meaning. Among the most commonly employed are:

S.O.P. This contraction of "Standard Operating Procedure" denotes any prescribed, preferable, or habitual method of doing a thing.

Z.I. Home is called the "Z.I." (Zone of the Interior) nearly as often as it is called the States, or Stateside.

Redeploy. To go home. Note that the verb, although transitive (*i.e.,* "the soldier is redeployed"), is used as an intransitive (*e.g.,* "I'm gonna redeploy next month").

Fraternize. To have close relations, usually sexual, with a female enemy national. By extension it is used also with respect to the female population of allied countries and even American girls. On the other hand, I once saw a soldier charged with "fraternization" because he had philanthropically sold a prisoner of war a pack of cigarettes for $12.

By the Numbers. In training, certain fundamental operations, such as putting on a gas mask, are taught by the numbers—at the count of one, the carrier is unfastened, at the count of two the mask is removed, and so forth. To do anything "by the numbers" is to do it in a practiced, routine, semi-automatic manner.

G-2. Used as a verb, this is roughly the equivalent of "to case"—*i.e.,* to size up a situation before deciding on a course of action. G-2 is, of course, the staff division responsible for intelligence.

VII. MISCELLANEOUS

Beat up. An adjectival phrase of all work meaning damaged, worn-out, or of unimpressive appearance.

ETO-happy. Describes one who has been in the ETO too long, talks to himself, or even appears to like it. It is probably related to "stir-dippy."

Liberate. To scrounge or steal; to loot. (The French, with rather more justice and less cynicism, use *récupérer.*) "I liberated a swell gold watch in Mannheim."

Poop. Directives, staff studies, standard operating procedures, technical manuals, general orders, circulars, command letters, etc., etc., etc.

Repple Depple. Replacement Depot, a purgatory-like place where soldiers sweat out (*q.v.*) assignment to an organization. Early in the winter of 1944–45 the Army became alarmed by the gloomy connotations of "replacement" and officially substituted "reinforcement," but the new word never got farther than strictly official usage.

Sad sack. (A polite contraction of "sad sack of shit," sometimes contracted still further to "sack.") An inept, luckless, or stupid person. (Sergeant George Baker did not invent the term—he simply appropriated an established piece of slang as a name for his forlorn little private.)

Sack. Bed. To sack up or hit the sack is to go to bed. Sack time is sleep. May originally have referred to a sleeping bag or bedding roll, but now means any bed or substitute therefor.

Sweat out. To wait for or endure, usually under nerve-racking or monotonous conditions. Thus, one sweats out a promotion, a bombing, a chow line, or redeployment. This phrase occurs in *Tom Sawyer,* but its rise to prominence certainly dates from the war.

Shack up (*with*). To cohabit. Also used in the passive. "I'm shacked up around here" means that the speaker has found a friendly *fräulein* who in substance maintains a home for him. The *fräulein* herself is a "shack job."

See the chaplain. To resign oneself to the continuance of an unpleasant situation; to accept ill fortune without seeking to alleviate it. "See the chaplain" was the standard advice to one with a grievance about which nothing could be done—presumably because it was the mission of the chaplain, often a long-suffering man, to listen to the multitudinous complaints of soldiers who felt themselves misunderstood by the Army. Of course, in the vast majority of such cases the chaplain could do nothing except listen with more or less sympathy. The phrase was often expanded to "See the chaplain and have him punch ya T.S. slip." As a counter phrase, this was used in much the same spirit as "You've had it."

As I have indicated at the beginning of this article, it is possible that many terms have been overlooked in the foregoing discussion. But I believe that the preceding paragraphs represent a large majority of the new words and phrases added to the vocabulary of the average American soldier in Europe which have any chance of survival. According to a story printed in *Stars and Stripes* (Germany edition) of January 24, 1946, Dr. David W. Maurer, associate professor of English at the University of Louisville, believes that military slang may add a possible 100,000 new words to the American language. I think somebody has been kidding the professor; 100 words would be closer to it. (I leave out of account, as forming no part of the lexicon of the average G.I., the new technical words—but of these there can hardly be more than a few thousand, if that, and in any case they are not slang.) Nor has the American soldier "plundered almost every language on the face of the globe." The American soldier is probably less interested in other people's languages and customs than the soldiers of any other country, and he has done a remarkably poor job of picking up the language in the countries he has visited; he has preferred the easier course of letting the limeys or frogs or krauts or gu-gus, or whatever he calls the natives, learn American. I think it fair to say that in no respect has American provincialism been more clearly manifested than in that of language.

Index

Index

Hayden, Tom, 16, 132–37
Hearst Corporations, 56
Hegel, Georg Wilhelm Friedrich, 18
Helmstedt-Berlin railroad, 205
Himmler, Heinrich, 73, 154, 226
Hippies, 130–31
Hiss, Alger, 165
Hitler, Adolf, 3, 14–15, 71, 73–74, 93, 140, 161, 202–3
Ho Chi-minh, 136
Hobbes, Thomas, 19
Hoffa, Jimmy, 195
Hoffman, Abbie, 7, 15, 19, 23
Hoffman Julius, 11, 14, 21–22, 134
Holmes, Oliver Wendell, Jr., 54, 150, 188
Hoover, J. Edgar, 10
Hoppe, Willy, 57
Hopson, Howard, 126
House Un-American Activities Committee, 152–53, 173
Howe, Lt. Henry, 256
Howe, William S., 5
Hughes, Charles Evans, 96, 98
Hungary, 227

Illinois v. Allen (1970), 21
"Impartial inquiry," 35–36
Imprisonment, 41–42
Income-tax evasion, 34
Indonesia, 72
Insanity, 79–94
Integration, 104–5
"Inter-Allied Governing Authority," 203–4, 206, 208–9, 211
Internal Revenue Code, 123
Internal Revenue Service, 125

Irish, 40
Israel, 233
Italians, 40
Ivan the Terrible, 93

Jackson, Andrew, 97
Jackson, Robert H., 99
James II (King of England), 59, 146
Japan, 220–21, 225, 250
Jean Qui Pleure, 20
Jean Qui Rit, 19–20
Jefferson, Thomas, 191
Jeffreys, George, Baron, 20–21, 62, 156, 162
Jesuits, 84
Jesus Christ, 37, 82, 124
Jews, 40, 81
Johnson, Lyndon B., 140–41, 149, 155, 256
Jordan, 233
Joyce, William, 166
Jugurtha (King), 127–28
Justice Department, 125
Justinian, 49

Kaltenbrunner, Ernst, 30, 154
Katz v. United States, 189–93, 196
Keeton, Robert, 52
Kennedy, John F., 132, 200–201
Keyes, Lt., 243–44
Khrushchev, Nikita, 200–2, 219
King, Martin Luther, Jr., 15
Kirchwey, Freda, 151
Knipperdoling, 85
Komendatura, *see* "Inter-Allied Governing Authority"
Krokodil, 71

Joseph W. Bishop, Jr.

Joseph Warren Bishop, Jr., was born in Brooklyn, New York, in 1915. He graduated from Deerfield Academy, Dartmouth College, and Harvard Law School. After serving in the U.S. Army for four years during World War II, principally as a Judge Advocate in England, France, and Germany, he worked in the office of the United States Solicitor General, briefing and arguing cases in the Supreme Court. Later he served as Deputy General Counsel and Acting General Counsel of the Army—a position, he recalls, that earned him a denunciation by the late Senator Joseph McCarthy and his associates. After a spell as a Wall Street lawyer, which he found "rather boring," he joined the Yale Law School faculty in 1957 as Professor of Law, specializing in corporation, military, and international law. "Whatever may be said about life at Yale Law School," he offers as an *obiter dictum*, "it is not boring." He has been married for twenty years and has one son. He has contributed to *The New York Times Magazine*, *Esquire*, *Harper's*, *The New Republic*, and other general periodicals and to many law journals and other legal periodicals, and is co-author (with George T. Washington) of a legal treatise titled *Indemnifying the Corporate Executive*.